Frozen Institutions

"What do we have to learn from the Anglican church in Australia about how the church faces the challenge of the end of Christendom? The answer is that we have much to learn if our teacher is Bruce Kaye. Kaye is a no-nonsense theologian who makes these essays shine with clarity and wisdom. All who are trying to think through what it means to live as Christians after that is no longer a given will benefit from Kaye's book."
—Stanley Hauerwas, Duke Divinity School, retired

"Leadership through liminality requires re-embracing identity, recalling our formative story. Second, it requires courageous experimentation and imaginative exploration to discover how our identity might be expressed in changed circumstances. Finally, it involves discerning effective ways forward, consonant with our identity, as they emerge from experiments. In this collection of essays, Bruce Kaye offers this kind of leadership; with theological and historical acuity and insightful analysis, he creatively opens future possibilities."
—Phillip Aspinall, Anglican archbishop of Brisbane
 and former primate of Australia

"Frozen Institutions is a wonderful compendium of essays . . . . With insight and sharpness, Kaye brings his considerable skills as a wise and astute interpreter of the faith and fortunes of the Anglican Church worldwide as it grapples with issues of diversity and plurality in the modern world. A scholarly, penetrating, at times disturbing yet unfailingly gracious account of the ecclesia of God."
—Stephen Pickard, Charles Sturt University

"There is no better student of the life and witness of the body of Christ than Bruce Kaye. An Anglican theologian deeply committed to and thoroughly engaged in the church in Australia and globally, Kaye is a sharp critic of the forces that undermine the church's faithfulness to the gospel. These essays offer a hopeful future for both the Anglican Communion and Australian Anglicanism beyond Christendom and its divisive power politics. Good news indeed!"
—Ian T. Douglas, bishop of the Episcopal Church in Connecticut

"Ranging over Anglican, Australian, and ecumenical territory, Kaye shows that the institutional embodiment of religious faith is essential for its faithful transmission from one generation to another. But Kaye also

urges a process of ecclesial reform and development if faith is to remain a reality in the world. With its focus on structures of power and authority (and their abuse), this is a book to resource and reorientate our thinking."
—Paul Avis, School of Divinity, University of Edinburgh

Frozen Institutions

Questions for the Church after Christendom

Bruce N. Kaye

◦PICKWICK *Publications* · Eugene, Oregon

FROZEN INSTITUTIONS
Questions for the Church after Christendom

Copyright © 2022 Bruce N. Kaye. All rights reserved. Except for brief quotations in critical publications or reviews, no part of this book may be reproduced in any manner without prior written permission from the publisher. Write: Permissions, Wipf and Stock Publishers, 199 W. 8th Ave., Suite 3, Eugene, OR 97401.

Pickwick Publications
An Imprint of Wipf and Stock Publishers
199 W. 8th Ave., Suite 3
Eugene, OR 97401

www.wipfandstock.com

PAPERBACK ISBN: 978-1-6667-1348-0
HARDCOVER ISBN: 978-1-6667-1349-7
EBOOK ISBN: 978-1-6667-1350-3

Cataloguing-in-Publication data:

Names: Kaye, Bruce Norman, 1939–, author.

Title: Frozen institutions : questions for the church after Christendom / Bruce N. Kaye.

Description: Eugene, OR : Pickwick Publications, 2022 | Includes bibliographical references and index.

Identifiers: ISBN 978-1-6667-1348-0 (paperback) | ISBN 978-1-6667-1349-7 (hardcover) | ISBN 978-1-6667-1350-3 (ebook)

Subjects: LCSH: Anglican Communion.

Classification: BX5005 .K39 2022 (print) | BX5005 .K39 (ebook)

Scripture quotations are from New Revised Standard Version Bible, copyright © 1989 National Council of the Churches of Christ in the United States of America. Used by permission. All rights reserved worldwide.

For Louise, companion in arms

Contents

Acknowledgments xi
Introduction xiii

PART I *Anglicans Worldwide*

1. Sidelining of the Anglican Consultative Council in a Time of Turmoil 3
2. Plurality and Identity in the Modern World 15
3. Orthodox Anglicans and Catholicity 23
4. Reality and Form in Catholicity 32
5. Anglicanism's Uncertain Apostolicity 42
6. How Can We Speak of "Canonical Scripture" Today? 56
7. The Role of Eschatology in Recent Anglican Ecclesiology: A Study of Three International Doctrine Commission Reports 71

PART II *Anglicans in Australia*

8. The Landscape of the National Church 85
9. Anglican Theology in the Renewal of the Church 98
10. National Conferences and the Renewal of the Church 106
11. Changing the Context of Church Schools 112
12. Some Directions in the Anglican Church of Australia for Examining Chaplains 124
13. Purpose and Dynamics of General Synod 137
14. Conflict, Constitution, and Community: Cultural Change and Gender in the Anglican Church of Australia 151

Bibliography 187
Name/Subject Index 195
Scripture Index 207

Acknowledgments

THIS IS A BOOK of essays. All have been revised, some more than others. Some were written for the Journal of Anglican Studies as "Editor's Essays." Others were delivered as addresses at conferences or as papers at seminars, across the Anglican Church of Australia when I was the General Secretary of that church. These papers also reflect work engagement. They arose in the context of and were shaped by the requirements of my employment. For a theologian to have employments that allowed for, indeed encouraged, theological research and reflection has been a great privilege. As a result I wish to acknowledge the encouragement and support of colleagues with whom I have worked and who provided a stimulating context in which to think. Bill Lawton was the lateral thinking rector of a semi—rural parish on the outskirts of Sydney. He encouraged his curate to continue studies and at that time I began a daily habit of spending up to an hour each morning reading and taking notes on the Greek New Testament. It was a habit that continued, with some small breaks, and has deeply influenced my thinking, often in different ways and in changing directions. It certainly led to an early deliverance from the complacent literalism of the broader environment in which I began.

I had the benefit of some outstanding teachers at the University in Sydney: Bill Richie for patience and encouragement in the middle of a complex piece of Greek poetry, Bruce Mansfield, a master of elegant historical narrative, Edwin Judge, a terrier of attention to text and critical thinking, Marley Stevens, historian by engaging conversation, and John Anderson for philosophical engagement through the exegesis of Plato's Dialogues. At Moore College, Donald Robinson was a friend and exemplar in enjoying asking questions of the text of the New Testament. I owe a great debt to Bo Reicke during my doctoral studies in Basel and to Kingsley Barrett as a mentor to a young academic in Durham (UK).

These people helped me to grow out of the constrictions of my ecclesial origins and my own limitations and grasp something of privilege of being encouraged to think and imagine into the extraordinary wonders of the presence of God in the person of Jesus Christ.

My colleagues in both Durham and Sydney were also influential in helping me think Christianly about what I was doing in the institution in which I had some responsibility. At Durham John Cockerton for being a shielding hand and Ian Bunting for being a conservative looking radical and for being a close friend in hard times. At the University of New South Wales and New College, Randall Albury, Michael Birt, John Nevile, Conal Condren, and in the city of Sydney, Vincent Fairfax, who had initially encouraged me to go to Europe for further study. In the national office of the Anglican Church of Australia our wise and supportive Primate, Keith Rayner, and many colleagues throughout the Anglican Communion. I acknowledge the support of the Centre for Public and Contextual Theology in Charles Sturt University and its Director Stephen Pickard. These are all people who have shared with me the challenges of working in an institution which claims a higher calling. It can be a very frustrating experience, but it is where the hard work of theology needs to be done. Such thinking and insights as have come my way have been fostered and helped by Keith Mason and Hugh Mackay, not least in our regular monthly lunches for over the last twenty-five years.

I am very grateful to Wipf and Stock for once again publishing my book. They are a rare combination of innovation and old fashioned care and courtesy. It has been a special pleasure to work with the excellent team who have guided this book through to publication.

Someone said to me once that I was very fortunate to have been married to two wonderful women. They were right in so saying. They could also have said I have been fortunate to have had the company of two extraordinary children, Alison and Nigel and of their wonderful families. My first wife Rosemary died while they were still young when we were in Durham. These were hard times. Since 1983, my wife Louise has been central in our family and provided us with unbridled love and encouragement. She has been an articulate and spirited interlocutor and constant witness as a Christian person. This book is dedicated to her with profound gratitude and love.

Introduction

ENGLISH CHRISTIANITY EXISTED FOR fifteen hundred years as a Christendom which united civil and ecclesiastical together into one unity of government. The hubris of the seventeenth century Restoration settlement led to the dynamics that fractured the old national unity and led eventually over several centuries to the dissolution of the overt marks of the Christendom model. While most of the overt marks of Christendom have now gone, the effect of over a thousand years of Christendom has left traces of the tacit assumptions that underlay that socio-political condition. Coming to terms with the tacit assumptions of Christendom is not easy and is still a continuing challenge for Anglicans. This is the underlying context of these essays.

Christendom is just one form of the challenge for the church not to be conformed to the schema of this world. Christendom is a long running institutional connection between church and civil power in a polity. In a thought experiment we might imagine that the early church did not become part of a Constantine or a Roman Empire. That it continued in its natural minority group social and institutional development. Would there be the same issues of colonization of power perceptions that the encounter with Constantine raised. Institutional arrangements in the church would have developed. Perhaps they would have been similar to those that did arise in the Constantine experience. Either way such institutional evolution would eventually raise the problems of authority and power in the life of the church.

This is not a new idea. A classic statement of the corruptibility of ecclesiastical arrangements is provided in the 1662 Book of Common Prayer.

The question being addressed in the Of Ceremonies statement in the Book of Common Prayer is ceremonies, but the principle being enunciated is of more general import. In literary hermeneutics the point is commonly accepted and in more recent centuries is recognized in relation to the meaning of the texts in the Bible. In this context, however, I wish to relate it to the institutional arrangements that pertain in the church generally and their underlying values and assumptions. The form of the ecclesiastical arrangements may stay the same, or at least similar, but their operation can certainly be decidedly influenced by the changed value assumptions that influence their operation. Those tacit assumptions in the church change as much by the changes in the tacit assumptions of the culture within which the reader of the documents is located. The same thing can be said of institutional positions such as a bishop or a parish priest or deacons. The form of the office in each case may remain the same, but the substantive content of the exercise of the office has and will change. The question is, are these underlying changes for the good or do they represent some kind of corruption of the meaning of the office. The essays in this volume are ploughing some furrows in this field.

> Of such Ceremonies as be used in the Church, and have had their beginning by the institution of man, some at the first were of godly intent and purpose devised, and yet at length turned to vanity and superstition: some entered into the Church by undiscreet devotion, and such a zeal as was without knowledge; and for because they were winked at in the beginning, they grew daily to more and more abuses, which not only for their unprofitableness, but also because they have much blinded the people, and obscured the glory of God, are worthy to be cut away, and clean rejected: other there be, which although they have been devised by man, yet it is thought good to reserve them still, as well for a decent order in the Church, (for the which they were first devised) as because they pertain to edification, whereunto all things done in the Church (as the Apostle teacheth) ought to be referred.[1]

The questions raised in these essays, particularly those in Part I, are not new. Indeed they are both important and also perennial. Though broadly Anglican in range these essays are nonetheless concerned with a number of particular themes that have arisen over a long period of time. Various aspects of Anglican thought and practice clearly are present. Furthermore these topics have presented themselves to me in the course of my work as a theologian in the church. In the early 1970s I was asked to

---

1. Church of England, *Book of Common Prayer*, "Of Ceremonies."

teach a new course in Durham for ordinands in the Church of England on the Use of the Bible. This challenged me to look in detail at the history of the interpretation of the biblical texts, especially the New Testament. That history was itself evidence of the changing character of Christian understanding and of attempts to sustain some place for the text of the New Testament in succeeding generations, or in Troelstch's terms, "totalities." Underlying my work on hermeneutics lay the pervasive themes of epistemology and history. Lecturing on hermeneutics to ordinands and on the life and thought of the apostle Paul to graduates in the university constituted a great learning experience that left deep marks on my thinking generally.

In 1972, I had the pleasure of an extended conversation with Charles Vereker, Professor of Political Theory and Institutions at Durham. It began, by chance, on Durham railway station and continued on the train until we reached London Kings Cross. It raised in a fresh and general way the question of institutions. What were they? What purpose did they serve in human existence? How did they serve specific purposes or sustain particular values? How were they corrupted or sustained? What kinds of social relations did they facilitate? Indeed, what counted as an institution? What role did institutionality have in ecclesiology and, in the context of the New Testament documents, was institutionalization in the early Christian groups best thought of as, in Käseman's phrase "early Catholicism" or something less historically pejorative. And why were they inevitable in social groups that survived changing generations? How does a general conception of institutions help in dealing with such enduring questions of ministerial orders and the idea of a canon? If institutions are broadly conceived of as attempts to maintain across generations some continuity of patterns of relationships between people and or things, then it clearly will have relevance to any attempt at ecclesiology. It certainly will have something to do with the emergence of regulated job descriptions or of defined locations of authority.

Relating to all these questions was the character and location of the origins of Christianity. If Jesus was indeed Immanuel, God with us, and was unique and singular in that respect, how did that particular gain relevance and accessibility to later generations and ages? These questions are at the heart of the Christological endeavors of the earliest Christians and rightly have been preeminent ever since. Christianity exists out of the truth contained in how we understand and respond to Jesus as the Christ. Within this framework the themes of epistemology, history, continuity, and institutions have for the past fifty years been ever present in my endeavors to understand what it means to be a Christian, or part of a Christian community, in the here and now of my existence.

After sixteen years absence in Europe, I returned to the very different intellectual environment of Australia, and Sydney in particular, to take up a position as Master of New College within the University of New South Wales. Eleven years later I was invited to be the General Secretary of the Anglican Church of Australia. In both these responsibilities I was given quite specific institutional tasks. As the Master of a University College I was charged with developing the college to be more manifestly an academic institution accessible to and engaged with every level of the intellectual life of the wider university. That involved changes that expressed values appropriate to the idea of an Anglican university college and New College in particular, and institutional changes to secure those values. In my last employment, as General Secretary of the Anglican Church of Australia, a similar task was set before me. The task was to promote policies and changes that would enhance the church's engagement with Australian society. This change agenda affected everything that was done in the General Synod Office. My position in the Australian church brought me into the world of the Anglican Communion and extensive engagements with its life and challenges.

The essays in this volume are drawn mainly from this last decade of my working life and further activity and thinking after that. The essays set in the context of worldwide Anglicanism are in Part I and in Part II are essays concerned with matters Australian. The essays in Part I have mostly been previously published in one form or another. A number were published in the Journal of Anglican Studies which grew out of the projects initiated in the General Synod Office. Those in Part II were originally speeches given on a variety of occasions in Australia. These all refer to some aspect of Anglican church life in Australia and relate to the renewal agenda being pursued from the General Synod Office. Each part has its own introduction.

The last and longest essay in this second group is a paper prepared for the national, or inter-diocesan, debate in the Australian church about the blessing of same sex marriages. In 2017, the Marriage law was changed in Australia to extend marriage beyond heterosexual relationships. The diocese of Wangaratta passed a regulation allowing, under certain conditions, for a service of blessing of any marriage contracted under the new Commonwealth law. The diocesan regulation was referred to the Appellate Tribunal which, under the constitution of the church, is the final court of appeal for an opinion on the meaning of the constitution. The Tribunal found the regulation to be not inconsistent with the constitution. This essay explores what is at stake for the Anglican Church of Australia in this matter. It serves to highlight the constitution of the Anglican Church of Australia as being a loose federal union between the dioceses. The dioceses retain very high levels of independence. The structures of the national church are minimal in the extreme. The question raised by the Wangaratta move is whether this kind of national church constitution might be helpful in confronting divisions on this question. We shall see.

Lying behind these biographical experiences is a growing conviction about the influence of the assumptions of the Christendom period. It is easy to miss the political point of the history of western Christianity when it is dealt with as "church history." Often in seminary curricula this church history is pursued with only slight reference to the wider historical context in which that narrative is deployed. A classic example of this is the way in which the Council of Nicaea is treated as a domestic debate about Christology, without recognizing the formative influence of the emperor Constantine on both the calling of the council and its debates and conclusions.

A Christendom church inevitably conducts relations within the church in ways that are influenced, if not conditioned, by the patterns and character of power in the political elements of that Christendom. Furthermore the ecclesiastical elements in the Christendom are necessarily involved in the exercise of power and authority in the political realm. That involvement has in the long history of the English Christendom meant being party to brutalities and violence which fall well outside the normal Christian morality. Here the sense of the divine presence in the life of the Christians of this Christendom has been colonized by the power and authority of the "kingdoms of this world" rather than the kingdom of Jesus which is not of this world.

Anglicanism has been shaped by a very long period of life as the English Christendom. The separation of churches from the Church of England in new places with different political arrangements and different pattens of church sate relations has not meant that the ghosts of the English Christendom have disappeared from Anglicanism generally. Sometimes they have united with "imperial looking" elements in the new host culture. Sometimes they have grown their own power politics.

Using the Christendom pattern as background in contemporary church life sharpens some of the issues at stake for modern Anglicans.

When looked at in this way the deep ambiguity of power in the life of the church becomes apparent. The importance of power in the Christian community was manifest even in the group of Jesus' disciples. It became important, not because it constrained the freedoms of others, or hindered the production of an ordered and moral Christian community. It gained its importance by Jesus framing it as an instinct that was contrary to the nature of his kingdom and of the kind of community he envisaged.

Mark tells a story of two disciples, James and John, sons of Zebedee, asking Jesus to grant them "to sit, one at your right hand and one at your left, in your glory" to which he replies that this is not his to grant. Jealousy angered the other disciples. Clearly conflicts and jealousies were to be found in this group of disciples who had been following Jesus for some time and at close quarters. This group response prompts Jesus to provide one of the most important statements of Christian group practice.

> When the ten heard this, they began to be angry with James and John. So, Jesus called them and said to them, "You know that among the Gentiles those whom they recognize as their rulers lord it over them, and their great ones are tyrants over them. But it is not so among you; but whoever wishes to become great among you must be your servant, and whoever wishes to be first among you must be slave of all. For the Son of Man came not to be served but to serve, and to give his life a ransom for many."
> (Mark 10:41–45)

Here in simple but stark terms Jesus lays out the contrast between two ways in which a community might live: power that lords it over, and tyrannizes others, or the guiding principles of humility and service. Clearly humility and service are the way for a Christian community to operate. Clearly Christendom is a liaison that flirts with what Jesus calls the way of the gentiles. Just as clearly officers in an institution can use their position to increase their power and distort the exercise of their responsibilities. The recent Royal Commission on Institutional Responses to Child Abuse in Australia specifically drew attention to this problem under the heading of "clericalism" and referred to the Anglican Church.

Groups and communities that last longer than one generation of membership naturally seek to provide for some kind of continuity in the life of that community. They do this by laying down arrangements that will provide the kind of community they wish to sustain. This is what institutions do and we see them emerging in the early generation of Christians. In a Christian community such institutions would therefore serve the values and character of the Christian community. Institutions are really attempts to sustain some similarity of relationship between people and or things over time. Such institutions are clearly susceptible to change and corruption. An office of service in an institution can, without a lot of difficulty, be turned into an opportunity to acquire priority and to exercise power. This process has the effect of freezing the office and its proper functioning in favor of the deployment of the power of the incumbent. It is this issue that lies behind the notion that the church should be always reforming.

The essays in this book have been written during the long period when I was working on *The Rise and Fall of the English Christendom*. Prior to that work I had spent a lot of time with Richard Hooker and came away with, amongst other things, a profound sense of the centrality of Christ in all theological thinking. In that book I drew attention to Hooker's Christological framework for his exposition of the sacraments.

> Forasmuch there is no union of God with man without that mean between both which is both, it seems requisite that we first consider how God is in Christ, then how Christ is in us, and how the sacraments do serve to make us partakers of Christ.[2]

His discussion of the early church Christological debates focusses on the misrepresentations of the heresies as they tend to move between an extreme emphasis on the humanity of Christ at the expense of the divinity or the other way around. He says therefore that we need to "keep warily a middle course shunning both that distraction of persons wherein Nestorius went awry, and also this later confusion of natures which deceived Eutyches."[3] The sacraments are Hooker's immediate concern in this section but the argument applies also to such claims to an immediate and absolute authority for the presence of Christ in the life of the church.

The old polarity of the religion of Protestants being the Bible and that of the magisterium of Roman Catholics corrupts the central characterization of Christianity. The religion of Christians is Christ who, though we have not seen him yet, we believe. Claims of absolute present authority for later institutions are a serious derogation from the core of the faith. The description of Anglicanism as a via media between Rome and

2. Hooker, *Lawes*, Book V, 50.2.
3. Hooker, *Lawes*, Book V, 53.3.

Geneva is misleading unless it is seen in the Christological framework identified by Hooker. In one sense Anglicanism has represented a middle way between an absolute Pope and an absolute Bible. In both cases the absoluteness is moderated and those sources kept in their proper place by rigorous attention to the historicality of God's presence in Jesus Christ. These essays move in this area of theological conversation.

Part I

Anglicans Worldwide

Introduction

THE ESSAYS IN THIS part are concerned with questions that have arisen generally in the Anglican Communion. They are in roughly chronological order of composition and refer to themes that were important in the dynamic troubles faced by the institutions of the Communion mainly at the beginning of the present century. The first refers to a shift in the centre of action in the Communion from the ACC to Lambeth and the Primates. The 1998 Lambeth Conference was a somewhat traumatic event especially in its final stages. The final encounters included mutual abuse and strong disagreement on what should be said about same-sex relations. A group of bishops took the unprecedented step of publishing after the conference a joint letter dissenting from the final resolution. Nonetheless senior figures began describing this resolution LC 1998, 1.10, as the accepted teaching for Anglicans, which clearly was not the case. In this crisis the freshly minted Primates Meeting became the focus of activity. "Leadership" eclipsed "consultation" as the way to think about the role of the instruments of the communion. It is an interesting example of institutional power and authority creep. Using resources not available to me Alex Ross has recently examined this period and calls it the Age of the Primates.[1]

Chapter 2 is concerned with some of the complexities of imagining what sort of community the Anglican Communion really is. Chapters

---

1. See Ross, *Authority and Polity*.

3–6 are directed to the conduct of the debate about gender relations. Some began first calling themselves orthodox Anglicans and others as heretics and most recently others who took a different view on same-sex relations as being apostate. This extraordinary rhetoric was justified on the grounds that those who differed from them did not accept their rather particular view of the character of scripture and its authority and its, to them, obvious entailment of a view against same-sex relationships. Leaving aside the obviously rhetorical deployment of these terms, the principles of orthodoxy, catholicity, apostolicity and scripture require more careful reflection in a post Christendom world. Even the 1662 Book of Common Prayer identifies the contingency of its arrangements in the short essays on Ceremonies and Preface. If there is to be any serious connection between later generations and the historical figure of Jesus and any sense of incarnation in his person and work, then historical contingency cannot be escaped in any configuration of Christianity and hence of the church and its institutions.

The last essay in this section concerns an issue that, it seems to me, has been somewhat absent from the ecclesiological debates. The three Inter-Anglican Theological and Doctrinal Commission reports are examined from the point of view of eschatology. Its absence has meant a loss of perspective about the contingency of ecclesial institutional arrangements.

1

Sidelining of the Anglican Consultative Council in a Time of Turmoil[1]

THE DECADES ON EITHER side of the turn of the century were quite dramatic in the world of Anglicanism as significant conflict came to public notice. During this period the various groups within the Anglican Communion acted in different and surprising ways which had the effect of sidelining the Anglican Consultative Council (ACC). From the point of view of legitimate roles this was rather surprising since the ACC was the only formally constituted Communion body with a constitution approved by the Provinces. Furthermore, the ACC was the only institution with a membership of laity and clergy elected by the Provinces.

During this period the ACC met on fourteen occasions. The ACC had taken initiatives in mission consultation and the terms and operation of the first Inter-Anglican Theological and Doctrinal Commission whose brief was directed at contextualizing mission. At the end of the century a storm of institutional conflict over sexual ethics erupted. Provinces took actions on both sides of this conflict and so it became not just a conflict about opinions or even policies, but of provincial action. The conflict was between provinces. The ACC was a leader in the earlier phase of mission and contextualization, but was sidelined in the heat of this conflict. It failed to fulfill the expectations of its constitution when preempted by actions taken by the Archbishop of Canterbury and the Primates.

Within the Anglican Communion there had been early signs of the coming storm. The 1988 Lambeth conference had debated the ordination

1. An earlier version of this essay appeared as Kaye, "Sidelining."

of women as priests and as bishops and the Eames Commission was appointed to set out guidelines for respect between provinces on this issue. There was also a short debate about homosexuality and a call for further study. This all began to get complicated when Bishop Jack Spong in the USA ordained an openly homosexual man in 1989 and then in 1990 retired Bishop Righter also ordained an openly homosexual man. 1990 was Archbishop Robert Runcie's last ACC and the occasion of the announcement of the appointment of George Carey as Archbishop of Canterbury. It was also the last meeting of the then chair of the ACC, the widely experienced Yong Pin Chung. Clearly these were times of change as well as challenge.

In his presidential address at that ACC meeting Archbishop Runcie reflected on the character of the Anglican Communion and how it sustains affection, friendship, and diversity. He went on to declare that

> the creation of the ACC was our Communion's boldest attempt to match the need for coherence and order with the wide degree of freedom and autonomy our Provinces enjoy. It provides a vehicle for addressing issues, of which one of the most pressing is our difficulty in maintaining communion without abandoning the principle of autonomy.[2]

He looked for some flexibility in the way in which the ACC, the Lambeth Conference and the meeting of Primates operated, but in general he thought "that in the Anglican Communion we have the least unsatisfactory way of leading a world Church,"[3] a statement that contains so many assumptions that it is hard to know where to begin.

During the course of the meeting an extra section was added to consider a document on Unity and Authority in the Anglican Communion which had been prepared during the course of the previous ACC and amended before going to the Lambeth Conference in 1988. The group at ACC 8 were unable to do anything constructive with this document revealing in the process a significant confusion as to the remit of the various instrumentalities of the Communion. It was the beginning of movement in the organizational initiative and power in the Communion. The Eames Commission had already been appointed, the new Inter-Anglican Theological and Doctrinal Commission (IATDC) had also been appointed

---

2. ACC, *Broken World*, 32.

3. ACC, *Broken World*, 34. Perhaps an allusion to Winston Churchill's *bon mot* about democracy

with Robin Eames as the chair. The issue of women and ordination was moving away from the ACC. It was something of an irony since the ACC had been the body in Anglicanism in 1979 that had taken clear decisions and leadership on this matter.

In 1993, the ACC met jointly with the Primates in Cape Town. The usual matters were canvassed and resolutions passed. The document *Belonging Together*, which had been commissioned out of the previous Lambeth Conference, was considered and a new IATDC was appointed to continue the work of the consultation which had produced *Belonging Together*. This was the commission that produced *The Virginia Report* that has provided much of the conceptual basis for subsequent debate on the institutions of the Anglican Communion. The new IATDC was to be appointed by the Archbishop of Canterbury, though it was to be responsible to the Archbishop and the ACC. At the next ACC in 1996, there was no mention of the sexuality issue, despite the fact that in the US Bishop Righter had been acquitted of a charge for ordaining an openly homosexual man. There was no report from the IATDC which had been established and there was no report on the responses from provinces to the proposals in the document *Belonging Together* which the previous ACC had requested.

In 1999, the ACC continued its distant interest in *The Virginia Report* with a bland resolution calling for arrangements for study of the report. The resolution noted that the report had been introduced to ACC10 (Panama 1996), though no mention of this is made in the resolutions of that meeting, nor of the fact that the Lambeth Conference in 1998 had received the report and asked the Primates, not the ACC, to monitor a decade of study in each province on the report. It then went on to ask the Primates to ensure that opportunity be given at provincial and diocesan level for careful and critical study of the report. The ACC also asked for some simple language texts to be made available and for seminars to be organized for training leaders to conduct seminars on the report.[4]

Why did the ACC at its 1996 meeting not deal with the report more substantially? After all, the IATDC had been appointed on terms that made it responsible to the ACC and the Archbishop of Canterbury who was ex officio the President of the ACC. The constitution of the ACC makes such communication and inter provincial engagement one of its main tasks. Despite this, in 1996 the ACC left it to Lambeth, which gave it

---

4. ACC, *Communion We Share*.

to the Primates who immediately decided to meet annually following the hotly contentious 1998 Lambeth Conference. There was an extensive presentation of *The Virginia Report* in 1999 at ACC XI, but the resolutions of that meeting show no engagement in doing anything on this subject.

Was George Carey beginning to feel that the Primates were a more comfortable group with whom to meet? Did it seem that the disasters during the 1994 genocide in Burundi and Rwanda called for some more decisive and authoritative action by the church and that maybe would be best done through a Primates' group? Those considerations certainly influenced the formation of the Anglican Communion Trust of the Archbishop of Canterbury at this time. Whatever the reasons, the effect was the ACC was left out of the loop in regard to the ordination of women issues and the organizational recommendations of *The Virginia Report*. This was despite the fact that they had originally led on the former and that they were constitutionally responsible for the latter.

However, the absence of gender issues from the agenda and resolutions of the 1999 ACC is even more astonishing. The meeting had a presentation from gay and lesbian people as part of a listening process called for at the 1998 Lambeth Conference. There is no reference in the report to the ACC by the Secretary General of the growing storm over gender issues and the subject is completely absent from their resolutions.

Even at the meeting of the ACC in September 2002 there was no resolution on this matter. The only reference is the general resolution of thanks which includes the words,

> For the informal talk organized and given by the Rt Revd Michael Ingham and panelists to members of the ACC on the decision by the Diocese of New Westminster (Anglican Province of Canada) to authorize the blessing of same-sex unions.[5]

Michael Ingham had announced that he would authorize such blessings if the synod of the Diocese agreed to them and the synod had in fact agreed to them in June 2002 three months before the meeting of the ACC in September. Why did the ACC not engage with that action? The ACC was in reality already sidelined. What should have been before the ACC was now being dealt with from Lambeth Palace. What did this mean for the ACC or for the relations between the Anglican Communion Office and Lambeth Palace? Silence was a screen to the changes taking place.

---

5. ACC, "Resolutions," no. 44.

Moreover, since the previous meeting of the ACC in 1999 Chuck Murphy and John Rodgers had been ordained in 2000 as missionary Bishops to the USA by Archbishops Kolini of Rwanda and Moses Tay of South East Asia. A year later these two Bishops ordained a further four men as Bishops to work in the USA. In 2000, the Anglican Mission in America was formed in Amsterdam as a mission to the US from Rwanda. The Bishops working in the US would be part of the House of Bishops of the Church in Rwanda. These "cross border" actions were entirely related to the conflict over the place of homosexuality in the public life of the Church; could same-sex couples be given liturgical blessings and could openly homosexual people be ordained as priest or bishop? Again, the ACC had clear actions prior to its meeting which would naturally fall within its purposes as set out in its constitution, the only properly constituted body in the Anglican Communion which had the specific approval of the Provinces. But the action had moved elsewhere by covert changes and somewhat passive acceptance.

By the meeting of the ACC in June 2005 in Nottingham in the UK the role of the ACC as commentator from the sidelines of the conflict had been completely fulfilled. Here the resolutions simply note the actions taken by the Primates and endorsed them. They agreed to the withdrawal of the US and Canadian representatives from participation in the meeting of the ACC, though they received a presentation from both Churches for which they expressed thanks but made no comment nor resolved on any action as a consequence. The Council did ask the Secretary General to allocate resources to collate responses from the Provinces on the "Listening Process" and also to provide research and study material for the next Lambeth Conference and the next meeting of the Council.

In 1990 at ACC 8, Robert Runcie, the then outgoing Archbishop of Canterbury, described the creation of the ACC as "our Communion's boldest attempt to match the need for coherence and order with the wide degree of freedom and autonomy our Provinces enjoy."[6] He had good reason to describe it in this way. The ACC had set the pace in addressing initiatives such as the ordination of women and the challenges and complexities of mission in the different provinces around the world by the terms it had set for the first IATDC.[7] The ACC constitution had won the support of the provinces and had brought together lay, clerical, and

---

6. ACC, *Broken World*, 32.
7. ACC and IATDC, *For the Sake of the Kingdom*.

episcopal representatives from the provinces in a new and constructive way.

But step by step after 1990 the ACC became marginalized in the vital institutional issues that concerned relations between the Provinces in the Anglican Communion. Even the question of the ordination of women was taken over by others and the sexuality issue hardly ever hit the agenda. Why this happened is hard to know. But it might help to observe how and by whom these issues were dealt with in the period from 1990 to 2005. The ordination of women proceeded in the various provinces at their own local pace. Hong Kong acted in 1971, but nothing more happened until the "uncanonical" ordinations in the US in 1974 and 1975, which were regularized by the General Convention of the Episcopal Church in 1976. Ordinations proceeded slowly in other places thereafter. The question before the Anglican Communion was how to manage the disagreements amongst the provinces on this, disagreement that amounted to serious conflict over the ordination of women as Bishops. The process of managing that conflict was handled by the Eames Commission, which had been established by the Archbishop of Canterbury on the basis of a resolution at the 1988 Lambeth Conference. It was officially named The Archbishop of Canterbury's Commission on Unity and Women in the Episcopate.

The issue of gender relations in the public life of the Church became a more serious conflict in the Communion and it was handled in its most recent form by the Archbishop of Canterbury in response to a meeting of the Primates. That action was not taken until 2003 in response to two things. First, liturgical blessings for gay couples were authorized for use in the Diocese of New Westminster in the same week in which the Primates' meeting was taking place in Brazil in May 2003. Secondly Gene Robinson, a man in an openly homosexual relationship, was nominated to be the diocesan Bishop of New Hampshire in June 2003. The General Convention in The Episcopal Church confirmed this nomination and the Archbishop of Canterbury called an emergency meeting of Primates in October 2003 to address this development. Following that meeting the Archbishop of Canterbury created The Lambeth Commission on Communion. The commission was to report within the year in preparation for the ensuing meetings of the Primates and the ACC. The Commission was to look at various forms of episcopal oversight and especially the possibility of a role for the Archbishop of Canterbury within provinces other than his own. The Windsor Report was published in October 2004.

It is interesting to note the terms of the statement issued by the Primates in October 2003. They appeal to a resolution of the 1998 Lambeth Conference calling for a greater role for the Archbishop of Canterbury as the basis for their request to the Archbishop to establish a commission for that purpose and add to the terms of reference matters arising from recent developments. The mandate of the commission accurately reflects these questions. However, in doing this they make two important claims. In taking these steps they are:

> As Primates of our Communion seeking to exercise the "enhanced responsibility" entrusted to us by successive Lambeth Conferences. Secondly, we also re-affirm the resolutions made by the Bishops of the Anglican Communion gathered at the Lambeth Conference in 1998 on issues of human sexuality as having moral force and commanding the respect of the Communion as its present position on these issues. . . . Therefore, as a body we deeply regret the actions of the Diocese of New Westminster and The Episcopal Church (USA) which appear to a number of provinces to have short-circuited that process, and could be perceived to alter unilaterally the teaching of the Anglican Communion on this issue. They do not. Whilst we recognize the juridical autonomy of each province in our Communion, the mutual interdependence of the provinces means that none has authority unilaterally to substitute an alternative teaching as if it were the teaching of the entire Anglican Communion.[8]

This is really a new doctrine of the role of the Lambeth Conference and of the Primates' meeting. The idea that the Lambeth Conference could declare the definitive teaching of the Anglican Communion is entirely novel, and to suggest, as this claim does, that it could restrict the capacity, juridical or otherwise, of provinces to declare the belief of that Church flies in the face of the constitutional arrangements in most of the provinces of the Anglican Communion. They are entirely correct to say that the actions in North America do not change the teaching of the Anglican Communion. What the Anglican Communion believes is only what is embedded in the constitution of the ACC, since that is the only document that has been agreed by all the provinces. Some political observers saw this communiqué as a grab for power. It is certainly a novel institutional move that purports to empower a group within the Communion to

---

8. "A Statement by the Primates," no. 5.

do things as if they were institutionally warranted when in fact they were not. It is certainly a form of creep by a group within the Communion to enhance their own power. The Primates' actions do suggest some institutional panic in the face of serious conflict. In the rush of that panic the only properly constituted body in the Anglican Communion, the ACC, was swept aside to the role of commentator from the sidelines. Not only was the ACC the only body properly constituted by the provinces it was also the only conciliar body with elected representatives from the provinces, of bishops, clergy and lay people.

The Windsor Report went in due course to the Primates meeting in February 2005. In general, they encouraged the direction of the report, though they were cautious of any development of the role of the Archbishop of Canterbury "which would seem to imply the creation of an international jurisdiction which could override our proper provincial autonomy."[9] They asked the Archbishop of Canterbury to establish "a panel of reference to supervise the adequacy of pastoral provisions made by any Churches" where there were "groups in serious theological dispute with their diocesan Bishop." At the same time, they committed themselves "neither to encourage nor to initiate cross-boundary interventions."[10] There are serious contradictions in all this. The Primates want to protest the autonomy of their provinces which are territorially defined and within which the province holds the juridical role. They also asked the Churches in Canada and the US to voluntarily withdraw from the Anglican Communion bodies and also to attend the meeting of the ACC with a presentation of their position. If provincial autonomy and integrity are significant ecclesiological principles, why did they not recommend some appropriate discipline for those bishops who were clearly violating those principles by setting up alternative jurisdictions in other provinces. On the contrary this group was given the merest slap on the wrist, in reality an effective green light to continue and the churches in the US and Canada were purportedly administered a discipline they could not exercise without contradicting their own ecclesial principles. They therefore asked one group to voluntarily adopt some "apparently disciplinary" steps themselves. This is not principled ecclesial formulation. It is just politics.

9. The Anglican Communion, "Primates' Meeting," no. 10.
10. The Anglican Communion, "Primates' Meeting," no. 15.

In March 2005, the Joint Standing Committee of the Primates meeting and the ACC asked for a document on the preparation of a covenant. The ACC meeting two months later noted and endorsed the decisions of the Primates at their meeting earlier in the year. In May the following year the Joint Standing Committee decided to establish a covenant design group. The Archbishop of Canterbury appointed the Covenant Design Group in May 2006.

At its meeting in June 2005 the ACC changed the membership of the Council to include Primates as the Episcopal members of the ACC, subject to the approval of two thirds of the Provinces. The Council also agreed to refer to the Archbishop of Canterbury as a focus of unity rather than an instrument of unity. We notice again that the ACC meeting comes at the end of the procession of meetings and endorses what others have already decided.

But at this meeting there was little movement on these organizational matters—or are they really power issues? The ACC Standing Committee is to include the five members of the executive of the Primates meeting, the ACC Chair and Vice Chair and six others. They also ask for a meeting of the ACC Standing Committee to meet at the same time as and with some joint sessions with the Primates. It was hard at the time not to think of these amalgamations as a one sided affair with the Primates gaining more power in the organization of the communion. The organizations of the Anglican Communion were already highly clericalized. These changes increased that trend and, not surprisingly, within the ACC itself there was a modest push back from lay people with proposals for voting by orders, and special meetings for the lay members.

The ACC did not meet again until June 2009, presumably because of the Lambeth Conference in 2008. However, the Primates did meet in February 2007 and made some extraordinary and almost certainly canonically illegal, demands of the bishops of The Episcopal Church. Not surprisingly their demands were not met. The Lambeth Conference of 2008 was an altogether different affair and the Global Anglican Future Conference (GAFCON) came and went.[11] The Primates met again in February 2009 and repented of their previous offensive behavior and conducted themselves with becoming restraint. A note of humility crept into their meeting. In terms of action on the homosexuality conflicts they say,

---

11. See Kaye, *Conflict*.

> We affirm the recommendation of the Windsor Continuation Group that work will need to be done to develop the Instruments of Communion and the Anglican Covenant. With the Windsor Continuation Group, we encourage the Archbishop of Canterbury, the Anglican Consultative Council and the Anglican Communion Office to proceed with this work.[12]

They are not appointing their own group and they want to work with the ACC. The ACC 14 met in Kingston Jamaica in June 2009. It is noteworthy that on the Windsor Continuation Group's report the ACC affirmed its recommendations and encouraged the Archbishop of Canterbury to work with the ACC Standing Committee and the Secretary General to further the recommendations of the group. In relation to the latest version of the covenant (Ridley Draft) there was a good deal of complicated debate focused on section four which contained material on organizational sanctions and levels of membership. In the end, the ACC thanked the group for their work and

> b. recognises that an Anglican Communion Covenant may provide an effective means to strengthen and promote our common life as a Communion;
>
> c. asks the Archbishop of Canterbury, in consultation with the Secretary General, to appoint a small working group to consider and consult with the Provinces on Section 4 and its possible revision, and to report to the next meeting of the Standing Committee;
>
> d. asks the Standing Committee, at that meeting, to approve a final form of Section 4;
>
> e. asks the Secretary General to send the revised Ridley Cambridge Text, at that time, only to the member Churches of the Anglican Consultative Council for consideration and decision on acceptance or adoption by them as The Anglican Communion Covenant;
>
> f. asks those member Churches to report to ACC 15 on the progress made in the processes of response to, and acceptance or adoption of the covenant.[13]

---

12. Primates Meeting Communique, "Anglican Communion News Service," sec. 11.

13. ACC, "Resolutions of ACC - 14."

What is noteworthy here is that the ACC has taken charge of the action on this matter. Its Standing Committee will approve the final form of Section 4 and the Secretary General will send it to the provinces for consideration and adoption. Of course, in one sense the ACC is the provinces' body. It is made up of their elected representatives and it would be astounding if they were not the body to handle this aspect of this matter. But the manner of these resolutions of the ACC is a return to an earlier phase. These are not resolutions from the sidelines, or commentary on the actions already taken by others.

In the years leading up to this situation there have been new noises coming from the organizational groups in the Anglican Communion. If 1998 marked the embarrassing nadir of the Lambeth Conference, 2008 marked a return to something more like the original pattern and more attractive in terms of the professed faith of its participants. If the 2007 Primates meeting marked the bottom of the barrel of indulgence in power and hubris, the 2009 Primates meeting marked something of a resurrection to Christian humility and grace. If ACC 9 (1993) to ACC 12 (2002) marked a time of alienation and sidelining of the ACC from the action, ACC 13 (2005) marked the beginnings of a change and ACC 14 (2009) showed that change in fuller and clearer form.

How these changes have come about will fall to later historians to investigate in relation to more detailed resources than are now available. Nonetheless at this stage we can note two things. Institutions change from time to time and not always from a rediscovery of the movement's originating vision or its values but sometimes from power creep from some participants. Institutions cannot provide for every possible aspect of the life of a community. Those who inhabit the institutions must inevitably act out of discretion and judgement to respond to particular situations. If those actions are informed and shaped by the values and purposes of the community that is served by these institutions then the life of that community is enhanced and its purposes advanced. That "discretion space" also provides the opportunity for groups or individuals to take to themselves more positional power and then to consolidate their initiative into the institutional life of the movement. Poguntke and Webb[14] have pointed out that in populous democratic countries in the twentieth century there has been a general "presidentializing" of politics and thus of power. In a voluntary association like an Anglican church, or even

---

14. Poguntke and Webb, *Presidentialization*.

more in a fellowship of Anglican churches, that tendency to presidentialize power is all the more available. In this turn of the century period that tendency was well on display, particularly from the Primates.

What is at stake in the Anglican Communion is the resilient and persistent dynamics of the long standing provincial ecclesiology that is so deeply embedded in the Anglican story. Provincial autonomy is not just about local independence. It is about the primary locus of the presence of God being in the lives of Christians which, in the Anglican story, is served by the ecclesiastical arrangements. In that sense Anglicanism has no basis for thinking it might become a world church. Rather it has correctly thought of itself as a fellowship of churches and in that context has a strong tradition of provincial jurisdiction for the provision of an ordered ministry of word and sacrament.

2

Plurality and Identity in the Modern World[1]

WE LIVE IN A world of strange contradictions. On the one hand modern technology through the internet brings people together in astonishing and unprecedented ways. Yet at the same time people are diminished in their relationships because of the very nature of the technology. We see that our fully engaged three dimensional personal encounters are squeezed out in favor of two-dimensional bytes. At one and the same time we are connected in a vast and expanding plurality yet have our more immediate and coherent social identity corroded and changed. These social phenomena provide the context within which ecclesial reflection can and must take place. The issue of how plurality and connecting identity hold together is no less a question in the church than it is in the broader political life of humanity at large.

In 1996, that late and great scholar Adrian Hastings gave a series of lectures at the Queen's University in Belfast, Ireland, which were published the following year under the title *The Construction of Nationhood*. Hastings put forward a fresh and better understanding of the nation and nationalism than was available at the time in what was known as the modernist view of nationalism.[2] In broad terms that view contended that nationalism grew during the course of the eighteenth century within the framework of the new nation state. On the contrary, said Hastings, nationalism can be found coming to a high point in England in the late sixteenth century. He portrayed England, though he sometimes refers to Britain, as being the prototype of the nation and nation state.

---

1. An earlier version of this essay appeared as Kaye, "Plurality."
2. The view was mainly represented by Gellner, *Nations*; Hobsbawm, *Nationalism*.

He envisaged nationhood emerging out of one or more ethnicities.[3] Nation he said "is a far more self-conscious community than an ethnicity."[4] A "nation possesses or claims the right to political identity and autonomy as a people, together with the control of specific territory." "A nation-state is a state which identifies itself with one specific nation."[5]

Hastings makes a further point about the way in which peoples become communities, ethnicities, states, and nations. "By far the most important and widely present factor in this process is an extensively used vernacular literature."

> Some may be disturbed by the idea that, in a sense, texts can produce peoples. But there is really no alternative. A community, political, religious, or whatever, is essentially a creation of human communication and it is only to be expected that the form of the communication will determine the character of the community.[6]

The nation-state was not the only political form that Hastings thought was available in the modern world. Hastings extends his argument that Britain pioneered the nation-state; it also pioneered the non-national world empire. While France's empire was conceived, if unrealistically, as an extension of its nation-state, Britain's was not. That does not make it less modern. Indeed it may be the political reality of Britain's global empire which looks in another fifty years' time more like the real prototype of the political structuring of modernity.[7]

This conception of the British Empire as non-national was highlighted to me when I was visiting the Anglican Province of the Indian Ocean to speak at its General Synod in 2002. I arrived first in Mauritius as the guest of the Anglican bishop, Ian Ernest. Mauritius was probably first discovered as an uninhabited island by Arab sailors in the tenth century. A recorded discovery was made by Portuguese sailors in 1507. It had been controlled by the French from 1715 to 1810 when it was taken over by the British on terms that allowed French settlers to keep their property and use the French language. The law of France was to be used in civil and criminal matters. It became independent in 1962 and a

---

3. Hastings, *Construction of Nationhood*, 2.
4. Hastings, *Construction of Nationhood*, 3.
5. Hastings, *Construction of Nationhood*, 3.
6. Hastings, *Construction of Nationhood*, 20.
7. Hastings, *Construction of Nationhood*, 6–7.

republic in 1992. Today the population is a mixture of Indian, African, Chinese, French and English ethnicities. Despite one hundred and fifty years of British control less than 8 percent of the population are Anglicans while 24 percent are Roman Catholic, 17 percent Muslim and 48 percent Hindu. Mauritius is now an independent nation-state fully cognizant of its plurality and a growing national identity.

The General Synod was to be held on the small island of Reunion about 270 kilometers south west of Mauritius. Reunion was first claimed by France in 1638 and has remained in French control ever since, apart from a brief period during the Napoleonic wars. It is now an overseas Department of the French Republic and elects representatives to the National Assembly in Paris. The language is French and the public institutions are all French. It is part of France. The contrast with Mauritius could hardly be greater. The Republic of France retained its connection with the former colony of Reunion by incorporating it into the metropolitan nation-state. The former colony of Britain became an independent entity with a working mixed national identity.

This pattern is similar, or at least analogous, to the constitutional incorporation of former "colonial" or mission dioceses into The Episcopal Church in the United States of America. These churches constitute Province Nine in The Episcopal Church.[8] They send representatives to the General Convention and are in many respects like the overseas departments of the French Republic. It is a very different pattern from that found in the overseas Anglican churches from the time of the British Empire. What Hilary Carey has recently said in relation to settler churches generally in the British Empire is true also of the Anglican churches, despite lingering nostalgia in some quarters. "Yet, the Christian churches of the settler empire were, eventually, both nationalized and internationalized. In the former colonies, they acquired organizations and religious characteristics that increasingly owed less to empire and more to rising nations, with their independent legislatures and constitutions, into which they had been planted."[9]

Inevitably within a larger society that is held together by institutional structures or shared social habits, the accommodation, even cultivation, of diversity within that society can create significant political

---

8. "Province Nine. The Ninth Province shall consist of the Dioceses of this Church in Colombia, the Dominican Republic, Ecuador, Honduras, Puerto Rico, and Venezuela." Episcopal Church, *Constitution and Canons*, Canon 9, p. 42.

9. Carey, *God's Empire*, 380.

and relationship problems. The vast movement of people across the globe and across the borders of nation-states during the course of the twentieth century has left many nation states much more diverse and multicultural than they were at the beginning of the century. That pattern is likely to continue. The experiments in a government policy of multiculturalism in Canada, the United States and Australia illustrate how the diversity can be shaped differently in different circumstances.[10] There are other examples of different patterns of empire. The relationship between the Roman Senate in the period of the republic was quite mixed and more like a traditional Roman client relationship. In the period of the empire this changed and provinces were more controlled directly by Rome.

In 1995, just after I had become General Secretary of the Anglican Church of Australia, I had the opportunity to take afternoon tea with the vicar of Littlemore in the diocese of Oxford in England. I had read most of the publications of the Revd David Nicholls and it was therefore with great anticipation that I knocked on his front door and spent an enchanting afternoon amongst his books listening to his ruminations on politics and the church. David Nicholls was an historian and political scientist, a graduate of the London School of Economics and Cambridge University. He taught in the University of West Indies in Trinidad and returned to Oxford to continue teaching. He had written extensively on pluralism and the book I had found the most interesting was *The Pluralist State*. The book deals with the political ideas of John Neville Figgis and his contemporaries. In the book Nicholls reports favorably on Figgis's suggestion that the principal bulwarks against ecclesiastical tyranny were "the devolution of power and decision-making to small groups within the church, and the ultimate supremacy of conscience. 'Within the Catholic society let there be groups as many as you will' he declared."[11] This neatly expresses David Nicholls' concerns with the way in which plurality within the church is fundamental to its life and health as indeed it is to human society generally.

As Benedict Anderson[12] has rightly pointed out, there are many other nations or communities besides those housed in nation-states. Besides those more ethnically shaped communities discussed by Anderson we may note, in a slightly different key, the nation state characteristics of

---

10. See Lopez, *Origins of Multiculturalism*.
11. Figgis, *Hopes for English Religion*, 120, quoted in Nicholls, *State*, 95.
12. Anderson, *Imagined Communities*.

the great trading companies in the empire period such as the Dutch East India Company and the East India Company.[13] The business corporation, either in its local form or as a multi-national enterprise, as an example of such a nation or community. How the modern business corporation is structured has been debated in a long and extensive literature with views ranging from the multiunit hierarchical model of Alfred Chandler Jr.[14] to the more open-ended flexible circular network model of David Limerick.[15] To a large extent the design of such an institutional arrangement depends upon the founding circumstances and the purpose for which the enterprise exists. Non-government organizations that provide services in all parts of the world similarly are designed in ways that represent their origins and their purposes. Activist groups such as Greenpeace also shape their structure in order to achieve the purposes for which they exist. Community groups within society are similarly shaped in order to relate effectively to the wider society in which they operate and the purposes for which they exist.

These are matters that arise in the human condition. They not only form an important part of the context within which the church lives and operates, they inevitably influence the way in which Christians are able to think about the life and structure of their ecclesial communities.

This is the more so for Anglicans who have such a distinctive and powerful heritage of the church in relation to the state. The long centuries when Anglicanism was the religion of the English state have inevitably left their mark for both good and ill upon Anglican sentiment. But Adrian Hastings is correct in pointing to the fact that Anglican churches born outside the English state soon found that they could not replicate the precise structures of the relationships with the state that existed for the Church of England. This became very apparent after the American War of Independence when Episcopalians sought to put together a constitution for themselves in the light of the new political arrangements that pertained in their land. They could not establish their church on the basis of a church state relationship such as they remembered from England. Yet, in a bold experiment in contextualization and in principle not too distant from the establishment thinking in Anglican England, they established for themselves a constitution that in many respects mimicked

---

13. See the recent discussion in Dalrymple and Fraser, *The Anarchy*; Phillips and Sharman, *Outsourcing Empire*.

14. Chandler, *The Visible Hand*; Chandler and Daems, *Managerial Hierarchies*.

15. Limerick, "Shape of the New Organisation."

the constitution of the new American Republic. The particular character of the constitution of the Anglican Church in Nigeria similarly shows the influence of local social political and cultural forces. The same is true in the Anglican Church of Australia. When constitutions for dioceses were established, they reflected the independent political attitudes which prevailed in the different colonies in Australia at that time.[16]

These questions of innovation and continuity have become strikingly important in the last fifteen years for relations between Anglican churches scattered around the world. Various international institutional arrangements have been tried and are regularly changed. In recent times some of these institutional arrangements have been called "Instruments of Unity," though other arrangements and institutions continue without this kind of special designation. The question before Anglicans around the world, not only within their own provinces, but also in relations between these churches, is therefore not unprecedented either in the way in which Christians have thought about the political life of humanity at large or the way in which Anglicans have thought about the institutionality of their Christian communities.

How that institutionality is shaped has a great deal to do with both the character of that community and the purpose for which it exists. The character of the community is not adequately defined by its being made up of Christian people who subscribe to certain doctrines. Rather the function and character envisaged for the actual relationships involved is what defines the community. There is a world of difference between the Evangelical Fellowship in the Anglican Communion (EFAC) and The Anglican Church in North America (ACNA). EFAC is a voluntary society of individuals who join together to promote activities such as bursaries, newsletters and conferences, in support of their evangelical point of view. ACNA presents itself as a Province of dioceses, networks and clusters (regional or affinity based). Its constitution provides for a Provincial Council, the appointment of an Archbishop and a range of other things which make it clear that what has been established is an ecclesiastical structure to provide a disciplined ministry of word and sacraments. In other words, it is a church, indeed an Anglican church.[17] The doctrinal commitments they make simply tells us what kind of a church this is. What makes it a church is what it sets out to do.

16. See Kaye, *Introduction to World Anglicanism*.
17. See ACNA, "Constitution and Canons."

Within the mainstream Anglican ecclesial pattern there are clearly different patterns of relationships at different places in the community. The structure of the organizational arrangements will depend upon what kind of community those structures are designed to serve and in relation to what purpose. The purpose in a parish might, for example, be taken from the terms of the ordinal. The purpose of the ministry within the parish is to bring the community to maturity of Christian life and faith.[18] That is a different purpose from what is properly espoused by, for example, a church welfare organization. It is also necessarily different from the purpose for which a diocese exists and significantly different again from the purpose of the more scattered community of a province.

So the question for Anglican churches around the world in the present circumstances has a great deal to do with what we think that "imagined community" of Anglican churches around the world actually is and the purpose for which it exists. The way in which plurality lives with some degree of identity will be an important aspect of that question. Generally speaking, the diocese sustains an appropriate and disciplined ministry of Word and Sacrament in the parishes and takes jurisdictional responsibility for the clergy for that purpose. In most provinces jurisdictional responsibility for bishops is taken by the provincial structures. Each step in this movement from parish to diocese to province to national church to Anglican Communion envisages different institutional arrangements that are appropriate to the purpose of each entity and the different relationships each supports. The questions at stake are fundamentally relational in character rather than jurisdictionally determined.

Adrian Hasting's reference to the texts that create communities and shape the character of the nation applies a fortiori to the church. However, the texts of the New Testament do not provide blueprints for the specifics of our present arrangements or the particularity of our present challenges, even though they do address some of those things for their own day. Paul's letters are mostly aimed at the moral and behavioral character of the Christian communities to which he writes. The practical arrangements for the life of the community are not much dealt with. How the Christians behave towards each other is critical and similarly

---

18. I have in mind here the exhortations in the ordination services in the 1662 Book of Common Prayer, a document that is embedded in most Provincial constitutions. Later Anglican prayer books have tended to substitute this description of the goal of the ministry with a job description of the clergy somewhat in the style of modern employment arrangements.

how they live generally in a way that is recognizably Christian. His letters really offer an insight into the formation of what a Christian community might reasonably look like and how Christians should live in the circumstances to which they were addressed. A key question is how, in both individual and community relations, these Christians can live in a manner appropriate to their Christian character. In that, Jesus warning was apt: "By this shall all know that you are my disciples, if you love one another" (John 13:35), repeated in a different form by Tertullian, "See, they say, how they love one another."[19] Love exists and prospers in diversity as well as adversity and is often corrupted in uniformity. The much spoken of quest for unity in the church is fraught with ambiguity and misconception. What is central is that we love one another and display the moral qualities of this love as seen in Christ.[20]

---

19. Tertullian, *Apology*, 39.
20. For a fuller exposition of this theme see Kaye, *Colonial Religion*.

3

Orthodox Anglicans and Catholicity[1]

WHEN BASIL GEORGE MITCHELL died on the 23rd of June 2011, English academic life and Christians generally lost one of the most important voices of the twentieth century in public philosophy. Just a few years after he became Nolloth Professor of Christian Religion at the University of Oxford in 1968 he went to Durham in the north of England to give a lecture in the university. His predecessor at Oxford, Ian Ramsey, was then the bishop of Durham. These were heady times for the public profession of Christian faith. Ramsey had contributed extensively to the debates on science and religion and the nature of religious language. Mitchell wrote on politics and law and the place of Christian faith in a secular society. In the wider community secularization was popularly thought to be coming to its fulfilment[2] and for Anglicans in England their pattern of faith seemed to be particularly old hat. Student unrest had arrived from France and Germany in 1969 and in a form that engaged even the generally conservative theological students. The debate often polarized and older academics were dismissed as simply "not getting it." Institution was challenged in the name of community and rationality challenged in the name of experience.

Mitchell's lecture was entitled *How to Play Theological Ping-Pong*.[3] The lecture was packed out and I attended not only as a keen ping-pong

1. An earlier version of this essay appeared as Kaye, "Orthodox Anglicans."

2. See the analyses of Brown, *The Death of Christian Britain*; McLeod, *Religious Crisis*.

3. It was later published as Mitchell, *Theological Ping-Pong*. John Heywood Thomas, who taught Philosophy in the Department of Theology, was present at the lecture and gave the subsequent published form a favorable review.

player (in the more literal sense of using a ball and bat at a table) but also as a recently appointed Tutor and Lecturer in New Testament. Mitchell took to task the manner of public debate on theological matters. You could win an argument by showing that your opponent's position was fatally flawed on the assumption that therefore by default your own position was established. Mitchell's point was that such a binary picture of argument about theological issues was not just naïve generally but that it seriously misrepresented the complex nature of the subject. There needed to be a more serious presentation. Underlying his sometimes satirical, but consistently entertaining lecture, was another point, namely, that there was a serious conversation going on in academic and church circles and that conversation should be given more attention than was contained in the popular public debate.

This rather simple point could easily be applied to a number of phases in public life. Complex issues are difficult to represent in a popular mass media environment. Mitchell was addressing a vital issue in the understanding and practice of Christian faith in a social environment where plausibility assumptions were changing. In such a context where Christian identity was at stake the Christian community has a particular responsibility to foster serious conversation. In the forty years after Mitchell's Durham lecture Anglicans and also other Christian traditions such as the Copts and various Orthodox families have been facing the challenge of defining their Christian identity. Dramatic political changes, mass migration and globalization have forced these Christians to work out the terms of their identity in new and different contexts. It is a particularly difficult issue for them because their ecclesial traditions have been so enmeshed with their "home" environment, just as indeed is the case for Anglicans.[4]

The current Anglican debate about identity raised to some extent by the changing notions of gender and of appropriate relations between the sexes, has produced some interesting rhetorical moves. Some participants refer to themselves as "Orthodox Anglicans" and those with whom they disagree on this subject as "heretics." Others see the issue before Anglicans worldwide as a question of catholicity over against local independency. There are other elements in the rhetoric of the current confusions that are both interesting and warrant investigation, but these

---

4. Anglicans were confronted with this in missiological terms by the first IATDC established by the ACC, but alas the report has not been given the attention it deserves. ACC and IATDC, *For the Sake of the Kingdom*.

two seem to me to stand together in interesting ways and also appear to proceed without much attention to the serious theological conversation that is being neglected. They also raise some of the questions Basil Mitchell highlighted in the early 1970s.

At the time of Mitchell's lecture New Testament studies were at something of a turning point with the waning of the influence of Rudolf Bultmann and a move from the rather precise form critical analysis of texts in the New Testament to a consideration of the documents as a whole and the communities to which they were addressed. The diversity of approach reflected in the different gospels was just the most obvious starting point for an examination of the diversity to be uncovered in the New Testament generally. This was the time of redaction criticism in the gospels and of the rhetoric to be found in the letters of Paul. The issue became not so much whether particular documents were written by Paul as to the different ways in which he expressed himself in writing to different communities. The great conflict between Judaism and Christianity, made so prominent in the nineteenth century by F. C. Baur, was now widened to see other conflicts and diversity within the New Testament. Writing on Romans presents a classic example of the different ways of reading a particular text which might or might not have been written out of a knowledge of the conditions in Rome.[5]

As a young New Testament lecturer these issues claimed my attention and Mitchell's lecture crystallized a set of questions that was both disturbing and challenging. The challenge was focused sharply by the publication of Walter Bauer's *Orthodoxy and Heresy in Earliest Christianity* in 1971 in the US and in 1972 in the UK. Bauer had published this work first in Germany in 1934, but it gained little notice in the politically preoccupied Germany of the time. It was reissued in German in 1964, but it caught the flow of the times in 1972 in the Anglo-Saxon world not least because it challenged a traditional view of the authority on which Christianity was based.

During the nineteenth century the reliability of the text of the Bible had been questioned where the assumption had been that Christianity was founded on reliable historical events reported in historically reliable texts. Bauer addressed a different question. He challenged the idea, long held in Christianity, that authentic Christianity was that taught by Jesus

---

5. The classic text in this movement had been originally published in German in 1930. Schweitzer tried to overcome the problems with a radically Lutheran interpretation of Paul generally and of Romans in particular.

to the apostles and then passed on by the apostles and embedded in the New Testament. Divergence from this original norm came later and was construed in varying degrees as heresy over against the originating orthodoxy. This was how to construe orthodoxy and heresy. Bauer claimed that this picture was a later construction and served the purposes of the emerging institutional church.[6] He proposed looking at both sides of the argument without prejudice as to which side "won" the argument within the church. Bauer did not deal with the New Testament material but rather later documents and those areas of the ancient world not covered by the New Testament material.

It was inevitable that these questions of orthodoxy and heresy should be taken up by New Testament scholars, though the issue was discussed in the more open ended terms of diversity and unity. While the New Testament guild of scholars could reasonably see this task in descriptive and analytical terms, the task itself and its results created a significant set of theological issues. If the text of the New Testament did not speak univocally, and if the differences were not simply different ways of putting something, but rather ways of putting something different, then the role of the New Testament as a classic text of authority in Christian faith became a serious theological question. A collection of texts seen as coherent and displaying a high level of detailed agreement could more easily be thought to provide a more or less univocal authority. In the context of demonstrable and significant diversity within the New Testament collection of texts such a univocal authority was less available.

The establishment of a canon of scripture turns out not to provide an authoritative coherent notion of authority but rather the identification of the character of earliest Christianity marked by diversity and conflict. On a broader theological perspective any serious reflection on the extraordinary notion of incarnation and the promise of divine presence through the Holy Spirit might well have suggested a more nuanced and complex sense of authority in Christian faith and practice rather than simply a univocal text. The diversity embedded in the New Testament turns out to point to a richer and more theologically integrated notion of orthodoxy and its companion heresy.

The year before he was elected as Archbishop of Canterbury Rowan Williams contributed a paper on "Defining Heresy" to a collection of essays on *The Origins of Christendom in the West*. He notes the early use of

---

6. This has clear echoes of D. F. Strauss. See Kaye, "D. F. Strauss and the European Theological Tradition," 172–93.

the Greek term *haeresis* to mean simply a faction or a party and then, referring to the work of Walter Bauer, goes on to refute, as Bauer had done, the older picture of "Christian history as the record of a single coherent belief community from which dissident groups broke away because they believed different things."[7] On the contrary he claims that "the history of the early Christian period suggests less a pattern of primitive ideological protest against a clearly defined orthodoxy than a story of the gradual fragmentation of communities originally rather loosely defined as far as commonly accepted belief goes."[8]

While theological uniformity was slow to develop, the tendency to reject varieties of Gnostic teaching was clear very early. Moreover deviant behavior was more likely to concern these networked Christian communities. This issue becomes more important when "traditional markers of identity have been challenged or destroyed."[9] Williams instances the fall of Jerusalem and the destruction of the Temple as just such an example of this challenge. The great achievement of Tannaitic Judaism was to give an enduring way of dealing with identity beyond this great tragedy and thereby to sustain a future for Judaism. The disappearing use of the 1662 Book of Common Prayer by Anglicans is another occasion of boundary uncertainty and identity disorientation. Thus concludes Williams "This is how *haeresis* turns into heresy: when a sectional interest or emphasis offends against hardening criteria of belonging, particularly in a period of general disorientation."[10]

Williams envisages a process whereby at the end of the first century a number of groups associating themselves with the name of Jesus felt the need to develop closer and tighter criteria for belonging. They have circulated texts and traditions and they seem to be marked by practices of baptism and Eucharist. Anxiety about boundaries arises because of pressure from the state and the need to identify the terms of communication between the groups. So a cluster of practices emerged; sharing martyrdom stories, criteria to discern legitimacy of travelling teachers, testing prophets. In all of this "increasing significance is given to the role of tangible links with the history of Jesus and to the idea of a *universal* interpretation of the traditions about Jesus that can be applied from community

---

7. Williams, "Defining Heresy," 316.
8. Williams, "Defining Heresy," 316.
9. Williams, "Defining Heresy," 319.
10. Williams, "Defining Heresy," 320.

to community across (and beyond) the Roman world."[11] There are some, notably Gnostics, who fall outside this growing "catholic" network and they become increasingly regarded as aliens.

At this point Williams pauses to make a crucial point for his argument. Embedded in the Christian foundations is a dynamic of disruption. Jesus comes to announce the kingdom of God, not to repristinate the faith of ancient Israel. Fulfilling the law involves both continuity and also what turns out to be revolutionary discontinuity. "Christianity is self-consciously both innovative and universalistic; that is to say, it is aware of beginning in a rupture from existing systems of meaning, and it moves consistently and rapidly away from any localized, ethnic or political criteria for belonging."[12] "In short, Christianity is fundamentally disruptive of preexisting forms of religious meaning and social belonging. . . . The generative moment of Christian language and practice is one of dissonance and difficulty."[13]

Making this point enables him to show that the same question about discontinuity and continuity applies to those who became heretics and those who did not. The emerging "catholic" network of recognition did not escape this foundational element in Christian faith; indeed this very fact became a serious challenge in the process of institutionalization already beginning in the so called "catholic" network.

That process in the course of the third and fourth centuries turned out to involve the creation of a sense of recomposing the world in an ordered and Christian way. So, continuity between old and new covenant, creator and redeemer, become key themes in the rerunning of the arguments of the second century in a new phase in which Christianity was coming to terms with the world as it was. In this context the emerging institutions of Christianity, particularly the *regula fidei* and the sacramental system, were strong enough to cope with divisions that appeared not to be based on fundamental difference of belief. One could live with schism, but not heresy. Heresy was "whatever pushes Christian speech over from its precarious balance into a rhetoric of cosmic fragmentation."[14]

On the basis of this analysis Williams sees the ongoing task as tied necessarily to the disruptive character in Christianity itself. It has to do

---

11. Williams, "Defining Heresy," 321.
12. Williams, "Defining Heresy," 322.
13. Williams, "Defining Heresy," 323.
14. Williams, "Defining Heresy," 334.

with power and "securing the authority of Christian leadership" and this is important because of the anxieties that inevitably lie within a community "that is self-consciously challenging the prevailing norms of meaning and coherence in the social and cosmic environment."[15]

> The actual Christian "norm" is not so much in the steady overcoming of all this in a fully reconciled metaphysic, as in the continuing labor of engagement between the disruptive narrative and the conventions making for historical intelligibility—the institutionally positive aspects that make it possible to see the act of God in Jesus as fulfilling as well as overthrowing, aspects such as ministerial validation and succession, iconography, sacramental theologies and so on.[16]

Added to this Williams claims that the peculiar form of the intellectual life of western Christendom has been of intensifying disunity and skepticism.

This is a powerful analysis that provides the basis for an approach to Christian mission which takes seriously the eschatology embedded in the foundation of Christianity and recognizes the inevitable processes of institutionalization at work in any community that exists over time and has to come to terms with generational transmission.

However it seems to me that there are some things missing in the story. Institutional development in earliest Christianity can be seen within the New Testament documents themselves not only through the pattern of handing on traditions received from others but also in the patterns of church life reflected in Paul's letters and in such things as the passing on of his "ways." The association of the narrative of Jesus' last supper with his disciples with the disorderly fellowship meals in Corinth has the effect not only of providing a rationale for more seemly order, but also of establishing a link between the meals and an aspect of Jesus' story. The general emergence of the institutions of ordered ministry and the practices of baptism and commensality in remembrance of Jesus' death, each seen eventually as sacramental activities, took place over a significantly longer period of time and in different ways and in different places.

The idea of a select list of Christian documents is first referred to in a second century document, but the final form of the process in anything like a canon of agreed texts takes several centuries to appear and gain

---

15. Williams, "Defining Heresy," 334.
16. Williams, "Defining Heresy," 335.

general acceptance. These institutions of sacrament and associated offices of ministry and a canon only develop in the context of increasing inter-local connection. The situation seems to me to be more complex and multi-faceted than Williams' suggestion that the development of notions of identity and heresy and associated doctrines that "mirrored the mechanisms of episcopal authority."[17]

Missing also from this analysis is the influence of the social structures of contemporary society in the formation and apprehension of emerging institutionalities in Christianity. Not the least important in this process was the adoption of Christianity as the religion of the empire and the reflex effect which this had on Christian institutional perceptions, not least conceptions of authority and power.[18] Anglicans are not without experience in this phenomenon. We can see it in the changing patterns of ecclesiastical relations with political powers from Wilfrid through Alfred, Lanfranc and others to the Tudor Royal Supremacy and the emergence in the twentieth century of stages of quasi democratic models in the Church of England. Outside England the process is more clearly visible in the post-independence Episcopal Church in the USA with a constitution that is virtually a mirror image of the new Federal Constitution of the USA, or the Westminster Parliamentary style of synods that emerged in former British colonies such as South Africa, Canada, Aotearoa New Zealand, and Australia. Making these comparisons does not denigrate the point in relation to the early church, but it does point to the contextual character of the modelling that emerged from this interaction and the essentially contingent character of these institutions.

In this context it seems to me that Latin Christendom left a heritage in the modern world that characteristically sees the holy in the church in primarily institutional terms. One can see this most acutely in the papal claims to exclusive representation of Christ from Gregory VII up to the present via Vatican I. It is also visible in the debates about the validity of ministerial orders that marked a good deal of Anglican Roman Catholic relations in the nineteenth and early part of the twentieth century.

Rowan Williams helpfully refers to iconography and the Greek Christological debates of the seventh and eighth centuries which seem to me to present an alternative to Western institutionality that is more vernacular in its conception of the divine presence and resonates with

---

17. Williams, "Defining Heresy," 313.

18. There is a wide literature on this. For a recent account see Rieger, *Christ & Empire*.

aspects of lay authority which dominated the first millennium of English Christianity and is still found in Anglicanism.

Williams' article, emphasized by these comments, shows clearly that notions of orthodoxy are not simply about bodies of doctrine that can be regarded as normative in all places at all times. Heresy has ecclesial connotations which require engagement with some sense of catholicity. Such a catholicity would provide for a dynamic interaction between the various locals that go to make up that network of churches that has emerged in history from English Christianity and that go by the name of Anglican.[19]

Claiming the title "orthodox" or "catholic" in the present uncertain times of Anglicanism seems to point to something like the kind of theological ping-pong to which Basil Mitchell objected so long ago even though in a different context. In Mitchell's terms the game probably begs too many questions to be helpful in the formation of any future ecclesial shape for Anglican churches around the world. Whatever the supposed rhetorical value of the language of "orthodox" it does not really advance the needed conversation beyond a Mitchell style game of ping-pong. A sad aspect of the emergence of this usage is that it reflects something of the character of the debate as it is actually conducted. It suggests a trend to rhetoric and assertion rather than argument and engagement. From a church that professes Jesus Christ something better is surely to be expected.

---

19. See the use of this idea in IATDC, *Communion, Conflict, and Hope*.

4

Reality and Form in Catholicity[1]

THE WORD "CATHOLIC" HAS had a varied and often controversial history in Anglicanism. Its ordinary English sense is that of general and universal. One sees this historically in the growing medical literature of the seventeenth century in relation to cures or treatments that are said to be generally or universally applicable. Of course, it had a specific application to Western Christianity after the Great Schism in 1054 when the Eastern churches generally became known as Orthodox and the Western as Catholic. At the time of the Reformation in England catholic was somewhat self-consciously used to mean all Christians in distinction from those churches under the jurisdiction of the Church of Rome. Elizabeth's injunctions in 1559 stated: "You shall pray for Christes Holy Catholique church, that is, for the whole congregation of Christian people dispersed throughout the whole worlde, and especially for the Church of England and Ireland." Similar usage is retained in the 1662 Book of Common Prayer. More convoluted usages appear in the nineteenth century in the context of the Oxford movement and the ritualist controversies. This phase has influenced current usage.

The term is used by Anglicans to refer to a particular tradition within Anglicanism and it thus became a sub group demarcating term. This is a loss, since catholicity properly belongs as a vital element in the life of the church. Two elements are worth recovering. First, the idea that the local church belongs to a wider fellowship as part of its vital life of faith. The second element is that the wider church, whether within a specific

---

1. An earlier version of this essay appeared as Kaye, "Reality and Form."

tradition like Anglicanism or more generally, represents the reality of Christian life in the inter-relation of local churches with others.

A brief narrative of these themes might help us to see how the reality to which catholicity refers relates to the infinitely varied form of organizations by which it has been facilitated.

The word "catholic" does not occur in the New Testament at all yet it was a word commonly available at the time of the writing of the New Testament documents. J. B. Lightfoot drew attention to other examples of the use of the word to describe something that is general or universal, all encompassing, the whole.[2] Ignatius's letter to the Smyrneans (8.2), probably written about AD 134 is the first use of the term in a Christian document.[3] "Wherever the bishop appears let the congregation [*plēthos*] be present; just as wherever Jesus Christ is, there is the whole church [*katholikē ekklēsia*]." Lightfoot points out that the meaning in this text is of the general or universal church as opposed to a particular body of Christians, a meaning that is obviously required by the context. The bishop, Ignatius argues, is the focus for each individual church as Jesus Christ is the focus of the universal church. Clearly in this letter the argument is directed to the group of dissenters in Smyrna who were arguing for a more docetic understanding of Christ. Cyril of Jerusalem uses the term in a similar way when he claims the church is denominated "catholic because it is spread throughout the whole world from one end to the other."[4] But in the latter part of the second century the term "catholic" began to be used to designate what was sometimes called the "Great Church" in contrast to the heretical sects against which the churches were reacting. Similarly, as apostolic texts were being collected into a canon of recognized texts, a New Testament, one criterion was that the texts were those received by the Catholic Church, that is the generality of Christian churches. We can see this formulation in the earliest such list of texts in the Muratorian fragment which probably dates from the second half of the second century. The use of the term "catholic" in early church creeds appears only in the fourth century and, according to J. N. D. Kelly, it retained in many cases the simple meaning of all Christians scattered throughout the world.[5]

2. Lightfoot, *Apostolic Fathers*, II, 310.
3. Lightfoot, *Apostolic Fathers*, II, 310–11.
4. Cyril, *Catechetical Lectures*, 18.2, cited in Lightfoot, *Apostolic Fathers*, II, 310.
5. Kelly, *Early Christian Creeds*, 385–86.

But this "Great Church" itself is a reasonably loose-limbed affair especially in the East. There were priests and many congregations and we know there was a church building in Edessa in AD 201 because it is mentioned in an account of a flooding tragedy in that year recorded in the Chronicle of Edessa.[6] However, we have no text before the end of the second century that refers to a bishop[7] and "it is difficult to prove the historic existence of ruling bishops in Eastern Syria and Mesopotamia before the year 300."[8] In 401 Isaac was elected Catholicos, a term roughly equivalent to Patriarch, and in a synod in the same year the creed of Nicaea was adopted on the suggestion of a visiting Western bishop, Marutha. They also agreed on some organizational matters: one bishop per diocese, consecration by three other bishops and dates for major festivals of the Christian year. The synod went on to agree twenty one canons on church order using Western examples but adapting them to local Eastern needs.

The Eastern churches were demonstrating friendly independence from the west.[9] A later synod (AD 424) called by Catholicos Dadyeshua, included six metropolitans and thirty bishops from Persia and set the tone of the independence of the Eastern church and its relations with the West:

> By the Word of God we define: that Easterners cannot complain against their patriarch to western patriarchs; that every case that cannot be settled in his presence must await the judgment of Christ [and] on no grounds whatever can one think or say that the Catholicos of the East can be judged by those who are below him, or by a patriarch equal to him; he himself must be the judge all those beneath him, and he can be judged only by Christ who has chosen him, elevated him and placed him at the head of his church.[10]

This declaration focused on jurisdictional issues and was aimed at retaining integrity of the Eastern church both internally and in relations with the West.

So the "Great Church" did not have a unified coherent organization as might be suggested by the narrow Western historiography which

---

6. Moffett, *Christianity in Asia*, 58.
7. Moffett, *Christianity in Asia*, 59.
8. Moffett, *Christianity in Asia*, 118.
9. Moffett, *Christianity in Asia*, 155–57.
10. Moffett, *Christianity in Asia*, 162.

Eusebius did so much to shape, not least with an heroic focus on the emperor Constantine as protector of that church.[11] Philip Jenkins has recently drawn attention to the narrow scope of this Western-focused historiography of early Christianity.[12] Much later in the middle of the fifth century Christianity was split across the whole known world by the Arian and Nestorian disputes. The Eastern churches remained Nestorian long after the Council of Chalcedon, which was supposed to have settled matters.

These inter-relationships in the early centuries of Christianity illustrate clearly how the identification of catholicity with definition and jurisdiction meant that the understanding of catholicity in the sense of mutual interdependence became ambiguous. The notion was further complicated after the Arab invasions of the Mediterranean world in the seventh and eighth centuries. These invasions meant that many Christians came to live under a Moslem Caliphate. Christians in Syria, Palestine, North Africa and Spain, where churches were not obliterated, found themselves having to live under very different political constraints. In this context the notion of a "Great Church" as being the single and coherent repository of orthodoxy became extremely difficult to sustain. Peter Brown points out that in this period many Christendoms could be found in the northern perimeter of Europe including in Britain, each with their own traditions and sense of identity.[13]

The political landscape of Western Europe was changed dramatically by these Arab invasions. Fragmentation was apparent on all sides and the capital of the "Roman Empire," Constantinople, was besieged by Arab forces. In the West, by the end of the eighth century, the Frankish rule under Charlemagne had extended its reach over most of Europe. Charlemagne had halted the Arab invaders at the Pyrenees. Gradually what appeared to be a new hegemony began to emerge in Western Europe, namely the rule of Charlemagne. But this was a different kind of empire from that to which ancient Christianity had so conveniently accommodated.

---

11. See the discussion in Herrin, *Formation of Christendom*.

12. Jenkins, *Lost History*.

13. Peter Brown treats this material in both editions of his work *Western Christendom*. The second edition was significantly revised and the chapters reorganized. The material relevant to this paragraph appears at different points in the two editions as follows: Brown, *Western Christendom* (1996), ch. 13; Brown, *Western Christendom* (2013), chs. 14–16.

When Pope Leo crowned Charlemagne in Rome as emperor, the event was full of complications and ambiguity.[14] Divers interests were at stake and these differences, as they came together in the event in Rome on Christmas Day AD 800, illustrate the changing character of the politics of late antiquity in Europe and the role of the church in these changes. Charlemagne as the central figure came with a number of concerns. This pious man saw his rule as in succession to that of the kings of the Old Testament and his rule as being legitimated by his judging justly. That is to say it was the quality of his rule rather than the consequences of his conquests that gave his kingship its integrity. He disliked the Byzantium habit of treating him simply as a king who had conquered rather than as a king with a divine and providential heritage of action. Charlemagne saw himself as a collegial ruler alongside the Byzantium emperors rather than a mere rex of derivative dignity.

He had political advisers in his capital Aachen who were more brutally realistic and saw him as an Emperor in the Roman tradition since he had sway over all the old centers of rule of the Roman emperors. The English scholar, Alcuin, on the other hand, was active in the affairs of the court of Charlemagne and saw him as the protector of a Western Christendom. In 800, Pope Leo was preoccupied with his own position in Rome and in fear of threats to his own position. In different ways the coronation served these interests in large part by its very ambiguity. Leo gained Charlemagne as protector because he had crowned him and Charlemagne himself found recognition on a par with the emperor in the East.

But the central issue of what the coronation actually recognized in the West remained unresolved. Over what kind of empire was Charlemagne emperor and thus what kind of emperor was he? Alongside this, and for our purposes here, the equally important question was what kind of Christendom was signified. Peter Münz puts it this way:

> what was the meaning of the "Empire" thus founded by a Christian city of God, a new universal Roman Empire, a mere rival to Byzantium, a Frankish overlordship, or a simple dominion over the city of Rome. It seems to me that all attempts to explain what the "Empire" was, are based upon the fallacy of misplaced concreteness for they assume that the "Empire" then established existed apart from the mind and intentions of the people who established it and that it had a meaning over and above that

---

14. I am indebted in this analysis to the important essay of Peter Münz on this issue: Münz, *Carolingian Empire*.

imputed to it by the people concerned. By itself, the "Empire" had no existence, and therefore no meaning.¹⁵

It seems to me that Peter Münz somewhat overstates the point here. It is not that it had no meaning. It did not represent an existent and visible empire, but it did provide a basis for the different parties involved to claim roles for themselves and others in the ongoing political and ecclesiastical development of this new Western and European phase. We might today call the coronation a rhetorical reality that provided a basis for understanding the present in multivalent ways and for shaping the future in different ways according to the interests of different parties. This coronation really marks the beginning of the Western Christendom which in due course was an important element in shaping the transition of Europe from late antiquity to early modernity.¹⁶

Robert Markus pointed to the end of the sixth and the beginning of the seventh centuries as marking the end of an epoch he called "Ancient Christianity." This turning point marked the "end of the Western Empire and its fragmentation into the barbarian kingdoms of Europe."¹⁷ Charlemagne's coronation in 800 marked the beginning of a move to the formation of Western Christendom shaped by the very different kind of hegemony of Charlemagne and inbuilt different interests and centers of power, not least those of the Pope.

In many respects the new Christendom of Western Europe which emerged on these foundations was less coherent politically than Constantine's empire. The character of ecclesiastical life as seen in the papacy of Gregory the Great (590–604) contrasts importantly with the vastly more extensive institutional shape of the Roman church during the papacy of Gregory VII (1073–84). This contrast shows how far things were able to move institutionally for both church and politics in Western Europe. In time this new Western Holy Roman Empire disintegrated as political life was shaped by the emergence of the nation state. On the other hand, the international reach and character of the Roman Church was consolidated, pursuing where it could the vision of Gregory VII and

---

15. Münz, *Carolingian Empire*, vii.

16. For a consideration of the Muslim and Arab influence in relation to commercial practices and institutions see Heck, *Charlemagne*.

17. Markus, *Ancient Christianity*, xiii.

Innocent III in which the Pope was seen as the successor of Peter and the representative of Christ on earth.[18]

Similar changes can be seen at work in the experience of the English Church. On the one hand there was national consolidation and acceptance of the idea of the nation and its national church as being self-sufficient. The recitals of the Henrican legislation in the sixteenth century represent simply an extreme example of a process which had begun eight hundred years before.

We can see this nicely expressed in the contest between King William I, aided by his archbishop Lanfranc, and Pope Gregory VII. Gregory was in trouble politically with the Holy Roman Emperor. The Pope sought financial support from William and also a declaration of fealty. William's reply is brief and to the point. In a letter probably written in 1080, he reports that he had been asked to pay the back amounts of Peter's pence and "to profess allegiance to you and your successors." He will pay Peter's pence because while he had been away the collection had been slack. However, "I have not consented to pay fealty, nor will I now, because I never promised it, nor do I find that my predecessors ever paid it to your predecessors." He goes on to say in the best diplomatic terms that "it is our most earnest desire above all things to love you most sincerely, and to hear you most obediently."[19]

It is remarkable how William has entirely declined the terms in which Gregory put his case. Peter's pence is not a feudal obligation. It is help. Fealty is a question of tradition and it fails altogether on that score. "We long to hear you obediently" but, by implication, this means that we need to hear you in terms and on assumptions that are appropriate to the tradition of our relationship. William will have nothing of Gregory's revolutionary papal empire.

This correspondence between William and the Pope illustrates a significant distinction between a respectful relationship and a jurisdictional one. William accepts respect and fellowship and indeed is willing to pay back payments of Peter's pence, but he will not give fealty to the Pope. That is to say he will not submit himself as a Christian king of a Christian country to the jurisdiction of the Pope.

In British Christianity, the antecedents of what could later be called Anglicanism, the political entanglement of the church with the state

---

18. For an elaboration of this aspect of Gregory VII's approach Cowdrey, *Pope Gregory VII*.

19. Douglas and Greenaway, *Historical Documents*, Doc. 101.

has been a central issue for well over a thousand years. As the political framework has changed over the centuries so the conception of what is an appropriate entanglement for Anglican Christianity has had to adjust. It has been a mixed story. Indeed, it could not have been otherwise. For in its own national tradition this Anglican Christianity must of necessity relate to the society and politics within which it lives out its Christian and ecclesial life. What is thinkable in one century may not be thinkable in another. The domestic imperialism of the Tudors shaped the understanding of the nature of ecclesiastical polity at the time of the Reformation. Even such a resourceful theologian as Richard Hooker could not get his mind beyond a national horizon to a universal sense of the church with which there might be some kind of interdependent relationships.

This long and ambiguous narrative illustrates very well that institutional arrangements can shape interdependence of the kind we find in the earliest days of Christianity for both good and ill. The issue is not that there must be a certain form for these interdependent relationships but that the reality of the relationships and the attitudes of the local church are the keys. It is not the existence of a single great church to which others relate and on which they depend. Rather it is the universality of the Gospel which expresses itself in different circumstances and creates an ecclesial life in those local circumstances which needs the influence of catholic interdependence for its prospering and faithfulness.

In other words, catholicity is a dynamic of church life that is necessarily local. It contradicts the autonomy of the life of faith of a church in a particular locality. Rowan Williams has consistently over the years made this very point in his appeal for the enhancement of the life of the Anglican Communion. He returned to it in his 2011 Christmas letter to Primates in the Anglican Communion.

> Throughout the time of my service as Archbishop I have tried to keep before my own eyes and those of the Communion the warnings given by St Paul about the risks of saying "I have no need of you" to any other who seeks to serve Jesus Christ as a member of His Body. I make no apology for repeating this point. Advent is a good time to recall that we all live in imperfect churches, that we all must draw together in hope for the fuller presence of Our Lord, and that we all therefore must be willing to receive from each other whatever gifts God has to give through them.[20]

---

20. Williams, *Letter to Anglican Primates*, no. 11.

This theme can be found in the report of the first IATDC, *For the Sake of the Gospel*, and was revisited in the last report of the IATDC, *Communion, Conflict, and Hope*. Under the heading of dynamic catholicity the recent report states, "From the first, the local church has had a catholic dimension; it relates to the wider body of churches in space and time. Without such relationship it cannot function healthily as a local church."[21]

This kind of catholicity contradicts the autonomy of the life of faith of any particular church in Anglicanism. That means any particular parish, diocese or province. It assists the gift of faithfulness in the diversity of locals that need other locals in order to nourish and sustain the life of Christian faith in their own local church, parish, diocese, or province. The framework for this kind of catholicity in the life of the Church underlines that this life is marked by Grace—what we have we have received from God—and Humility—what others have they have also received from God. Such a conception of catholicity as interdependence inevitably entails argument as to the nature of faithfulness. Such argument is an enduring feature of such interdependent ecclesial life. Unity, in the sense of agreement on a wide front, is not the crucial issue, though from time to time it might be an outcome of the central and vital mark of church life. The central mark of faithfulness in our confession of Jesus Christ in personal and ecclesial life is the gospel virtue of love.

In this context catholicity is a quality of the life of the local church and is a vital means for the cultivation of the virtues of humility and love. Such an ecclesial insight means that any local arrangements for the cultivation of an effective catholicity should be shaped so that they promote these virtues.

The text "I have no need of you" used by Rowan Williams comes from 1 Corinthians 12 where Paul famously uses the image of a body for the life of the local Corinthian church. In that body the various parts, and the way they work together, is a metaphor for the exercising of individual contributions in the church. The church as body says that the ecclesial community does not consist of one member but of many. God, Paul says, has arranged each member of the body as he chose. So where there is one body and many members, one of those members may not say to another "I have no need of you." Towards the end of 1 Corinthians 12 Paul goes beyond this image of the body in order to indicate that there is a certain

---

21. IATDC, *Communion, Conflict, and Hope*, no. 45.

priority in the gifts that have been given by God in the church. He tells his Corinthians friends to strive for the greater or higher gifts.

Clearly the body image is one way of looking at the church, albeit a somewhat static one and he wishes to move beyond that point to make a further and more fundamental point, namely that the essential character of the church's life is the central gospel virtue of love. He says "And I will show you a still more excellent way" and thereby introduces what we know as chapter 13. In that chapter, love is what gives each of the gifts their significance, indeed their very character as gift. Love itself is also characterized as patient, kind, not envious or boastful, arrogant or rude. It does not insist on its own way; it is not irritable or resentful, it does not rejoice in wrongdoing but rejoices in the truth. Love never ends, indeed it goes beyond our final days, so he says faith, hope and love abide, but the greatest of these is love.

The unity which makes the church community a Christian community is the practice of love. The test of institutional arrangements within the church and between churches from this perspective is, will they facilitate these dynamics and virtues? If the question is will they reach agreement, then the arrangements are very likely to complicate matters and deflect the community from its more fundamental Christian vocation.

From one point of view, the peaceable kingdom of a Christian community may often look like a shambolic confusion of arguments. What makes it a peaceable kingdom is not the absence of agreement but that these Christians love each other. That is the unity which makes a church community Christian. The interdependence between churches, and indeed between Christians, is a catholicity that derives from the effectiveness of the gospel in different circumstances and it is a manifestation of the gift and grace of God. The truth of that catholicity can be seen when it produces the virtues of love and humility. To put it more bluntly, it is the reality of catholicity as mutual interdependence that matters. The form taken at any given time or place by institutional arrangements to facilitate such catholicity is secondary and variable. It is the reality that counts, not the form.

5

Anglicanism's Uncertain Apostolicity[1]

IN 2012, I WAS in the University of Southern Queensland for a conference on the history of the British World. Many of the papers were concerned with historiographical issues and addressing the different ways in which events and conflicts in the history of the British world have been handled. Quite a few were designed to challenge a received interpretation by deploying a rereading of the relevant sources and setting them in a different interpretative context. A number were concerned with Anglican issues such as the restoration, Archbishop Sheldon and witchcraft, and recasting the role of clergy in colonial New South Wales. Of course, this is very much the bread and butter work of historians as they try to make sense of the past for succeeding generations.

During the conference I had a conversation with a scientist in the university who referred to the difference as he saw it between the humanities and what he called the "hard sciences." By coincidence that was the day that the European Council for Nuclear Research (CERN) announced the identification of the Higgs Boson. The New York Times headlined "Signalling a likely end to one of the longest, most expensive searches in the history of science, physicists said Wednesday that they had discovered a new subatomic particle that looks for all the world like the Higgs boson, a key to understanding why there is diversity and life in the universe." However, it noted that some physicists were referring to

---

1. An earlier version of this essay appeared as Kaye, "Anglicanism's Uncertain Apostolicity."

a "Higgs like particle." Peter Higgs and Francois Englert were awarded a Nobel Prize in Physics for their work in this field.

The hard scientists seemed to be struggling with similar issues of certainty as the historians in the humanities. The scientists were actively canvassing the question as to whether the discovery of this "Higgs like particle" would confirm or question the standard theory of the sub-atomic world that had prevailed in scientific work for the last thirty years. The historians were debating how far the material sources being brought forward, sometimes for the first time, would challenge a prevailing theory.

In the hard sciences the absence of absolute certainty did not stop them, or us, doing things as if we were frozen in the face of a sea of uncertainty. I recall a researcher reminding a group of engineering professors at a university seminar that we did not fully understand some key aspects of the fundamental science in heavier than air flight. He also pointed out that this did not stop him flying on a jumbo jet across the very wide Pacific Ocean. The historians went home from their conference and continued to get on with their lives and their work as historians. If anything, in both cases, uncertainty prompted action and engagement rather than resignation and passivity.

My Queensland conversations prompted me to reflect on how far these issues of uncertainty and action have worked in Anglican faith and practice. There are practical every day markers of Anglican identity whose significance we can easily forget because of their familiarity. Two institutional continuities come to mind very easily in this regard; the ordained ministry and the canon of scripture. Both relate to the Anglican claim that the tradition preserves an apostolic faith. In each case there is confidence that these institutions of canon and ministerial order contribute to and secure the apostolicity of Anglican beliefs and practices. They provide a reliable connection between the faith of the apostles and succeeding generations down to the present time. On a shorter horizon that is what the hard scientist might call the received theory.

A form of the received theory on apostolicity is to be found in both Anglicanism and Roman Catholicism. The two traditions have been at odds over the theory for many centuries, more especially over the last century. There is a rich tradition of literature on this century of conflict a great deal of it prompted by currents flowing from the Anglo Catholic revival in the nineteenth century. In 1989, Paul Avis[2] provided a system-

---

2. Avis, *Anglicanism and the Christian Church*.

atic review of Anglican ecclesiology for the modern period from the sixteenth century to the present and Stephen Pickard[3] has returned to the debate in 2009 with a more thematic focus on the nature of ministry in the church. Stephen Pickard in particular draws attention to the influence of ecumenical conversations on the understanding of apostolicity as encompassing

> the whole life of the church and its "exemplified" and "embodied" in "marks" or "elements": canon of Scriptures, creeds, confessional writings, liturgies, activities of preaching, celebrating sacraments, exercising pastoral care and oversight, common life of the church, engagement in mission. Apostolicity thus encompasses faith, sacrament, ministry and service.[4]

These are interesting developments and show how interaction with other Christian traditions can influence Anglican self-understanding.[5] However here I wish to focus on several incidents in the debate between Anglicans and Roman Catholics on the particular issue of apostolicity. These incidents offer a glimpse into an interesting aspect of Anglican institutional identity.

In 1974, I had the privilege of a German Academic Exchange Fellowship in the Catholic Faculty of Theology in the University of Freiburg im Breisgau to work on the history of Roman Catholic interpretation of the New Testament. Here, I found reports of the meetings of Roman Catholic New Testament scholars. Regular biennial conferences of these scholars began in 1957 and during the 1960s the conference spread beyond Germany both in terms of its location and its membership. It came to be called *Tagung der deutschsprachigen katholischen Neutestamentler*. Each conference considered a particular theme. Reports of the meetings were usually given in the journal *Biblische Zeitschrift*. These meetings reflected the liberation of Roman Catholic biblical scholars from Papal constraints on the free investigation of the Biblical texts perceived to have been implied in the Encyclical Letter of 1895 *Providentissimus Deus* of Pope Leo XIII. This Encyclical established the Pontifical Biblical Institute and placed it in the hands of the Jesuits. In 1943, Pope Pius XII issued an Encyclical Letter *Divino afflante Spiritu, which* revisited this question. The Pope noted the major developments in scientific critical

---

3. Pickard, *Collaborative Ministry*.
4. Pickard, *Collaborative Ministry*, 196.
5. See also Cross, *Influence*.

biblical studies made mostly by Protestant scholars and encouraged the adoption of these methods by Roman Catholic scholars.[6] The result was an abundant flourishing of Catholic biblical scholarship.

A large number gathered for the 1963 meeting of the *Tagung der deutschsprachigen katholischen Neutestamentler* to discuss the Form-critical method. In 1969, the theme was Church office in the New Testament. There was vigorous debate amongst the forty people present and a wide range of views was expressed. Because the debate was inconclusive the subject was set down for the next meeting in 1971. Again, the debate was very lively but this time there was some kind of resolution. In his report Werner Bracht formulated four theses as the result of the conference.

1. The New Testament does not yet speak of church office in the later sense of permanent and legal. The office appears more as a "service function" of the church.

2. This office is Christological and based on the sending of Jesus, but it is also ecclesiastical and to be seen in combination with and in the service of the church.

3. The recognition of Paul's apostolic office is from the church, and also from his own self-understanding, which is eschatologically orientated.

4. From a purely historical point of view the New Testament shows a gap in the succession of the office of apostle, which does not allow the view of a direct succession. However, it is not possible to exclude an actual context between the later office and the original apostolic office.

These conclusions were highly controversial within the Roman Catholic Church because they clearly stood in sharp contrast to the claims made by Pope Leo XIII in 1896. Implicit in these historical conclusions are some serious questions about the character of the continuity between the ministerial order of the church and the apostles.

---

6. Pius XII, *Divino afflante Spiritu*, no. 31: "Moreover we may rightly and deservedly hope that our time also can contribute something towards the deeper and more accurate interpretation of Sacred Scripture. For not a few things, especially in matters pertaining to history, were scarcely at all or not fully explained by the commentators of past ages, since they lacked almost all the information which was needed for their clearer exposition."

Following some moves towards unity between the Church of England and the Roman Catholic Church in the late nineteenth century Pope Leo XIII initiated a consultative investigation to clarify the matter of Roman recognition of Anglican orders for priests and bishops. The conclusions were set out in a letter (*Apostolicae Curae*) from the Pope on 15 September 1896 which concluded, "We pronounce and declare that ordinations carried out according to the Anglican rite have been, and are, absolutely null and utterly void."[7]

The Letter argued this on two grounds. First that historically, with the ordinal of Edward VI, "the true Sacrament of Order as instituted by Christ lapsed, and with it the hierarchical succession." The ordinal of Edward VI was defective both in terms of form and content. It did not purport to ordain priests to celebrate the eucharist in its proper and full sense. Even the slightly amended 1662 ordinal with the addition of the words "for the office and work of a priest" did not adequately remedy the situation. Furthermore, the use of this ordinal for a long period of time meant that the apostolic succession of order had irretrievably been lost in the Church of England.

It is this latter argument to which I draw attention here. The argument arises out of a claim that the line of actual historical succession of ministry goes back from the present Pope to Christ himself. It is the certainty of that connection that makes the Pope's office effective sacramentally. Not only his office but all those whose sacramental standing relate to his in the ordered hierarchy of what is regarded in this argument as the one true Church.

The following year the two English archbishops, Frederick Temple and William MacLagan published a reply entitled *Saepius Officio*.[8] The appeal made by the archbishops to the apostolic tradition in sections 18 and 19 makes two things quite clear.

The fundamental appeal is to "the Lord and his apostles." "'Our Fathers' fundamental principle was to refer everything to the authority of the Lord, revealed in the Holy Scriptures" (Section 18). They claim the English ordinal "expresses more clearly and faithfully those things which by Christ's institution belong to the nature of the priesthood and the effect of the Catholic rites used in the Universal Church" (Section 19). They conclude with a revealing and trenchant comment "We also gladly

---

7. Leo XIII, *Apostolicae curae*, no. 36.
8. Church of England, *Saepius Officio*.

declare that there is much in his (Pope Leo XIII) own person that is worthy of love and reverence. But that error, which is inveterate in the Roman communion, of substituting the visible head for the invisible Christ, will rob his good words of any fruit of peace" (Section 20).

There was of course a lot going on in the background and the exchange grew out of conversations about the possibility of some rapprochement between the two traditions.

Almost exactly one hundred years later Pope John Paul II issued in 1998 a personal letter changing certain elements of canon law. Canon 750, paragraph 1, stated that the faithful are to believe those truths set out in the Word of God and "at the same time proposed as divinely revealed"[9] by the solemn or ordinary magisterium, that is to say the Pope. At the same time the Congregation for the Doctrine of the Faith issued a commentary written by then Cardinal Ratzinger in which he identified some of the doctrines that were to be regarded as divinely revealed under this heading. He included in his list the letter of Pope Leo XIII *Apostolicae curae*, which had declared Anglican orders null and void.[10]

The publication of this commentary without any prior notice caused some ruffling of feathers in the ecumenical nest, but in fact it simply restated what had clearly been the case since 1895. It showed with the utmost clarity that the certainty of the Roman Catholic Church's apostolicity relied on the historical continuity from Peter to the Pope, and that the order of bishops went back to the apostles in continuous succession.

Throughout the last century the Roman Catholic Church has remained consistent in its conception of the nature and basis of the apostolicity of its ministry and gospel. It is not as if this was a matter that

---

9. John Paul II, *Ad tuendam fidem*, Canon 750 § 1: "Those things are to be believed by divine and catholic faith which are contained in the word of God as it has been written or handed down by tradition, that is, in the single deposit of faith entrusted to the Church, and which are at the same time proposed as divinely revealed either by the solemn Magisterium of the Church, or by its ordinary and universal Magisterium, which in fact is manifested by the common adherence of Christ's faithful under the guidance of the sacred Magisterium. All are therefore bound to avoid any contrary doctrines."

10. Congregation for the Doctrine of the Faith, *Profession of Faith*, no. 11: "With regard to those truths connected to revelation by historical necessity and which are to be held definitively, but are not able to be declared as divinely revealed, the following examples can be given: the legitimacy of the election of the Supreme Pontiff or of the celebration of an ecumenical council, the canonizations of saints (*dogmatic facts*), the declaration of Pope Leo XIII in the Apostolic Letter *Apostolicae Curae* on the invalidity of Anglican ordinations."

concerned only theologians and ecclesiastical bureaucrats in Rome or Canterbury. It was an issue felt in the far reaches of each of the traditions.

For example these self-same conflicts were felt in the distant colony of New South Wales nearly sixty years earlier. William Grant Broughton, the high church bishop of Australia, found himself fending off criticism of the status of his episcopal orders from local Roman Catholics. He was accused of being simply a tool of the government and that his authority arose from his relationship to the crown and the force of his Letters Patent. Broughton determined to demonstrate the error of these criticisms. To do that he needed a territory not under British sovereignty where the jurisdiction of his Letters Patent did not apply. A window of opportunity appeared for him in relation to New Zealand.

In 1837, William Hobson had been sent from Sydney to protect settlers in the Bay of Islands in New Zealand. He returned and recommended New Zealand be brought under the jurisdiction of the British crown. This was a matter of considerable interest and discussion in Sydney. On December 13, 1838, Broughton sailed for New Zealand to visit Church Missionary Society missionaries in the Bay of Islands. In doing so he preempted William Hobson's return visit in 1840 as the government representative to negotiate with the Maoris an acceptance of British sovereignty.

In response to a welcome address from the missionaries Broughton declared,

> For myself, my brethren, I come among you without other commission or authority than that which being first lodged with the Apostles, is derived in succession from themselves to everyone rightfully and canonically consecrated to the episcopal charge. Whatsoever directive functions I may exercise here are traced to no other origin than this; and your acceptance of me in that character is an unconstrained purely spiritual act.[11] In this I rejoice, as it may have the effect of rendering more apparent the true apostolical foundation, constitution and character of this blessed Church of England, to which we all belong.[12]

---

[11]. Many years before Broughton had made use of such a distinction in explaining the authority of the New Testament documents. On the influence of Herbert Marsh and Broughton's historical approach see Kaye, *Colonial Religion*, ch. 1.

[12]. Address of the Lord Bishop of Australia, 5 January 1839. British Library Add MS c n/o 13A/3.

Within the year Broughton found he had to respond to Tract 90 from the Oxford revivalists, which had become available in the colony. In his charge to the clergy of New South Wales in October 1841 he dwelt at considerable length on the apostolic foundations of the ministerial order of the Church of England. On the one hand he declared that this ministerial order should not be deprecated, but on the other hand it should not be made the subject of too inordinate claims. The strongest affirmation of the apostolic character of the ministerial order should not lead to the conclusion that there is "no validity in any divine ordinance administered by mere laymen, or by such as do not partake of that successional appointment to the ministry."[13]

Broughton in colonial New South Wales, the Pope in Rome and the Archbishops in England were all struggling with the same underlying question. On what basis can there be certainty about the apostolic character of the contemporary ministerial order of the church, or more generally the identity of a particular church. How and in what way can Anglicans be said to have an apostolic faith?

Somewhat in the same spirit as Bishop Broughton, J. B. Lightfoot in his famous essay on the ministry published in 1868 as a separate essay in his commentary on Paul's letter to the Philippians, drives to the same conclusion, though in somewhat more pointed terms.[14] Like Broughton, Lightfoot was responding to what he referred to as the sacerdotal interpretation of the ministry. Of the eighty-eight pages of the essay he devotes twenty-five pages to what he describes as "one of the most striking and important phenomenon in the history of the Church."[15]

He opens the essay with a powerful statement of what he calls an ideal that needs constantly to be kept in mind.

> The Kingdom of Christ, not being a kingdom of this world, is not limited by the restrictions which fetter other societies, political or religious. It is in the fullest sense free. Comprehensive and universal. . . . Each individual member holds personal communion with the Divine Head. To Him immediately he is responsible, and from him directly he obtains pardon and draws strength.[16]

---

13. Broughton, *Charge to the Clergy*, 15.
14. Lightfoot, *Philippians*.
15. Lightfoot, *Philippians*, 244.
16. Lightfoot, *Philippians*, 181.

Nonetheless he says all human societies cannot exist over time without officers, rules or institutions. In the case of the church such rules and institutions are simply means to an end. The apostles he said waged war against "the principle which exalted the means into an end, and gave intrinsic value to subordinate aids and expedients."[17] Nonetheless the principle of a "universal priesthood, of the religious equality of all men" has "hitherto been very imperfectly apprehended; that throughout the history of the Church it has been struggling for recognition."[18]

Lightfoot then goes on to set out the origins of the threefold order of ministry. Deacons were a new order of service which spread from the Jerusalem church to gentile churches where the early Christian churches would have been regarded by contemporaries as a confraternity. Presbyters were not a new office but adopted from the synagogue, and these were also called bishops in gentile churches. These presbyters were "rulers and instructors of the congregation."[19] These two orders were "firmly and widely established" at the close of the apostolic age. He rejects the idea that bishops replaced apostles. Rather "the episcopate was formed not out of the apostolic order by localization but out of the presbyteral by elevation: and the title, which was originally common to all, came at length to be appropriated to the chief among them."[20]

Lightfoot goes out of his way to reject the view of Richard Rothe[21] that the order of bishops arose in response to the destruction of Jerusalem and thus the center of reference for the church was removed and "out of this need the Catholic Church arose." He then goes on to survey evidence from the various centers around the Mediterranean and the East to show how bishops grew out of the order of presbyters. The bishop was one presbyter set over the rest in a locality, though he remained still a presbyter.

Lightfoot's general conclusion about apostolic succession is very instructive in terms of how we imagine our connection to the apostolic beliefs and practices.

17. Lightfoot, *Philippians*, 184. Compare this to the expression used by the Archbishops of England at the conclusion of their response to Pope Leo: "But that error, which is inveterate in the Roman communion, of substituting the visible head for the invisible Christ" (Church of England, *Saepius Officio*, sec. XX).

18. Lightfoot, *Philippians*, 183.

19. Lightfoot, *Philippians*, 194.

20. Lightfoot, *Philippians*, 196.

21. Rothe, *Anfange*.

It has been seen that the institution of an episcopate must be placed as far back as the closing years of the first century, and that it cannot, without violence to historical testimony, be dissevered from the name of St John. But it has been seen also that the earliest bishops did not hold the same independent position of supremacy which was and is occupied by their later representatives.[22]

The chief causes of the emergence of bishops were the struggles with a hostile society and of conflict within the church about the gospel. He examined three key representatives of the development from the end of the first century, Ignatius, Irenaeus, and Cyprian. In regard to Ignatius he declares that the language used by him if taken literally would be "subversive to the true spirit of Christianity."[23] With Irenaeus "the episcopate is regarded now not so much as the centre of ecclesiastical unity but rather as the depository of apostolic tradition."[24]

With Cyprian we come to something quite new. "If with Ignatius the bishop is the centre of Christian unity, if with Irenaeus he is the depository of the apostolic tradition, with Cyprian he is the absolute vice-regent of Christ in things spiritual."[25]

In trying to understand the character of the relationship between the contemporary and the apostolic age, that is to say, the apostolicity of the Church of England, Lightfoot puts the whole matter under a wholly contingent heading. The ministerial arrangements are part of the pragmatically required arrangements for the life of the church. Those arrangements never take any precedence over the ideal he set out at the beginning. The historical origins of the threefold order led to a very early and approximate historical connection with Jesus.[26] The threefold ministerial order in his understanding is apostolic in the sense that it serves the apostolic ideal of the church and also that it can be traced historically back very close to the apostolic age. The first reason means that the

22. Lightfoot, *Philippians*, 234.
23. Lightfoot, *Philippians*, 237.
24. Lightfoot, *Philippians*, 239.
25. Lightfoot, *Philippians*, 240. It is interesting to note that Broughton in Australia had been working on a translation of Cyprian's *Epistle to Rogation concerning a Deacon Who Had Set Himself in Opposition to His Diocesan*. He unsuccessfully appealed to Cyprian in the bishops' conference of 1850 in their discussion of the relationship between a bishop and a synod. See Shaw, *Patriarch and Patriot*, 238.
26. See further Kaye and Treloar, "Lightfoot and New Testament Interpretation"; Kaye and Treloar, "Lightfoot on Strauss."

second, historical continuity, cannot have any determinative force on the main question. On this reading the apostolicity of the ministerial order of Anglicans based on continuous historical connection, is thus not absolutely certain, even though it is of very ancient pedigree.

Lightfoot is making a clear distinction between those things which stand secure and certain, such as the ideal of the church he sets out at the beginning of his essay. On the other hand there are those arrangements in church life like the ministerial order he describes which exist for practical reasons to serve the fundamental ideal of the church as a community of people who belong to Christ's kingdom which is not of this world.

Both these episodes, Lightfoot and Broughton, occurred in the nineteenth century in the context of the influence of the Oxford revival led by Newman and others, and in particular their appeal to the bishops of the Church of England to exercise their apostolically grounded authority. Broughton had been a keen supporter of the Oxford revival. Through the late 1830s he began to doubt their extreme claims for apostolicity through episcopal orders. Tract 90 finally forced him to depart the ranks of Oxford supporters. Like the Oxford reformers Broughton found himself engrossed in the tensions of church state relations which in both cases acted as a catalyst to seeking a strengthened sense of church integrity and authority. For some this meant separation of the church from the state, and for some separation from the Church of England, usually to join the Roman Catholic Church. In colonial New South Wales Broughton saw the point of the first of these moves but could not bring himself to act systematically on it. In relation to Rome he remained a lifelong confirmed critic.

Lightfoot also was responding to the Oxford revival, but a later and different aspect of it. Similarly, Leo XIII and the Archbishops were responding to the long running currents of the Oxford movement. All three examples reveal a struggle to formulate an apostolic pedigree for Anglican ministerial orders in a time of immense social change in England and Europe and when many of these changes directly affected the institutional credibility of the church, especially the Church of England. Their task was not an easy one. Both Broughton and the Archbishops were also confronted by a Roman Catholic Church that expressed itself with increasing confidence about its institution of ministry.

The doctrinal position of the 1998 revision of canon law and the authoritative commentary of then Cardinal Ratzinger, later Pope Benedict XVI, provide a clear assertion of the universal authority of the Pope as the successor of Peter. The apostolicity of this Christian tradition is set in terms of absolute certainty by the presence of a magisterium and the confident claim of historical institutional continuity. Of course, the Roman Catholic community is too large and diverse for there not to be dissent and divergent views on this point, though this dissent is set within a very clear official confidence. Quite remarkably the conclusions of the German New Testament Scholars in 1969 very closely follow those of Lightfoot one hundred years before. More than that they place a question mark against the historical claims implicit in the Ratzinger commentary on the recent papal revision of Canon Law.

On the other hand, the apostolicity of the Anglican tradition of Christianity is set in much more contingent terms and in a different key. The approach to continuity is made through the early church up to the New Testament so that scripture is the ultimate authority for such matters.[27] The contrast with the role and status of the magisterium in the Roman Catholic tradition accentuates the more obviously contingent character of the orders of ministry in Anglican churches and their apostolicity. The historical antiquity of this ministerial order probably makes it difficult to imagine any widespread departure from this pattern in Anglicanism. The authority of the pattern is not based on some kind of tactile physical succession, but rather on the basis of a general sense of length of practice. That consideration is framed within a deeper principle that Lightfoot identified in the terms of his day, namely that the church exists as a community whose true commonwealth is "in heaven not on earth." It is reasonably clear that the apostolicity of Anglican orders of bishops priests and deacons is uncertain in the sense that it is not institutionally connected with the patterns of the apostolic period and thus, of course, with Christ himself. That does not mean it has no connection with the apostles, just not that one. More fundamentally the contingent character of these arrangements gives to them a more appropriate Christian identity in the service of Jesus' kingdom that is not of this world. They necessarily exist in order to serve a purpose beyond themselves.

Of course, institutions operating over long periods of time find it easy to consolidate themselves. Thus, by the accretion of power and initiative the orders of ministry in Anglicanism can attain a level of authority that can easily compare in practical terms with those in the Roman Catholic tradition. In such circumstances it can easily become a natural,

---

27. A good example of this method can be seen in Archbishop Cranmer's essay on the Lord's Supper in Cranmer, *Defence*.

even proper, thing for office holders to protect the institution. The recent Australian Royal Commission into Institutional Responses to Child Sexual Abuse drew attention to this phenomenon in the Anglican Church of Australia. Institutional creep is not a new thing in human societies. The Preface to the 1662 Book of Common Prayer begins with a general assertion, "There was never any thing by the wit of man so well devised, or so sure established, which in continuance of time hath not been corrupted." The Book of Common Prayer is more expansive in referring to the ceremonies in the church:

> Of such Ceremonies as be used in the Church, and have had their beginning by the institution of man, some at the first were of godly intent and purpose devised, and yet at length turned to vanity and superstition: some entered into the Church by undiscreet devotion, and such a zeal as was without knowledge; and for because they were winked at in the beginning, they grew daily to more and more abuses, which not only for their unprofitableness, but also because they have much blinded the people, and obscured the glory of God, are worthy to be cut away, and clean rejected: other there be, which although they have been devised by man, yet it is thought good to reserve them still, as well for a decent order in the Church, (for the which they were first devised) as because they pertain to edification, whereunto all things done in the Church (as the Apostle teacheth) ought to be referred.[28]

The sixteenth century authors were, of course, embarked on significant changes in church and state. The more fundamentally contingent character of the institutionality in Anglicanism has two important implications. First, it means that the dangers of creep and accretion are much greater. There is no overarching authority or office to restrain power creep or to facilitate it.[29] The rather open systems make it easy for officers of the church, principally clergy of all three orders, to exploit this openness in order to accrue advantage and power. Secondly it places more reliance on the active engagement of the whole church to sustain those values that are important to the identity of the church. This makes a dynamic emphasis on catholicity a more practically important reality in the life of the church, a point argued for by the IATDC in 2012.[30] The uncertain

---

28. Church of England, *Book of Common Prayer*, "Concerning Ceremonies."
29. Chapter 1 of this book provides an interesting example of this process.
30. See IATDC, *Communion, Conflict, and Hope*.

apostolicity of Anglicanism is in fact an institutional advantage. Not only does it point effectively to the historical origins of the faith in the life and death of Jesus of Nazareth, but it also places the active engagement of the whole church more centrally in its life and witness. It is however, a more risky pattern of ecclesiology because it leaves open possibilities for institutional creep.

6

How Can We Speak of "Canonical Scripture" Today?[1]

IN JULY 2012 A great Anglican New Testament scholar, Christopher Evans, died at the venerable age of one hundred and two. He had a long and varied church and academic life and many remember his ministry with affection and gratitude. I recall a great stir that he created in 1971, when he was professor of New Testament Studies at Kings College London. He published a collection of papers entitled *Is 'Holy Scripture' Christian? And Other Questions*. It was a book for its time. Not only did it resonate with emerging trends in biblical scholarship, but also it landed in the ferment of the "long 1960s" with its revolutionary impulses, most powerful amongst which was a revulsion against institutions of all kinds. Institutions were the guardians of the oppressive past which the young protesters wanted to put behind them. "Holy Scripture" was one such institution and so it seemed urgent to ask if this institution in the church were really Christian. In this essay I want to pursue some aspects of this question. How can the institution of the biblical canon be understood in the light of the dramatic changes that have taken place since the "long nineteen sixties" especially in the social and political location of Anglicans, and the significance of the historical particularity of the origins of Christianity?

In 2007, one of the United Kingdom's preeminent historians, Hugh McLeod published *The Religious Crisis of the 1960s*. This is one of the most important books on the contemporary crisis in Christianity in the West. McLeod goes so far as to say in relation to the period 1958–74 in

---

1. An earlier version of this essay appeared as Kaye, "How Can We Speak?"

Europe that "In the religious history of the West these years may come to be seen as marking a rupture as profound as that brought about by the Reformation."[2] He identifies three issues in the broad society that are relevant; more religious options became available, perceptions of the character of the society changed from religious to pluralist post Christian or secular, and the transmission of faith to the next generation weakened. He also highlighted internal church matters such as the reforming Second Vatican Council (1962–65). He argues that this brought Roman Catholics and other churches closer together, but at the same time divisions within churches increased largely turning on different ways of dealing with change, especially the changes going on in the wider society. This same pattern could be seen in Australia.[3]

McLeod sets this argument in the context of the decline of Christendom. Christendom, he says, "may be described as a society where there are close ties between the leaders of the church and secular elites; where the laws purport to be based on Christian principles; where, apart from certain clearly defined outside communities, everyone is assumed to be Christian; and where Christianity provides a common language, shared alike by the devout and by the religiously lukewarm."[4] I think such a kingdom or principality also acknowledged that theirs was a Christian nation. MacLeod shows that this Christendom declined in a number of stages: toleration by the state of a variety of forms of Christianity, the publication of anti-Christian ideas, and the separation of church and state. The loosening of the ties between church and society took longer and was more complex.[5]

The book investigates these matters in great detail. It was inevitably the case in such a Christendom that notions of power and authority exercised in the government of such a polity affected the way in which church institutions understood and exercised power. The very early notion of a beloved community shaped by service exercised in humility, was at first challenged by the processes of institutionalization of relationships and activity in the community. Later a more fundamental corruption occurred with the churches incorporation into the Roman Empire, and later medieval and early modern polities. In the twentieth century the

---

2. McLeod, *Religious Crisis*, 1.
3. See Hilliard, "Religious Crisis," 215–19.
4. McLeod, *Religious Crisis*, 18.
5. McLeod, *Religious Crisis*, 19.

residue of this Christendom mentality became one of the most ambiguous and corrupting forces in the assumptions of institutional church life. This has been especially so for Anglicans whose history has for such a very long time been subsumed in a Christendom embrace.

My purpose in referring to MacLeod's work is to draw attention to a curious confluence of movements in the middle of the twentieth century that has affected the question of the nature and authority of scripture for Christian people and in particular for Anglicans, and to which Christopher Evans pointed.

Deeply underlying the changing situation of the Church of England was the long slow death of the English Christendom. It is not surprising that it was taking a long time for the English Christendom to pass away for it had been the basic condition of English life for a millennium.[6] Early signs of this Christendom can be seen in Bede's description of the working relationship between Aidan, bishop of Lindisfarne (635–51) and Oswald, the king of Northumberland (634–42),[7] and institutionally more clearly in the relationship between William I and Archbishop Lanfranc in the establishment of the Anglo-Norman church settlement.[8] These relationships were not always smooth and were directly affected by the Gregorian reforms in the Papacy. Those struggles can be seen in the relationships between successive kings and archbishops, most notably between Archbishop Anselm and the kings William Rufus and Henry I[9] and then later between Thomas à Beckett and King Henry II.

The narrative of this Christendom reached its apogee in the Royal Supremacy of the Tudors with the laity in the church maintaining final control, as they had generally done throughout this English form of Christendom.[10] To this day, bishops in the Church of England swear an oath of homage to the Queen which acknowledges that the bishop holds the "Bishopric as well as the spiritualties as the temporalities therefor only of Your Majesty and for the same temporalities I do my homage presently to Your Majesty."[11] This is a kind of fossil remnant of what was once a relationship of very real power.

6. I have tried to characterize this rise and fall in Kaye, *Rise and Fall*.
7. Bede, *Ecclesiastical History* III.3–6.
8. See Cantor, *Church*; Cowdrey, *Lanfranc*, 185–205.
9. See the recent biography of Anselm in Vaughn, *Anselm*, especially chs. 4 and 6.
10. See the characterization of Cross, *Church and People*.
11. I am grateful to Dr. Colin Podmore for the text of this oath and to Bishop Christopher Hill for further information on the background and meaning of the oath.

The great disruption of the "long nineteen sixties" that McLeod describes had profound effects on the churches, including the Anglicans. After all the originating tradition of Anglicanism, the Church of England, had been the religious expression of this long running Christendom. This history has shaped the sentiment and thinking of Anglicans even though key institutional elements of the English Christendom have not survived in Anglican churches around the world, even in the Anglican churches in former British colonies.[12] In general, these churches adapted to the political framework in which they found themselves. Yet that very fact highlights the critical point that Christendom involved the investment of political power in ecclesiastical institutions and that very process had a flow on effect as to how those ecclesiastical institutions operated in the life of the Christian community and how that influenced its self-understanding.

This decline in Christendom not only affected the narrow issue of church state relations. What was changing was the complex pattern of relations between Christian organizations and the public institutions of society. In the process it also influenced the way in which authority and power in ecclesial institutions was practised and understood.

The Roman Catholic Church, with its much more concentrated institutionality, more visibly confronted, as a church, the rising modernity in Europe. Vatican I asserted its own authority, crystallized in the office of the papacy, by a declaration of Papal infallibility. More particularly in relation to Scripture Pope Leo XIII published in 1893 an encyclical *Providentissimus Deus* in which he set out guidelines for the way in which professors of sacred scripture in Roman Catholic seminaries should go about their work. They were to teach the text. He reserved a special place for the Vulgate translation and asserted that the divine writings were "free from all error."[13] He placed the teaching of scripture clearly within and subject to the official teaching of the Church. The Protestant responses to modernity have been much more variegated, though the emergence of a strong doctrine of *sola scriptura* acts as a kind of counter point to papal infallibility. In doing so it adopts similar categories of authority, even though it locates that authority differently.

However, things did not stand still. The world and the church continued to move and those movements are reflected in the encyclical of

---

12. See Strong, "Antipodean Establishment."
13. Leo XIII, *Providentissimus Deus*, no. 21.

Pius XII *Divino afflante Spiritu* published on September 30, 1943. This document was much more outward looking and confident about biblical scholarship. The Pope acknowledged the great advances made in archaeology, in linguistic studies and in the disciplines of literary criticism. He clearly signaled that it was time to go beyond the Vulgate as the single authoritative text for Roman Catholic theology. There is much stronger emphasis on the human form of the divine word in the written texts.

This encyclical opened the door for Roman Catholic biblical scholars to examine much more widely the character and form of the text of Scripture. Since the beginning of the eighteenth century Protestant scholars had engaged in much greater and more open examination of the Biblical texts in their historical and social environment. Now Roman Catholic biblical scholars engaged with their Protestant colleagues and the second half of the twentieth century witnessed an enormous flowering of Catholic Biblical scholarship.[14]

The Anglican narrative is more complicated and diffuse. At the time of the Reformation rejecting Papal authority was in the foreground of thinking and action. That the crown in England maintained its supremacy in the church was in stark contrast with the position of Roman Catholics. In the English Christendom the lay crown, evolving into other representations of the laity, stands in marked contrast to the clerical supremacy that had established itself in Roman Catholicism on the foundations of the "reforms" of Pope Gregory VII and the theology of Innocent III.

The absence of a central ecclesiastical magisterium in later Anglicanism meant that there was not that kind of institutional way of answering questions of doctrine or the nature of Christian life. Each of the Provinces or national churches in the Anglican Communion has its own constitution and canons. Within that framework there is certainly structural guidance as to what constitutes the Anglicanism of that province. Most of the provinces that belong to the Anglican Communion identify in their constitutions, in some form or other, a role for the tradition of the Church of England and many identify a role of some kind for the central documents of the seventeenth century restoration of the Church of England.[15]

---

14. See Kaye, "Recent Research."

15. There is some confusion as to what is an Anglican Province. The united churches of North India, Pakistan and South India are members of the ACC. The Anglican Communion web site also lists as provinces Bermuda, the Lusitanian Church, and the Reformed Episcopal Church of Spain.

These Articles might then attract some initial interest on the question of scripture and the canon. Article VI declares that scripture contains all that is necessary to salvation, and that what cannot be proved thereby is not to be required to be believed as an article of the Faith, or be thought necessary for salvation. This simple statement has been the subject of much interpretation from its first articulation. At least it can be said that the Articles set out the faith of the Church of England in a particular polemical context. It does not say that scripture provides everything that might be needed to decide in any or every particular question. Rather scripture contains all that is necessary to salvation. In this sense scripture has a limited role. It does not provide all the authorities that are relevant to a consideration of the Christian life. This same limited range is also in mind in Article XX on the authority of the church.

But there is more to be said of the role of scripture in the writing of the English Reformers. We can see this in Archbishop Cranmer's homily, "A Fruitful Exhortation to the Reading and Knowledge of Holy Scripture." Scripture encourages and forms the whole person, not simply the understanding of doctrine. "These books therefore ought to be much in our hands, in our eyes, in our ears, in our mouths, but most of all in our hearts."[16] He who is most inspired by the Holy Ghost will most profit. "There is nothing that more maintaineth godliness of the minds and driveth away ungodliness, than doth the continual reading or hearing of God's word, if it be joined with a godly mind and a good affection to know and follow God's will."[17] Such an engagement with scripture will move the Christian to be "daily less proud, less wrathful, less covetous, and less desirous of worldly and vain pleasures; he that daily, forsaking his old vicious life, increaseth in virtue more and more."[18] It is this instinct that drives the saturation of Cranmer's liturgy with scripture. That liturgy was designed to shape a Christian life and to form a Christian community in the Christian virtues. It did so by shaping hearts, sentiment and practice.

While this may seem at first sight to be simple and straightforward it leaves many things open that were not pressing priorities for these sixteenth century writers but which did emerge in subsequent centuries. Changing cultural and political circumstances brought to the fore issues

---

16. Cranmer, "A Fruitful Exhortation," 3.
17. Cranmer, "A Fruitful Exhortation," 5.
18. Cranmer, "A Fruitful Exhortation," 4.

such as changing notions of historical awareness and its impact on the use of biblical texts, cultural developments that changed ways of thinking, the rise of science as a default explanatory framework and the demise of the idea of a Christian society or state.[19] Such forces created disturbing questions about the nature and significance of ecclesiastical institutions.

All of these issues had been encountered by the time Anglicans came to that great "rupture" thought by Hugh McLeod to be potentially as great as that of the sixteenth century reformation. The "long nineteen sixties" witnessed widespread theological disturbance, publicly highlighted by the publication of *Honest to God* by Anglican bishop, John Robinson. Themes such as the death of God, secular theology and the new morality were on public display. The crisis of the nineteen sixties also contained a very strong current of antipathy to institutions. The institutions of the church came within this dynamic, as Hugh McLeod points out, along with other public institutions like universities. One of the central institutions in the church was the idea of a canon, an institutionally authoritative list of authoritative texts.

This was not a new question and during the first half of the twentieth century had been much discussed. A great deal of scholarship was devoted to uncovering the history of the formation of lists of texts that might be construed as scripture and of the emergence and meaning of the idea of a canon.[20] Foundational work had been done in the nineteenth century in England by the Cambridge trio Westcott, Lightfoot, and Hort. Hort produced a new critical edition of the text of the Greek New Testament and Westcott a history of the canon. Lightfoot published commentaries on the letters of St. Paul and detailed critical editions of the Apostolic Fathers.

The result of Westcott's work on the NT canon[21] and the monumental editions of the Apostolic Fathers by Lightfoot provided the backdrop for later work on the canon. One only has to look at the index of scriptural references in the Apostolic Fathers, provided by Lightfoot in each of his successive volumes, to realize the extent and range of the use of the NT texts by these later writers. It was this use that so impressed Theodore Zahn in Germany. These texts were scripture in the sense of reliable

---

19. For a useful survey of Anglican interpretation of scripture from the reformation to the present see Greer, *Anglican Approaches*.

20. See the collection of essays in McDonald and Sanders, *Canon Debate*; Metzger, *Canon*.

21. Westcott, *General Survey*.

information about Jesus and the faith of the apostles and the earliest Christians.

In the early discussion of the emergence of a canon as an "official" list of authoritative texts two alternatives shaped the debate. In Germany Theodore Zahn argued in his monumental work on the history of the canon that the canon arose as a natural outgrowth of some dynamics within the character of the Christian faith.[22] On the other hand Adolf von Harnack argued that the canon arose in response to external forces as part of a defensive self-definition.[23] He regarded the canon as the formation not so much as a list of documents read in church and regarded as "scripture," but rather as an official list of authoritative documents. This is a much more institutional and formal notion.

Recent scholarship from the middle of the twentieth century began to focus on this process in two phases. In the first instance from the earliest times Christians began to refer to certain texts as informative for an understanding of the faith. Early quotations such as those noted by Lightfoot in his edition of the Apostolic Fathers are of this kind. The early collection of gospel documents and Paul's letters reflect this activity. At stake here was the preservation of some continuity between the origins of the faith in the apostolic period and succeeding generations. This was clearly the way in which Irenaeus in the middle of the second century approached the challenge of the passing of time and the consequent loss of direct contact with the apostles and their preaching.[24] The same instinct can be seen at work in the development of early practices such as baptism and a "Lord's Supper" into more routinized institutional forms. The allied development of personnel arrangements to sustain these institutions can be seen in the emergence of ministries of order. The creation of church "practices" by Paul is but one part of the emergence of a variety of patterns in church life that can be seen as emerging institutions.[25] These institutional arrangements developed in response to local needs, growing numbers in the Christian communities and the complicating relationship with contemporary political and legal structures.

---

22. Zahn, *Geschichte*.
23. Harnack, *Origin*; Harnack, *Bible Reading*.
24. See Irenaeus, *Against Heresies*, III.1–4.
25. Kaye, *Web of Meaning*.

This process of growing institutions in early Christianity has been and is the subject of an enormous literature.[26] The toleration and then adoption of Christianity in the Roman Empire in the fourth century had a profound effect on all these developments. The tectonic shift from persecuted to privileged led to a struggle about the nature of power in the Christian communities. This was the beginning of the story of Christendom, the incorporation of the church into the power and structures of politics, in this case the Roman Empire.

Recent scholarship on the canon has sharpened the significance of this coincidence. Geoffrey Hahneman makes the dating point by distinguishing between "comments" as references to texts regarded as having authority and "collections" as gatherings of such texts and "catalogues" as "lists of scriptures with defined and established limits." This "move from collections to catalogues implies a conceptual change, a change which led to the formation of the Christian canon of scriptures."[27] There is early evidence of the use of texts as comments and also of the creation of collections of texts during the first three centuries. However, as Hanneman points out, catalogues suddenly begin to appear in the fourth century and he identifies the appearance of fifteen such catalogues by the early fifth century.[28] Clearly something was going on in the fourth century. Hahneman claims it "confirms a conceptual change in mind of the church."[29] Henry Gamble claims that "no ecumenical council in the ancient church ever ruled for the church as a whole on the question of the contents of the canon."[30] If this analysis is correct it suggests a correlation between the moves by the empire to integrate the church into its orbit and the status of these texts.

Nonetheless Eusebius was to have an important role in the identification and distribution of the New Testament texts. In 331, he was commissioned by the Emperor Constantine to prepare fifty copies of the sacred scriptures for the church in Constantinople.

---

26. For example, Campenhausen, *Ecclesiastical Authority*, and the older but still useful Hatch, *Organization*. On early Catholicism in relation to Lightfoot's unpublished lectures see Kaye, "Lightfoot and Baur."

27. Hahneman, "Muratorian Fragment," 412.

28. Hahneman, "Muratorian Fragment," 413.

29. Hahneman, "Muratorian Fragment," 413.

30. Gamble, "New Testament Canon," 291.

He reports in his history the triumph of the new Christian emperor in wiping the world clean of hatred of God.[31] At the end of the council of Nicaea in 325, Constantine urged the bishops to work for peace and they would thereby "be acting in a manner most pleasing to the supreme God, and you will confer an exceeding favor on me who am your fellow-servant."[32] In the great celebrations of the twentieth year of Constantine's reign Eusebius describes the scene of hospitality for the bishops in the imperial palace in overweening eulogistic terms. "One might have thought that a picture of Christ's kingdom was thus shadowed forth and a dream rather than a reality."[33]

Eusebius was Constantine's man and it is impossible not to observe the colonization of the bishops, and especially Eusebius, into the imperial firmament. Imperial notions of power and its institutional maintenance began to subvert the older domestic culture of the earliest Christian communities. In the nineteenth century Theodore Zahn thought the canon grew out of the internal dynamics of the church and Harnack thought of it as a response to heresy, but they both are focused on the church forces at work. This more recent work on the canon points to these changes in the context of the general colonization of the church by the empire and thus of a new way of thinking about the church and the practice of the faith.

By the fourth and fifth centuries, when the canon had a more precisely institutional authority, it had more determinedly contemporary and political significance. That transformation of the notion of scripture is thus seen as part of the authority of the developing institutional shape of the Christian communities underwritten by their engagement with the institutions of the wider society especially the authority of the Emperor as patron of the church. The formalization of an institutionally authoritative canon thus becomes part of the emergence of the Constantinian Christendom.

This mid twentieth century reconstruction of the emergence and nature of the canon fell gently in the good soil of the "long 1960s." The impact of the reworking of the history and character of the canon in twentieth century scholarship also collided in mid twentieth century with a recognition of diversity within the canon itself. This was not a new

---

31. Eusebius, *History*, 10.9.7. For a recent defense of Constantine see Leithart, *Defending Constantine*.

32. Eusebius, *Life of Constantine*, 3.12.

33. Eusebius, *Life of Constantine*, 3.15.

issue. It is reflected in Tatian's second century attempt to harmonize the differences and eliminate contradictions. The so-called canons of Eusebius of Caesarea (265–340) numbered the sections of the gospels and set out the differences and similarities in parallel columns of numbers corresponding to those in the margin of the text. The much later Muratorian fragment contains a comment on the four gospels. "And therefore, though various ideas are taught in the several books of the Gospels, yet it makes no difference to the faith of believers, since by one sovereign Spirit all things are declared in all of them."[34]

In modern scholarship the differences between the gospels was the driving question that led David F. Strauss to highlight differences in the resurrection accounts of the gospels His was essentially an attempt to show the continuity between the historical Jesus and the post resurrection Christ of faith.[35] However the modern form of this question focused on conflict and diversity within the earliest Christian communities generally. These themes can be seen in the work of F. C. Baur in Tubingen and J. B. Lightfoot in Cambridge. Lightfoot's commentaries on Paul's letters are a masterful elaboration of his sense of history as the increasing purpose of God.[36] Lightfoot was very aware of the conflicts in the church of his own day and his publications on early Christianity were written with a sharp consciousness of those conflicts. Indeed, he relates those conflicts to the conflicts to be found among the early Christians. He ends his essay on "St. Paul and the Three," in which he is obviously criticizing Baur, with a contemporary reference. "However great may be the theological differences and religious animosities of our own time, they are far surpassed in magnitude by the distractions of an age which, closing our eyes to facts, we are apt to invest with an ideal excellence."[37] Curiously his recognition of this conflicted character of early Christianity was not much noticed elsewhere during the nineteenth century.

However, in the middle of the twentieth century the question of conflict and diversity came decisively back on to the agenda. The English translation of Walter Bauer's radical new look on heresy in the early church gave prominence to that move. He attacked the idea that heresy was a corruption of a primary pure gospel. Christianity in its earliest

---

34. Gallagher and Meade, *Biblical Canon*, 179.
35. Kaye, "D. F. Strauss."
36. See the comprehensive treatment of this Lightfoot theme in Treloar, *Lightfoot*.
37. Lightfoot, *Galatians*, 374. See also Kaye, "Lightfoot and Baur," 216.

form simply displays significant diversity. His book was first published in Germany in 1934 and disappeared from notice in the political turmoil of that decade. It was republished in a new edition in 1964 and an English translation followed in 1971.

This thesis also fell into the rich "good soil" of the "long nineteen sixties" and immediately led to a rash of literature dealing with diversity and unity in the New Testament.[38] Close attention to linguistic usage and rhetorical style in Paul's letters had revealed a significant flexibility of expression.[39] Now it was clear that not only were things in the New Testament being expressed differently, different things were being expressed. This turn in New Testament scholarship seriously undercut the idea of "canonical scripture" representing a unity of thought and practice. The elemental diversity in earliest Christianity identified by Bauer came back to center stage just when the history of the canon was being reexamined in a volatile cultural context.

The idea that the canon of scripture could be seen as a coherent whole that spoke with one voice in the tones of a church-given authority now ran into serious intellectual trouble. That process was given force by the cultural changes in western societies described by Hugh McLeod. This was a more significant problem for Roman Catholics whose notion of the canon was more directly tied to their institutional center of authority in the magisterium. Anglicans, without such a central institutional arrangement of authority, were less tied, and perhaps more at sea in this situation. It is thus not surprising that theologians in this period asked how then might the Bible be used in Christian faith and practice. David Kelsey in the United States and Dennis Nineham in England were prominent exponents of the issue.[40]

In Basel the Swedish scholar, Bo Reicke, contributed to this discussion in a brief essay titled "Unity and Diversity in New Testament Theology." Reicke puts his finger on something simple and rather obvious.

> There is no question that all of the New Testament writings concern themselves with the *same Jesus Christ*, with the same events connected with him and their consequences.... Here is found the answer to the question concerning the unity of the New Testament message. The study of the content of the new Testament lies in the central idea of, the Christ—event. Because

38. For example, Dunn, *Unity and Diversity*.
39. See Witherington and Hyatt, *Romans*; Kaye, "To the Romans and Others."
40. Kelsey, *Uses of Scripture*; Nineham, *Use and Abuse of Bible*.

> the writings of the New Testament concern themselves without deviation with Jesus Christ, directly and immediately with the events connected with him, with the proclamation by him and about him, the unity of the content of the New Testament is given.[41]

The individual writers speak out of their own condition and context. The thing that is overwhelmingly important to them is the subject, Jesus. This is what is fundamental and different ways of telling this are simply varieties of experience and knowledge. The texts were created to point to and to inform or remind people about this Jesus. They are signposts to the Christ event.

The study of the history of the canon in both the nineteenth and mid twentieth century shows up the canon as a list of historically reliable documents for an insight into the life of the earliest Christians and marks that diverse and often conflictual life as a paradigm for subsequent generations. The great crisis of the "long nineteen sixties" has brought to bear cultural forces which, from the standpoint of cultural and political institutions, move in the opposite direction to those of the fifth century, which gave us a canon as an institutionally authoritative list of institutionally authoritative texts. That authority had been enmeshed in the political power of Constantine's imperial Christendom. The contemporary passing of Christendom, sharply highlighted by the crisis of the "long nineteen sixties," is having the effect of reversing the character of the political and cultural trends seen at the birth of the first Christendom and of shedding some of the tacit notions of authority and power embedded in that and subsequent empires. That is the cultural moment in which renewed study of the New testament forced a rethinking of the canon.

It was in this context that Christopher Evans had published his book *Is 'Holy Scripture' Christian?* This is not to suggest that such rethinking has not happened before. The understanding of Christianity as fundamentally created and shaped by the historical, particular and human presence of God in the person of Jesus has always been the magnet to draw us back to that historical reality. Of course the way back for the earliest Christians was different from Christians located in different cultures and places thousands of years later. When the Thirty Nine Articles describe scripture as containing whatever you need to be saved, they point

---

41. Reicke, "Unity and Diversity," 174–75.

to the originating events of Christianity in the person of Jesus who is the only really ultimate or fundamental authority for a knowledge of God.

The earliest Christians shaped their lives in ways that are not entirely available to later generations. Of course they were the first generation from the Christ event, but there is a considerable difference between the first and the one hundredth generation. In an introductory volume to a new series of commentaries on the New Testament the highly respected Anglican scholar, C. F. D. Moule published what was to become a very influential book, *The Birth of the New Testament*. After treating a wide range of issues, he concluded with a picture of how that early generation gained guidance about how to live as those who belong to Jesus Christ.

> It is tolerably clear that the most characteristic Christian way of guidance was in the kind of setting indicated in I Cor.XIV, where the Christians assemble, each with a psalm or a teaching or a revelation or an ecstatic outburst or ejaculation: *and the congregation exercises discernment*. This is how Christian ethical decisions were reached: informed discussion, prophetic insight, ecstatic fire—all in the context of the worshipping, and also discriminating, assembly, met with the good news in Jesus Christ behind them, the Spirit among them, and before them the expectation of being led forward into the will of God. And if there is one lesson of outstanding importance to be gleaned from all this, it is that only along similar lines, translated into terms of our present circumstances, can we hope for an informed Christian ethic for the present day.[42]

It is unlikely that repristinating the experience and practices of the first generation will suffice in the twenty first century. Historical distance has created quite serious and important differences. Nonetheless the picture given by Professor Moule reminds us of both the differences between our institutionalized church and at the same time the immanent presence of the risen Christ in the lives of Christians. To put it differently and more bluntly—Christology is always the heart of being Christian.

There are some interesting matters that come to the fore in this discussion. Institutions are essentially means of maintaining some degree of continuity through generations in relations between people and or things. They make the sustained life of a community possible over time. It was inevitable that institutions would emerge in the earliest generation of Christians. The shape of those institutions was in the hands of

---

42. Moule, *Birth*, 212–13.

the community and they existed to serve that community. They were contingent, in that they existed to serve the values and priorities of the community in which they emerged and the purposes for which they were created. But such institutions were also inevitably susceptible to corruption. Of course they could come to serve different values and purposes, as they have done in every generation since the first. The colonization of the church communities by the Constantinian Empire brought with it notions of authority and power, and thus character of community, that was at significant odds with the images given by Jesus, to say nothing of Paul of Tarsus. The tendency is already visible within the band of disciples, without the overweening influence of the later Roman imperium.

> You know that those who are regarded as rulers of the Gentiles lord it over them, and their high officials exercise authority over them. Not so with you. Instead, whoever wants to become great among you must be your servant, and whoever wants to be first must be slave of all. For even the Son of Man did not come to be served, but to serve, and to give his life as a ransom for many. (Mark 10:42–45)

This principle of relationships applies directly to the design and purposes of any institutions in a community of the disciples of Jesus. Furthermore, in a Christian community those institutions not only should reflect these conduct characteristics, but also do so under the fundamental and always acknowledged priority of Jesus whom Christians call Lord. Whatever we make of the seriously disaggregated notion of a fixed and absolute canon of scripture it will need to meet the test described of the New Testament documents themselves identified above by Bo Reicke, "the writings of the New Testament concern themselves without deviation with Jesus Christ, directly and immediately."

In any reconfiguration of the institutionality of the documents of the New testament the image of the early church seeking guidance presented above by Professor Moule might be a useful counter point in any ecclesiology that emerges. Given the history of Anglicans in the last fifty years some very serious conceptual reconfiguring is certainly needed as to how we imagine the character and shape of our tradition into a post twentieth-century era.

7

The Role of Eschatology in Recent Anglican Ecclesiology

A Study of Three International Doctrine Commission Reports[1]

EVER SINCE SCHLEIERMACHER IN the eighteenth century and Barth in the last century, it has been difficult if not impossible to contemplate doing theology without recognizing the dynamic relationship between the ecclesial tradition out of which the theological task is being undertaken and the shape and direction of the theological task itself.[2] Furthermore any consideration of ecclesiology that is to function in a particular church will need to engage with the particularities of the ecclesial tradition of that church. Different traditions of ecclesial practice and understanding emerged very early in Christianity and can be seen even in the documents of the New Testament.[3] The pattern of practices in Corinth was different from that in Philippi and in Thessalonica, and these churches were founded by the same apostle.[4] Different again were the patterns in

---

1. An earlier version of this essay appeared as Kaye, "The Role of Eschatology."

2. See Schleiermacher, *The Christian Faith*, and Karl Barth's opening declaration in Barth, *CD* 1/1:3: "As a theological discipline dogmatics is the scientific self-examination of the Christian Church with respect to the content of its distinctive talk about God."

3. See, for example, Dunn, *Jews and Christians*.

4. For differences in concepts and expressions see Kaye, "To the Romans and Others."

the Jerusalem church. Broader traditions emerged later and are part and parcel of any historical account of Christianity.[5]

The Anglican Project

In the case of Anglicanism its traditions go back to the formation of a more or less coherent Christian English nation and its subsequent occupation of the greater part of what we now call England. Adrian Hastings put the beginning of this English tradition in the eighth century with Bede, even though the nations of the land were not brought together until the ninth century under Alfred and then Harold.[6]

All Anglican churches around the world look to the long tradition of faith in this Church of England as the root from which they have sprung, one way or another.

The present historical moment for Anglicanism is shaped by this long pedigree but also by the imperial expansion of Britain and especially the dramatic decolonization of the British Empire in the second half of the twentieth century.[7] Alongside this decolonization process went also the development of independent Anglican churches in the new nations. The present Anglican Communion of Churches is made up of these new churches, along with some from older British colonies. It includes churches founded by missionaries from the United States, some later American dependencies which remain part of The Episcopal Church and the Anglican Church in Korea, which began with English missionaries acting under the protection of a treaty between Korea and the United States and Japanese missionaries when Korea was part of the Japanese empire, and some others.

They are also set within the dynamics of globalization with its varied colors of new empires, immediacy of contact across vast distances, and the struggle to find faithful local identity. The tension between local and global is inscribed deep in this moment of time and is reflected in the life of these Anglican churches around the world.[8]

---

5. For the period of late antiquity see especially Brown, *Western Christendom*.

6. Hastings, *Construction of Nationhood*.

7. Ward, *Global Anglicanism*; Douglas, *Fling Out the Banner*; Douglas and Pui-lan, *Beyond Colonial Anglicanism*.

8. Hassett, *Anglican Communion*; Radner and Turner, *Fate of Communion*.

At the turn of the century three international doctrine commissions were established in the Anglican Communion to examine aspects of ecclesiology. Their reports have come out roughly every ten years: *For the Sake of the Kingdom* (1987), *The Virginia Report* (1998), and *Communion, Conflict, and Hope* (2008).

Clearly the different tasks allocated to these three commissions inevitably moved them in different directions with different questions at the forefront of their reports. Even so, it is not unreasonable to ask how they each construe their ecclesiological discussion in the framework of eschatology. After all, the New Testament material is replete with notions of the Christian and the church living in the light of the coming kingdom of God. Within the Anglican tradition of liturgy and formularies, eschatology occupies a significant position. How did these commissions handle it?

For the Sake of The Kingdom (1987) was initiated by the Anglican Consultative Council[9] with the brief:

> Church and Kingdom in Creation and Redemption, being a study of the relationship between the Church of God as experienced and the Kingdom of God as anticipated, with special reference to the diverse and changing cultural contexts in which the Gospel is proclaimed, received, and lived.[10]

The Commission focused on context and difference, witness and mission, with the challenge of adaptation urgently faced in the new provinces, but they approach that question in a specifically eschatological framework.

The report began by asserting that their examination "of Gospel and culture, church and context, has had to return constantly to the question of the meaning of that promised kingdom."[11] They argue that the meaning of God's promise of his Kingdom is empty if it does not speak to the here and now of the multitudinous local contexts which they are addressing. Those local events are to be "seen as embodying and pointing to the

---

9. On the origins and role of the Anglican Consultative Council see Kaye, *Introduction to World Anglicanism*, 130–40.

10. The report is available online at http://www.anglicancommunion.org/ministry/theological/iatdc/docs/for_the_sake_of_the_kingdom_1986.pdf. ACC and IATDC, *For the Sake of the Kingdom*, Preface.

11. ACC and IATDC, *For the Sake of the Kingdom*, Preface. All three reports are divided into paragraphs and reference is made to the texts according to paragraph.

kingdom in this or that bit of actual human history."[12] In deploying the order of redemption language the report declares that the restoration of all things will be realized at the "coming of Jesus in power and glory, when the whole creation would be transformed."[13]

There is no yielding on the local as their point of attention and that in these specific local situations what "constitutes the ultimate basis of judgment for Christian believers is Christ himself. He is the one who represents and embodies the world's (and the church's) transcendent horizon, the Kingdom of God."[14]

They end up by saying that there is indeed a "sovereign" truth, something beyond our fashions and fancies, but that it is to be known only in the continuation of active human encounter. In this context there will be disagreement and conflict but in dealing with those conflicts they are very clear as to what is at stake. "If we refuse such listening, we need to be called by the Gospel to conversion and repentance, renewed attention to the Gospel and to one another in the presence of the Gospel."[15]

Throughout this report there is a clear preoccupation with the situation on the ground for churches caught up in the vast political changes arising from the decolonization process. It is concerned to help forge ways of dealing with those new circumstances in a way that recognizes both this reality and the challenge to be faithful in Christian witness. Eschatological categories function here as the ultimate point of reference for faithfulness and underline diverse responses in different local situations. The gospel is the sovereign truth that is to be embodied in each and every local situation. It is an emphasis on transcendence that shapes the argument and frames the interpretation of the challenge.

The Virginia Report (1998) was initiated through the Lambeth Conference and grew out of the Eames Commission on how to respond to the ordination of women in some provinces.[16] Its focus was on unity and institutions that could maintain that unity. They were asked to undertake this enquiry by reference to the doctrine of the Trinity.

12. ACC and IATDC, *For the Sake of the Kingdom*, no. 5.

13. ACC and IATDC, *For the Sake of the Kingdom*, no. 29.

14. ACC and IATDC, *For the Sake of the Kingdom*, no. 58. Of course within the church such an emphasis inevitably leads to different judgments and conflict. The Commission offers a lengthy discussion of pluralism and in the process rejects any relativism that is often associated with notions of plurality.

15. ACC and IATDC, *For the Sake of the Kingdom*, no. 78.

16. See Kaye, *Conflict*.

As a matter of urgency further exploration of the meaning and nature of communion with particular reference to the doctrine of the Trinity, the unity and order of the Church, and the unity and community of humanity.[17]

The terms of reference for the Commission were thus precise not only as to the subject matter, the understanding of communion, but also, they were to approach the question via the doctrine of the Trinity. Surprisingly for a group of theologians the Commission simply accepted this restriction as to theological method. The Eames Commission had shaped a strategy for "keeping the peace" and the IATDC followed this by making unity the key goal. They then addressed the whole issue of conflict in terms of containment and, in the process, unity came to be thought of in terms of agreement.

The argument of the report is finely tuned. Trinity is the key to ecclesiology. Communion is understood in terms of a fairly broad model of the Trinity, structures are necessary to sustain and develop communion, and so we arrive at the current structures of the Anglican Communion. These structures are denominated, following the Eames Commission, as "Instruments of Unity." A rather particular use of the idea of subsidiarity is deployed to move towards a legitimating framework for heightening the roles of these so called "Instruments of Unity."

There is a steady theme of development in this report, though it is highly selective and even "Whiggish."[18] It does not refer to earlier attempts at Communion institutions which were abandoned; strategies such as regional centers, a Communion theological center or congresses similar to those held earlier in the twentieth century. The regional centers did not last long nor did a Communion theological center, though there are centers for Anglican Communion study independent of the structures of the Anglican Communion. The Congresses were widely regarded as significant in building awareness beyond provincial borders. Things like the fallibility of the church are acknowledged, but are often qualified and the qualification then taken up as the main theme in the argument.

Something like this happens also in relation to the explicit notice of eschatology in this report. In the opening paragraphs of the section

---

17. IATDC, *Virginia Report*, Introduction. The report is available online at IATDC, "Meetings Communiqués and Documents."

18. See Butterfield, *Whig Interpretation*.

dealing with communion with the Trinity and the life of the church the report identifies the place of the church in history as the body of Christ.

> Because the Church as communion participates in God's communion of Father, Son and Holy Spirit, it has an eschatological reality and significance. The Church is the advent, in history, of God's final will being done on earth as it is in heaven. That will was revealed in the life and ministry of Jesus Christ and is continually inspired by the work of the Spirit in the life and mission of the Church. The Church is the icon of the future toward which God is directing the history of the world.[19]

The church participates in the life of the Trinity and, through the Holy Spirit, lives as Jesus lived his life. The eschatology here works as a framework for understanding the situation of the church as part of the divine plan and action and also as the ideal, or goal towards which history and the church moves. In an idealist move the church becomes the model of destiny, an icon of heaven.

There is remarkably little or no significant role here for failure, sin, redemption, corruption or restitution in the eschaton. Indeed, these things do not play a significant role in the argument of the report. The report is rather an extended framing for understanding church structures, and in particular the recently created structures of the Anglican Communion. The focus on the Trinity by analogy with the church leaves little room for any ongoing dynamic in the life of the church and such movement as there is appears as "development." The tone of the ecclesiology here is static and could be thought to echo something of the *analogia entis* that was so vehemently attacked by Karl Barth.[20]

Communion, Conflict, and Hope (2008) was appointed to continue the work on the meaning of communion started by *The Virginia Report*.[21] However, the new Commission focused on a quite different set of issues; conflict, fallibility in the church, catholicity and hope. The tone and character of this report could not be more different from *The Virginia Report*. It flags in the Preface its intention to go beyond Virginia and by implication to challenge it. "The current Commission wanted to explore

---

19. IATDC, *Virginia Report*, 2.14.

20. See Barth, *CD* 1/1:xiii: "I regard the *analogia entis* as the invention of the Anti-Christ, and I believer that because of it, it is impossible to become a Roman Catholic, all other reasons for not doing so being to my mind short-sighted and trivial."

21. The report is available online at IATDC, "Meetings Communiqués and Documents."

to what extent this model needed to be complemented with understandings which were more historical, pneumatological and eschatological."²² *The Virginia Report* provided the basis for the Windsor Process and a covenant for Anglican Provinces with some level of sanctions. *Communion, Conflict, and Hope* sets a question mark against the implied centralization of that approach, albeit in the genteel language of diplomacy. "If the outcome of the Windsor process should result in some definitive centralization of the Communion, then one function of this report may be to constitute an appraisal of that development."²³

The starting point of the report is the plain fact of endemic conflict in the church from the very beginning. There is a strong focus on the fallibility of the church and in the church. The report also underlines a local focus and identifies Anglicanism as generally having a provincial shape to its ecclesiology.²⁴

The response to such conflict and difference within and between provinces is a dynamic notion of catholicity. The local needs those beyond the local in order to sustain the rich fullness of the gospel. The local can easily be trapped in its own local terms and the wider engagement offered in a dynamic catholicity enables each to grow and to learn. Indeed, one of the themes in this report is that the church is a learning environment in which the virtues of Christian living are nurtured.

This framework provides the basis for conceiving of the church as on pilgrimage and engaged in experiments about the form and direction of its ecclesial life. Eschatology shapes this pattern and it is identified as hope. The connection with the present reality is identified in their comment on 1 Corinthians 13. "The 'more excellent way' (I Corinthians 12.31) is that such gifts should be exercised according to the gospel virtue of love. Faith and hope speak to the eschatological character of the Christian vocation; love speaks to the substantive nature of the Gospel in living form."²⁵ The role that this hope plays is properly manifest in conflicts.

> Sometimes we hear of Communion being broken, and often this language is used in rhetorical exchanges about particular

---

22. IATDC, *Communion, Conflict, and Hope*, no. 3.

23. IATDC, *Communion, Conflict, and Hope*, no. 18.

24. The Windsor Report and its parent *The Virginia Report* show no awareness of this provincial character and move in a contrary direction.

25. IATDC, *Communion, Conflict, and Hope*, no. 30.

issues in dispute. The greater reality, however, is the brokenness of the church within which communion can and does flourish. Communion flourishes when we accept that discipleship in the church is a call to the way of the cross in the brokenness of the church to which we all contribute. Such costly participation in the crucifixion and resurrection sharpens our sense of the hope we have in Christ. This hope will not permit the fallibility which we bring to handling our conflicts to be the last word. Within the day-to-day process of reconciliation and growth in mutual understanding we grow up into that unity in Christ which characterizes the catholicity of the church in all its fullness.[26]

The hope pointed to in the title of the report is set in the midst of conflict and failure and focuses on the cross and resurrection of Christ on the one hand and on the telos towards which the pilgrimage of the church is directed. Both are firmly located in the reality of history but are not contained by it. Set in this eschatological time as the driver for the character of church life is love energized by hope and enlarged by a dynamic catholicity. Communion is love expressed in failure, conflict and hope. This is an understanding of unity that is worlds away from *The Virginia Report*.

The Three Reports

These three reports are remarkably different in their approach to ecclesiology and also in the role of eschatology in that ecclesiology. There are resonances of *For the Sake of the Kingdom* in *Communion, Conflict, and Hope*, indeed *Communion, Conflict, and Hope* goes to some trouble to reinstate *For the Sake of the Kingdom* into the conversation. The *Virginia Report* did not refer to *For the Sake of the Kingdom* at all, and *Communion, Conflict, and Hope* referred to *The Virginia Report* only in its introductory section.

The differences between the reports can be highlighted by drawing attention to a number of issues.

---

26. IATDC, *Communion, Conflict, and Hope*, nos. 50–51.

	For the Sake of the Kingdom	*The Virginia Report*	*Communion, Conflict, and Hope*
BRIEF	Church and the kingdom of God in the context of diversity and plurality in and between churches	The understanding of the church as communion in the light of the doctrine of the Trinity and institutional structures in the Anglican Communion	Developing the idea of communion, a brief given at a time when conflict within the Anglican Communion had escalated over sexuality issues
CONTEXT	New independent Anglican churches following decolonization and globalization and the challenge of mission in multi religious societies	Conflict between provinces in the Anglican Communion over the ordination of women	Heightened conflict between Anglican Provinces
FOCUS	The witness and mission imperative for the church and belonging to the Kingdom of God	The doctrine of the Trinity as model for unity in the church and how that is sustained by organizational structures in the Anglican Communion	Living faithfully in a church marked by failure, endemic fallibility and conflict
THEOLOGICAL DRIVERS IN THE ARGUMENT	The kingdom of God as the transcendent reality that shapes local expressions of the gospel	The doctrine of the Trinity and church institutions	A dynamic conception of the catholicity of the church and the hope present in Christ and as the telos of the church's pilgrimage
ESCHATOLOGY	A transcendent kingdom of God a key theme	Providential development towards a telos. Incidental reference only	The hope arising from the death and resurrection of Christ and as the telos towards which the church moves. A key driver in the argument

In one way or another, these reports were all grappling with how Anglicans are to live in the real circumstances of their lives. This is most prominent *For the Sake of the Kingdom* which is concerned primarily with the local church and the province engaging in the task of mission. The *Virginia Report* and *Communion, Conflict, and Hope* are focused on the relations between Anglican provinces and how they can be understood in the light of inherited patterns of ecclesiology. How is the local to relate to the more distant? Are relationships between groups who are significantly separated from each other bound to be qualitatively different from relations between groups or individuals who are much nearer in life to each other? Do more distant relations, even in a faster communicating world, necessarily tend to be more formal and even authoritarian? Will they inevitably tend away from the persuasive authority that is more suitable to proximate engaged relationships? And anyway is globalism a hoax that has had its day?[27]

The Virginia Report lacks any forceful eschatological concerns. It displaces love as the primary gospel virtue with unity. It more comfortably thinks of institutional structures as vital to the unity they seek, or at least the particular structures they are supporting. The other two reports are much more relaxed about institutions and focus on relationships, especially relationships that are local.

If institutions are about continuity of relations between people and or things over time then they necessarily emphasize the reliability of that continuity.[28] There is a certain fixity in institutions and they thus tend to become important, even vital in understanding the community they exist to serve. This is not a new phenomenon in Anglican or more generally in Christian history. In earlier debates, the precise character of the threefold order of ministry was often the point under discussion. The great nineteenth century scholar of the early church, J. B. Lightfoot struggled with this issue in his essay on *The Christian Ministry* included in his 1868 commentary of Philippians. He famously affirmed the Anglican commitment to the threefold order while making it abundantly clear that the order has no historically verifiable absolute sanction or authority, though he is comfortable with an historical proximate connection with Jesus.

> If the preceding investigation be substantially correct, the threefold ministry can be traced to Apostolic direction: and short of an express statement we can possess no better assurance of a Divine appointment or at least a Divine sanction. If the facts do

27. As argued by Saul, *Collapse*.
28. There is a considerable literature on institution theory. See, for example, Goodin, *Institutional Design*; Lühmann, *Social Systems*.

not allow us to unchurch other Christian communities differently organized, they may at least justify our jealous adhesion to a polity derived from this source.[29]

While the context and the issues are different it is clear that Lightfoot was struggling to sustain a continuity and authority for the institution of a threefold ministry in the church while yet, for reasons he set out in the first section of his essay, wishing to insist that such continuity did not convey any absolute character to the ministerial arrangements he was discussing.

Different frameworks in handling ecclesiology tend to different evaluations of the institutions that are a necessary part of ecclesial life. Lightfoot's ancient ideal type in combination with a belief in history as the "increasing purpose of God" leads him to value the institution of a threefold ministry extremely highly, but not so absolutely as to be of divine sanction.[30] The framework adopted by the *Virginia Report* of analogy with a particular doctrine of the Trinity inevitably tends to invest the institutionality of the church more highly and with more significance than any eschatological frame of reference might suggest. If the framework is that of contextualization for mission, then the tendency is to a variety of forms of plurality, as can be seen in *For the Sake of the Kingdom*. If the framework is set in terms of conflict and "dynamic catholicity" then the institutionality will tend to be regarded as more malleable, as can be seen in *Communion, Conflict, and Hope*.

The point of this paper is to test these reports in terms of the theme of eschatology. To lay before these reports the assertion by Jesus that his kingdom was not of this world. If a community believes as an article of its defining faith that their citizenship is in heaven, that they live not for this world, but in the hope of the coming Kingdom of God, then that must surely affect the way in which they approach institutions. How will that conviction shape their design, change and operation. It will certainly have some impact on the fixity of institutions or any thought that any of them have some absolute authority. Any attempt to model an institution on some formulation of a doctrine of God, such as the Trinity, must beware of Barth's strictures on the *analogia entis*. The *Virginia Report* seems sadly unaware of these questions and does not reveal any vital sense of the eschatological character of Christian ecclesiology. While *For the Sake*

---

29. Lightfoot, *Philippians*, 267.
30. On Lightfoot's view of history see Treloar, *Lightfoot*.

of the Kingdom and *Communion, Conflict, and Hope* gave priority to an eschatological framework, they do not provide any detailed account of institutionality for an eschatologically shaped community in which the primary condition of its institutions is the radical contingency of their existence.[31] What remains from this discussion for Anglicans is the articulation of a serious theology of institutionality that can take seriously the issues of eschatology.

---

31. For a modern examination of this theme in relation to the theological work of Karl Barth, see Hauerwas, *With the Grain of the Universe*, chs. 6–7.

Part II

Anglicans in Australia

Introduction

THE FIRST SIX PAPERS in this part are a selection of papers and lectures given during my time as General Secretary of the Anglican Church of Australia. They illustrate a coordinated renewal project seeking to operate outside the confines of the strict diocesanism that normally drives the Anglican Church of Australia. The first sets out some general matters about the context of the church in Australian society and culture. The following five address particular elements in a program from the General Synod Office aimed at the renewal of the life of the church across the nation. The perspective throughout is national. The constitution of the Anglican Church of Australia is decisively diocesan. Most of the governance strength is with the dioceses and decisions about actual ministry or mission are made in the dioceses. This balance is not always helpful in dealing with broad based issues or Anglican institutions that are related to a national framework of funding and accountability because of the financial arrangements of the Federal Government. Schools are a good example of this as explained in chapter 11.

Chapter 9 deals with a consequence of the constitution balance. Theology is broadly taught in diocesan seminaries which are located in the Metropolitan cities. The staffs of these seminaries do not meet together at all. The conduct of theology is therefore constantly subject to the limitation of the local. In response to this pattern the General Synod Office established annual post graduate level seminars in Theology,

History and Mission. The first two to these were very successful and led to a number of significant publications and were the seed bed from which the Journal of Anglican Studies grew. Chapter 9 was addressed to one of the meetings of the Theology seminar. Chapter 10 was a paper given at the second National Anglican Conference and addresses the contribution that such conferences can make to the life of the church, drawing attention to the national dimension of the community of Anglicans in this country. Chapter 12 is an example of the promotion of networks driven from the General Synod Office as a way of forming connections across the country.

Chapter 13 is a little different in that it reports on the dramatic changes made to the processes of the meetings of the General Synod which were designed to provide a more appropriate and effective way of dealing with contentious matters on which there was likely to be significant conflict.

The final chapter, 14, is of a different order. It is a modified version of a paper written to responds to the Appellate Tribunal's judgement on a matter of blessing existing same-sex marriages. Its interest in this collection is that it highlights something of the way the constitution of the Anglican Church of Australia operates in a serious conflict into which the church has entered and which remains unresolved at the time of writing. An earlier form of this paper was circulated in the church as a contribution to the efforts to deal with the conflict.

8

The Landscape of the National Church[1]

THE LANDSCAPE OF THE national Church in Australia is changing. It is changing because of some recent events in the church and because of changes in the environment in which we live. The widespread use of the new prayer book (1995) is undoubtedly an important landmark in our national Church. The recent National Anglican Conference (1997) has quite significantly changed the landscape and has the potential to enable us to reconceive our church in more dynamic and appropriate terms.

But I believe we need to find a more acute and focused conception of what we actually mean by the national Church and, as a consequence, how we think about our mission in Australia as Anglican Christians.

Reconceiving the Church as the People of God

If you had asked someone standing on the shores of Port Jackson in 1820 what it meant to them to be an Australian, they would probably not know what you were talking about. If you asked someone who was standing in the same place at the time when the Australian contingent set sail to take part in the First World War in November 1914, they probably would have had a more precise idea of what it was to be an Australian. That view would probably have been a little different from the views of a characteristic subscriber to the Bulletin which was enjoying a heyday of popularity. It was at this time that Henry Lawson penned his famous poem about Australian identity, "A Song of the Republic."

---

1. This is a revised version of a paper given to the Clergy Conference of the Diocese of Grafton in New South Wales.

> Sons of the South awake! arise!
> Sons of the South, and do.
> Banish from under your bonny skies
> Those old-world errors and wrongs and lies
> Making a hell in a Paradise
> That belongs to your sons and you.

The image of a successful sporting nation was prominent in Melbourne in 1956. The Olympic Games had just been held and Australians had won more gold medals at these games than ever in history, and a kindly government had arranged for the nation to watch this national triumph by introducing television into the country. The bi-centenary celebrations on February 26, 1988 of the arrival of the First Fleet to establish a British colony was somewhat different. While a representative First Fleet sailed into Sydney harbor to the cheers of thousands of onlookers, on the other side of the city a large crowd of people were protesting for land rights for Indigenous Australians. There has been continuing arguments about the propriety of celebrating Australia Day on what many now regard as "Invasion Day." For my part I have boycotted the public holiday on January 26 since that day in 1988.

But during the twenty first century there have been an increasing number of residents who do not really think they belong to this community; asylum seekers and refugees who have been left in the lurch by Federal Government policies, and indigenous people who are not able to participate in the life of this community, who suffer health and livelihood conditions far below others and whose young people are dramatically over represented in the criminal justice system. We manage to work with the political reality of the nation as a federal union between the states, and a commonwealth of citizens. While we pay council rates, state excise duties, and commonwealth income tax, we are never not Australians in doing these things. We understand that there is a relationship between state and federal levels of government and municipal decisions. All of these interact in different ways upon how we live as Australians. We not only understand about these institutional manifestations in our society, but also conduct an ongoing discussion about the precise role each different kind of institution has to play in our lives.

If we ask different people what they think the Anglican Church is many will answer in terms of the local parish church or perhaps the diocese. If pressed to ask about the national church they are likely to have only a vague idea and probably think of it in terms of organizations such as the General Synod. Most commonly ordinary Anglicans think of their church engagement in terms of the local parish church and perhaps with the public statements or actions of bishops or clergy. There is no national church paper or news outlet so most news comes from the local and is focusses on the local.

However, being Anglican is not adequately defined simply by stating a relationship to the synodical, diocesan or even parish organizational arrangements. Being Anglican means being a Christian within the framework of a particular tradition of Christian faith. That belief commitment involves being associated with those who share that pattern of belief. These Anglican Christians sustain their faith through a series of institutional arrangements which are much broader than simply the synodical and parochial organizational structure. For example 35 percent of the clergy in the Diocese of Sydney are employed in non-parochial work. They work in agencies as chaplains in Home Mission Societies, educational environments and in a plethora of other institutional arrangements. A number of the Anglican Church Schools in Sydney have no constitutional relationship to the diocesan structure. In Melbourne almost no Anglican schools have any constitutional relationship to the diocesan structure. The majority of the welfare agencies in Melbourne have no connection constitutionally with the diocesan structure. In these two large metropolitan areas, the reality is that the Anglican community is broader and more diverse than the synodical and diocesan structures.

Benedict Anderson wrote a fascinating book some time ago entitled *Imagined Communities*. He asked the question what does it mean to be an Italian in the United States that is different from being an Italian in Italy? What does it mean to belong to a community that crosses over the territorial boundaries of other communities, to belong to such an imagined community? I want to suggest that the Anglican Church of Australia is something like such an imagined community. It is a community of people which exists in our imagination. Being Anglican means being Christian within this historical tradition of the faith. Being Anglican also involves what we do and how we interact with other Anglicans.

If we think of the church as the community of God's people then we are better able to understand that the various institutional arrangements, such as the synodical and diocesan structures, the parish structures, the mission societies and the welfare agencies, are all simply instrumentalities for the sustenance and development of the faith of that Christian community which we call the church.

When you think therefore of the national Church, think of that community of Christian people who are scattered around this continent and who name themselves as Anglicans. It is that community of Christian people who seek to fulfil their vocations as Christians in this Australian environment who rightly deserve the title, the National Anglican Church. The instrumentalities of that community, General Synod, its agencies, the diocesan structures, the parish structures, the voluntary societies the welfare agencies, the church schools, all of these things exist to sustain the faith and advance the witness of that Christian community of people. The constitution of the church, agreed by all dioceses in 1962, sets out the institutional aspect of the functioning of this community. The church of the constitution is thus not a community, but the organizational entity established and defined in the constitution and which in that context is called church. The constitution describes fundamental beliefs and ruling principles for decision making and an organizational structure of a General Synod and the dioceses. The constitution is focused on these organizational aspects. This institutional focus of the constitution can be seen in the fact that its disciplinary arrangements only apply to office holders in the organization, that is to say clergy in all three orders. There is no disciplinary procedure for lay people.

If we conceive of the national church in terms akin to the Anderson's imagined communities, then we are better able to identify what dynamics are influencing the way in which Anglicans live in Australia, both in terms of the Australian community, of which they are constituent members at all times, and of the Anglican community, of which they are also constituent members all the time.

Dynamics in the Australian Community

As a window into this question, I want to refer to two recent books which have been extremely helpful in elucidating what is going on in our community. The first is Paul Kelly's book *The End of Certainty*, which is an examination of our economic and political circumstances in Australia. In that book he argued that during the course of the 1980s, what he calls the Australian Settlement, began to collapse. The Australian Settlement was the set of generally perceived notions that had dominated Australian thinking since the formation of the Commonwealth at the beginning of the twentieth century. The key markers in those precepts were the white

Australia policy, tariff protection, central wage arbitration, state paternalism, and imperial benevolence.

The white Australia policy collapsed as a result of decisions by the Whitlam government, but more conclusively as a result of actions taken by the Fraser government. The internationalization of the world economy and weakening of Australia's imperial links first with Britain and then with the United States, are also the key elements which have undermined what Kelly called the Australia Settlement. Those forces, particularly the globalization of the economy, have brought an end to the certainty which has existed in Australia during the twentieth century. All of these changes have led to different perceptions of our place in the world and the importance of the institutions which had served the previous arrangements.

The second book to which I referred was Hugh Mackay's book, *Reinventing Australia*. Hugh Mackay addresses more personal questions, but the most important aspect of his analysis is his description of what he calls the big angst, the age of anxiety. It is in the context of that anxiety that Australia has gone through a process of redefinition in regard to the role and place of women and the consequent influence that this has on the structure of the family, the place of work, the development of the non-cash economy, finance arrangements, multiculturalism, law and order.

Both these books draw attention to changes in Australian society which principally became apparent in the nineteen eighties and nineteen nineties. Both writers agree that in this period Australia has been going through a period of immense change, both as to the perceptions of who we are and therefore of challenges to the institutions which have sustained the previous ideas of who we are. If you think of the major social institutions of our society, it is hard to find one which has not in some way been affected by these changes. Think of work and the economy; family and marriage; law and governance; knowledge in education and cultural associations, and sport. All of these areas of life, and the institutions that shape and sustain them, have been subject to immense change in the last twenty years.

That age of uncertainty has evoked a number of different kinds of responses. Some have withdrawn into more ordered and structured ideas about the way in which we should live. Some have wanted to assert that in this changed and fluid environment, what I believe is right, should be what happens, what Hugh Mackay calls the "authority of assertion," based upon a notion of radical individualism. This idea has influenced many of the ways in which public debate is conducted in our society today.

Dynamics in Australian Anglicanism

The changes that have been happening in Australian Anglicanism have not been as great as those that have happened in the Australian community. We have certainly had our public debates of which three in particular stand out; the debate about the formation of the Constitution, the introduction of the new prayer book, A Prayer Book for Australia, and the ordination of women.

Those debates have often been conflictual and disputatious, and they have been concerned with internal agenda questions in our church. One of the consequences of these debates has been that centrifugal forces have been accelerated in our church. There has been a flight to the edges. Those edges have sometimes been ideological ones, or have been embodied in institutions. People have said we will return to our parishes and ignore the rest. Others have said that we will build a fortress in our parish or our diocese and protect the things that we believe to be important. Most obviously, of course, has been the enlivened sense of state rights, or diocesan independence. The problem is not so much in the institutional relationships which these centrifugal forces affect, as the culture of the communities which inhabit those institutions.

All of the Anglican agencies concerned with welfare, education and industry, have become more self-consciously national. They have formulated different ways of keeping together nationally across diocesan boundaries because of the more national forces at work in the broader community. The welfare agencies of our church have formed themselves into a national network, initially called NACON, the National Anglican Caring Organizations Network, but now renamed, Anglicare. The welfare agencies are driven to this national liaison because they must increasingly deal with a federal government for funding and policy purposes.

The same is true in regard to the conferences and activities of the Anglican schools consultative committee. During the last few years the Inter Trade and Industry Mission has been organized on a national basis, and while this is an ecumenical group, the Anglican involvement is considerable and creates dynamics similar to the welfare and schools groups.

Interests in spirituality have similarly crossed diocesan boundaries and given people networks of awareness that are national in character.

All of these developments manifest the centripetal forces at work in the community of Australian Anglicans. They are currents which draw people towards each other and make them more aware of the central core elements in the faith of Australian Anglicans.

The landscape, therefore in my view, is currently subject to some quite different currents. There are the obvious and public centrifugal forces, more commonly associated with what has been happening in the synods of the church. But at the same time there have been the centripetal forces which have tended to be associated with those aspects of the life of this community in its engagement with Australian society. If we concentrate simply on the constitutional organizational elements, the General Synod, diocesan and parochial structures, we will, I believe, miss the main game. Yet it will become increasingly important for us to focus on the main game because of the challenges which lie before us as a church community in this nation.

- How we deal with the indigenous questions and indigenous people in our society.
- How we deal with the increasing contrasts between rural and metropolitan life.
- How our church avoids becoming an ethnic boutique church, rather than a church which embraces the whole of multicultural Australia.
- How we relate to the rising young generation.
- How we affirm and support lay vocation in this plural society.

In facing these important challenges in ways that are faithful to our own Christian faith tradition, we will have to confront, as Australian society confronts, the challenge of whether values or power will shape our living arrangements.

The National Anglican Conference

The National Anglican Conference in Canberra in February 1997 was above all a surprise to everyone. Eight hundred people registered for the whole of the National Anglican Conference in Canberra. Two to three hundred more attended on a day basis. No one expected such a huge response, many feared that very few would come. It tapped a nerve. It revealed something of what was actually going on in the community below the surface.

The conference had its origins in proposals from the General Synod Office to which the Standing Committee acceded in October 1994 and the General Synod endorsed in 1995. The purpose of the conference was to draw together Australian Anglicans to assist them in their engagement with Australian society. The conference set out to be a listening conference. A conference where people could come from across the country to learn from each other, as to how they might best pursue their engagement with Australian society as Anglican Christians. The program was structured in a way which gave priority to that engagement with Australian society and enabled people to listen to each other and to listen to what others were doing around the country.

Each day of the conference had its own theme.

- That theme began with society. Where Are We?
- Moved to our own Anglican identity. Who Are We?
- Then on the third and fourth days began to ask the questions. Where Are We Going? And So What?

The thrust of the program, in its timing, moved from the society in which we lived and with which we were called to engage as Anglican Christians to the future in which that engagement is to be sustained and amplified. Within each day the conference program began with listening to speakers in plenary sessions, but then in small groups listening to each other, discovering what was already going on and what were people's visions for the future. Listening Groups and Workshops constituted an important part of the interactive character of the conference program.

This conference was a conference for the national Church in the sense of that community of Australian Anglicans which is scattered across the continent. It was organized out of the General Synod Office. The Standing Committee of General Synod was reluctant. They agreed to a cash advance of $25,000 on condition that the conference did not make a loss and the cash advance was to be repaid soon after the conference. The General Synod agreed "on the nod" in a busy agenda. The Primate, Archbishop Keith Rayner, was a strong supporter and the conference would not have been a success without the enthusiastic support of the Bishop of Canberra, George Browning and the force of over one hundred and fifty volunteers who contributed to every aspect of the conference. The cash advance from the Standing Committee was repaid a month before the conference was held and in the end the conference made a profit of $50,000, which came back as seed money for a second conference. Of course the conference somewhat went against the grain of the run of church politics, which in Australia is so attached to the dioceses and their local traditions of habits and outlook. When we asked the Archbishop of Sydney, Harry Goodhew, to chair the conference planning committee we encountered those politics. A church politician from the diocese of Sydney, but politically different from those attached to Harry Goodhew, told me in no uncertain terms that having Harry Goodhew as chair of the committee in no way guaranteed that Sydney would support the conference. Harry Goodhew was an excellent chair and people from Sydney were the largest group at the conference.

Some said at the beginning of the planning that it could not happen and that it would not happen. No one would come. In fact almost twice as many came as were planned for. The event was therefore surprising. Surprising that it happened at all, because of the large number of people who came and surprising in the spirit of energy, engagement and interaction which marked the conference. It was a people event. It was a listening event. It was an event when people connected with each other, simply on the basis that we were fellow Anglicans who lived in Australia. In that sense the conference uncovered and made manifest some of the real and effective currents operating in the Anglican community in Australia.

This was the first conference of this kind held on any scale in the history of our church. It was therefore not surprising that some important questions were not addressed.

- We did not effectively address the multicultural character of our society.
- We did not effectively address the way in which Christian vocation in that multicultural and plural society could be sustained.
- We did not address in the conference as a whole the contrast of challenges between rural and metropolitan existence.

And there were others. But these were matters for subsequent conferences. What was important about this conference was that it did grapple with the notion that we are a community of Anglican Christians in this nation, and that we have a vocation to learn from each other, to belong to each other and to engage with this society. The conference was an assertion of catholicity, of mutuality and inter-dependence. The conference had the very dramatic effect of emphasizing the centripetal forces in our community rather than centrifugal ones, represented in the organizational structures of the church.

One conference participant suggested it was a reidentification and reaffirmation of the central ground. I think that is true in the sense that it reaffirmed that what constituted us as an Anglican community in Australia was the core beliefs of our Anglican tradition of Christianity. What then flows from the National Anglican Conference? What does it signify?

I believe that the National Anglican Conference, by the very character of the event that it turned out to be, has affirmed the identity of Australian Anglicanism as a community of people. When we think about the national church, we will need to think about it in terms of it being a community of Anglicans in Australia.

It further indicates that we can no longer dispense with the luxury of not addressing the question of how Australian Anglicans live in this plural society in a way that is realistic in the terms of the character of Australian society.

That, I believe, has certain significant consequences for the way in which we think about the instruments of the church. It is essential that we constantly ask ourselves the question, what does this particular instrumentality contribute to the faith of the Anglican Christian community in Australia and to the engagement of those Anglicans with society? That question needs to be addressed in terms of both the purpose of the institution and the processes by which that institution operates. It is a question that needs to be asked about everything that is done in the General Synod and the organizations which it has established. It is a question which has to be asked in regard to the synods of all the dioceses and their diocesan organizations. It is a question that has to be addressed in every parish and the organizations and activities which they sustain. It is a question which has to be asked in terms of every Anglican institution which exists within this country, whether those institutions are schools, welfare agencies or industry-based organizations. The questions and the challenges remain constant. Those institutions and organizations of whatever kind exist only as instruments to serve the faith of Anglicans and their vocation in this society. So how are they doing with this task?

When it comes to synods, there are certain things that can be learned about the processes by which we make our decisions. The conference taught us that real understanding was advanced only when there is genuine personal encounter between those people who have come to the event. The process is creative when it enables listening and learning to take place. In other words, they should be people events moved by the presence of God to discern what is God's will for his people through this particular instrumentality of the General Synod, or the diocesan synod, or the parochial church council.

During the conference the worship organized by the Liturgical Group of the diocese of Canberra and was a vibrant combination of new and old. In large measure it was conducted by young people. It was not only in itself a creative experience but also an important tone setter in the quality of the interactions of the event.

Surely the conference has placed a sign post on the landscape of the national Church. That our institutions need to be outward serving. That the inner dynamics of our institutional life need transformation in terms of genuine encounter and personal relationships. Institutions should be kept in their place.

I believe that the conference also suggests to us that the really creative things happen when we as individuals or as groups, travel light not encumbered by vast organizational arrangements or political alignments, but act freely taking initiatives and keeping in contact with our fellows. Perhaps one could encapsulate it by saying that the unity which we need, is not the unity of uniformity or of conformity, but the unity which holds us together in the bonds of peace in such a way that we are all encouraged to take initiatives for Christ.

The Strategies of the General Synod Office

Given these lessons from the National Anglican Conference, what is or should be the role of the General Synod Office.

The General Synod Office is a small organization. We have a staff establishment of five people.

- The General Secretary and his Personal Assistant.
- The Finance and Administration Manager and his Secretary.
- A Research and Communications Officer.
- We also employ a very part-time Archivist, in order to catch up on the extensive backlog of archival filing.

However, this small office has a clear mission statement. "We exist to assist the church in its engagement with Australian society." By the church, we mean the community of Australian Anglicans called to serve God in this society. It is that mission statement which directs the priorities of the office. Clearly, we have obligations of a constitutional kind in regard to the General Synod and its instrumentalities. Those are done in such a way that they promote the mission statement of the office. Each year we establish goals in the office. These are designed to make us more effective and more efficient. Our concern is for the renewal of the national Church. That is to say the renewal in faith of the community of Anglican Christians set within Australian society. We seek to assist that community in financial and administrative ways and in terms of reaffirming and renewing the identity of that community as Anglican and as Australian.

As a community we Australian Anglicans have lost sight of much in the story of our past. The memory elements of identity have to do with what we believe holds us together and what we can learn from our own history. So we have begun to establish groups and networks around the country, which will assist the renewal of our awareness of our faith and of our history.

The General Synod Office works very much on a low key networking basis. We seek to renew the culture of our church by taking strategic initiatives which contribute to that renewal. The office in that sense is deliberately and determinedly anti-centralist in organizational terms. Our role is to assist people to fulfil their vocations and to do their job, not to do it for them. Our role is not to do the work of parish councils or dioceses or church agencies or any of the General Synod agencies. It is to encourage and assist in the national dimension of this work.

What we look for are signs of creativity and renewal, which we can then encourage and assist.

So What?

In confronting the problems created by the dominance of large corporations in the United States J. K. Galbraith declared that the greatest challenge confronting Americans was what he called "an emancipation of belief." The belief that actually things could be different. The belief that it is possible to change. The belief that renewal is available and is a possibility.

There are many people in our church who are frustrated and bowed down because they cannot believe that renewal is a possibility. There are many clergy who feel tired and worn out by the demands that are thrust upon them. But the future holds bright prospects of renewal for this Christian community. Not because there are many good things going on in this community, though that is true. Nor because there is a great wind sweeping across the land renewing Anglican churches, though that is happening in a few places. Bright hopes are ahead because it is possible to change, and that possibility is encouraged by every sign of the presence of the Spirit of God in this community of Christian people.

There are serious challenges about the precise character of our identity as Australian Anglicans:

- About the direction in which we should be moving.
- About the way in which institutional arrangements should be made more effective in the service of the faith.
- About the vocation of Anglicans in Australia.

There are many such questions. But the most fundamental question lies within each one of us. If we are willing to reconceive of the national Church as a community of Christian peoples scattered around this land, served by institutional arrangements, then it is possible for us to open up new doors and new opportunities for renewal in this church. That I believe would be a great step forward. But even with such a reconception, and such a redrawing of the landscape of the national Church, we will be led nowhere if we do not believe in our hearts that it is possible for this church to be renewed, that it is possible for God to take us and to use us and to revive us, in his service. The answer to that question lies deep within the heart of each one of us and our answer to that question will have a great deal to do with whether renewal comes to this church.

9

Anglican Theology in the Renewal of the Church[1]

THIS IS THE THIRD meeting of the National Anglican Theology Seminar. The first meeting of this Seminar took place in Perth in 1996 under the general theme, "Where Is Anglican Theology Going in Australia." There were seventeen people present. It was a residential seminar held at Wollaston College and preceded the meeting of the Australian and New Zealand Association of Theological Schools (ANZATS) conference. It was decided at the seminar to keep meeting and to pursue a role developing a sense of Australian Anglican theology in the life of the Anglican Church of Australia.

The second Seminar took place in Brisbane in 1997 and twenty-four people were present. It was held at Banyo Theological College just before the ANZATS Conference. The theme of the Seminar was "Towards an Anglican Theology of the Laity." A general pattern of the operation of the seminar began to emerge at this meeting. There was a combination of plenary groups and small groups. It was also a residential seminar with worship as an integral part of the programme. My own reflection on this particular seminar was that I found the discussion on the concept of laity confusing. We seemed to go around in circles, or at least I did. It seemed as if the concept of a laity was a church, or ecclesiastical term. One might say a term defined by default in relation to clergy. That did not seem to me to be a helpful framework in which to discuss the sorts of concerns which the question raised. This possibly occurred to me because we were

1. This is slightly revised version of a paper given at the opening of the third National Anglican Theology Seminar.

a group of intelligent people, all concerned about the question but not finding a lot of direction. My personal conclusion to the seminar was to take a vow not to use the term "laity" for six months. It certainly forced me to talk in other ways about important questions in this area.

This 1998 Seminar in Melbourne is the third to be held. The theme is "Reconciliation in Church and Society." Again, it is being held just prior to the ANZATS Conference.

The first Seminar in 1996 arose from a conversation at the 1995 ANZATS Conference which revealed that the staffs of the Anglican Theological Colleges in Australia never got together to discuss theological issues. Furthermore, there was no inclination to do so. The principal of the largest college had said that he could see no benefit in such a meeting. This sad fact put this seminar into a wider context in the life of the church and was thus nationally significant. It has been caught up in a broader strategy emanating from the General Synod Office aimed at the renewal of the life of the Anglican Church in Australia.

The Australian Ecclesial Context

For a variety of reasons Australian Anglicans find themselves in the situation of not being very clear about their own identity as a discrete community within Australian Christianity. In part that has to do with our recent history during the course of the last century, and in part it is reflected in our uncertainty about our relations as Anglicans with other Australians. Recently I attended a parish consultation where the facilitator asked the question, "What did the parish think that it did well?" A number of items were mentioned. Then the facilitator asked the group, "What things could be done better?" Again, a series of items were mentioned amongst which was the suggestion that we could do better at reaching out to people beyond the church. When asked why the parish thought that it was not good at this, one person replied in terms which seemed to gain the assent of the group, namely, "We are not confident that what we believe and do here will work out there." That lack of confidence is in large measure an aspect of our uncertainty about who we are as Anglican Christians when we meet with people who are different.

It is that kind of question which has prompted some reflection on the question of identity and how identity for a group of people, like Australian Anglicans, is shaped. We concluded that there are three important forces which sustain and shape a strong sense of identity. Our awareness of our own story of where we have come from, an awareness of our core beliefs or values, and some reflection on the way in which we relate to others. These three identity shaping forces have provided the framework for the formation of three study groups. The three groups are:

- 1996 Anglican Theology
- 1997 Anglican History
- 1998 Anglican Missiology

These groups have been initiated from the General Synod Office, but they have all been self-funding, and are directed towards the formation of three discrete communities of people who will take responsibility for cultivating these identity forming forces within the Australian Anglicanism.

As a consequence, the focus of these groups needs to be truly Australian, and truly Anglican. They also need to be effectively comprehensive. There are in the Australian Anglican community both centrifugal forces and centripetal forces at work. The centrifugal forces are most manifest in our institutional relationships and often focus on specific issues or local theological distinctives. This centrifugal force is embedded in our strict diocesan structures.

The centripetal forces, which are now increasingly visible in our church, are about the desire of Australian Anglicans to establish some kind of personal connection with others. Those forces were seen at the strikingly successful National Anglican Conference in 1997, and were also visible in some aspects of the 1998 General Synod meeting when new procedures were adopted that facilitated close encounters with people from different dioceses for small group discussion of contentious issues. They can also be seen in the various networks of Australian Anglicans, which are beginning to emerge across Australia. People in these networks want to share and make contact with each other in relation to their particular areas of ministry and activity. It is a challenging conundrum that the tribunes of the centrifugal forces are the hierarchy in its various forms or more loosely the politicians of the church structures. The tribunes of the centripetal forces are mostly laity in separated circumstances, rural, urban, or suburban in our large metropolitan dioceses, those who work in schools or welfare agencies or other independent Anglican organizations or as chaplains.

All of this could be healthy and positive, but at the level of difference some real engagement needs to be fostered, some courteous argument in relation to those issues where there are clear differences of conviction and opinion. Increased and more open personal contact is not a substitute for confronting differences. Rather it provides a better basis for a healthy and engaged community. Australian Anglicans need to sustain an effective conversation about points of difference. At the same time there needs to be a greater measure of encouragement for the foot soldiers responding to the centripetal breeze.

The three identity shaping groups, stewards of theology, history and mission, that have now come into existence, need to be comprehensive in terms of the character of Australian Anglicanism. They must accept a responsibility to share with the church community in terms of the power of the ideas and the theology upon which they work. Such a process will contribute significantly to a better sense of our identity as Australian Anglicans, in order that we can live "out there" with some sense of due confidence.

Wider Ecclesial Context

However, there are wider contexts than just Australian Anglicanism in which these identity questions are relevant. Christianity in Australia calls for living traditions to be in concert with each other. The recent reconstruction of the Australian Council of Churches into the National Council of Churches in Australia is a good example of the changing environment in ecumenical affairs. Whereas the old ACC was an ecumenical body which thought of itself, and very often acted, as a separate entity alongside the churches, the new NCCA is a body of the churches. Of course, it has made a difference that the Roman Catholic Church is a full member of the new body. In the last quarter of the twentieth century in ecumenical relations there has been a move away from ecumenical bodies and activities to churches doing things together ecumenically. The question before Anglicans in that context quite reasonably might be, what is our contribution to this interaction and collaboration. It is not always clear.

- Some suggest we bring a particular ethos.
- Some that we are a liturgical church.

- Some that we have bishops.
- Some that we are part of a worldwide Anglican Communion.

Most commonly, and it is understandable in a year of the Lambeth Conference, people focus on episcopacy. I recall hearing a sermon in which Cyprian (bishop of Carthage 249–58) was described as an Anglican because he was so interested in episcopacy, and also because he had a different view from the more imperial notions of the bishop in Rome. However, that is a view of Anglicanism which is directed towards a particular horizon. In fact, it is an echo of the apologetic that the English reformers mounted to defend their retention of episcopacy particularly against criticism from continental reformers in Geneva. In other words, the notion that the characteristic marker of Anglicanism is episcopacy, actually represents the view from London to Geneva. That is not the only view. If one asks what is the view from London to Rome, then episcopacy in itself is certainly not distinctive. If one asks what is the view from London to Constantinople, then certainly episcopacy is nothing distinctive. There might be minor variations on the sort of episcopacy, or notions of primacy, even universal primacy, but episcopacy is not especially distinctive from the point of view of those two horizons and as a consequence episcopacy is not especially distinctive. The Anglican Church of Australia is committed to the three orders of ministry in its constitution, but without any rationale offered. We will "preserve the three orders of bishops, priests and deacons in the sacred ministry."

It seems to me that one distinction of Anglican ecclesiology is that it asserts that the responsibility for the church belongs to the whole church. From the seventh century church and state in England were indissolubly linked in governing the realm, though the crown was always sovereign in this arrangement. During the Tudor period this pattern reached an extreme form. The nation was constituted as one entity with a spiritual and temporal aspect to it. This was the strong theory of the Royal Supremacy. In the overseas colonies the Royal Supremacy collapsed in the eighteenth century in America after the War of Independence or in the first half of the nineteenth century in Australia after the adoption of elected representative government in the colonies. Within the Royal Supremacy the crown represented the lay element in the governance of the kingdom, including the ecclesiastical system. The collapse of the Christendom model thus raised the question of the lay element in church governance.

As a speculative aside, I mention the question as to why the monasteries were dissolved and not the cathedrals at the time of the English Reformation. Monasteries clearly had allegiances outside the "empire" of England, and some connections with Rome. It was not because the cathedrals did not have wealth, from which the Crown or its friends could have benefited. At least one of the consequences, if not one of the intentions of this exercise, was that it eclipsed for the purposes of ecclesiastical polity, notions of corporateness in the church aside from the Royal Supremacy. The monasteries were mostly not part of the episcopal structure. The episcopal structure was focused around the diocese and the cathedral. While there may have been theological attempts to justify the retention of episcopacy in the English Reformation, from the point of view of Tudor and Stuart political theory, there were very important reasons of power and authority which justified the retention of episcopacy and the cathedrals, but not the monasteries. When James I came to London and sought to deal with the Puritans at the Hampton Court Conference, his reaction to their desire for the recognition of presbyteries and prophesying, was sharp and clear.

> That they aymed at a Scottish Presbytery, which, sayth he, as well agreeth with a monarchy, as God and the divell. Then Iack and Tom, and Will and Dick, shall meete, and at their pleasure censure me and my councill, and all our proceedings. And then turning to the bishops, the king said, "If once you were out, and they in place, I know what would become of my supremacie. No Bishop, no king."[2]

If not the intention for the dissolution of the monasteries then certainly the effect was to eclipse a key element in English ecclesiological experience.

The emergence of synodical decision making in Anglicanism represents the principle that the responsibility for the church belongs to the whole church. The form which it took was of course drawn from the contemporary political construction going on at the time in the colonies. When the Australian bishops met in 1850 to discuss what they should do in the face of the demise of the Royal Supremacy, the critical question with which they struggled was, how to provide for the lay element in church decision making. In the eighteenth century in the United States of America, that lay presence was constituted with a parallel assembly of

2. Barlow, *Summe of the Conference*, 82.

deputies alongside clergy. In Australia in the nineteenth century, a significant step was taken which united both clergy and laity in one synod.

I suggest that this element in our ecclesiology is of real ecumenical significance. It is a contribution which we can bring to the table. However, we tend not to do so because of our lack of clarity about our own ecclesiology and because of the lack of theological analysis and interpretation about our ecclesial polity.

Whether this proposal gains acceptance or not, the question of what we bring as our contribution to the ecumenical encounter in Australia remains and that question will only be answered by some better, more rigorously clarified sense of our identity as a church community.

If one casts the trajectory in a different direction and asks in the horizon of the Anglican Communion what Australian Anglicanism might bring, then clearly from an historical point of view, it is the synodical form of government which emerged in Australia and became the prime model generally around the world. We do have a contribution to make, but we actually do not make it and it is not really heard. Books on the history of the Anglican Communion seem to be set within a framework bounded by the Wash in Lincolnshire and the Appalachians in the eastern United States. The Australian historical contribution is not heard because the literature is not there and the literature is not there because we have not studied our own tradition enough, nor have we critically reflected upon it, not only for our own purposes but for the benefit of others.

The Real Significance of These Seminars

I believe the real significance of these three study groups (Australian Anglican Theology, Australian Anglican History and Australian Anglican Missiology) is quite profound. It is the formation of a living identity for Australian Anglicans, in order that we might live "out there," so that it is not "out there," but is in fact where we truly see we belong and where we are called by God to be the Christians we profess to be.

Work to Be Shared

This particular group is concerned with Australian Anglican Theology. That is our stewardship. We have to work to the highest standards of intellectual rigor and of being informed. In other words, it is a group of scholarly commitment in the service of others.

The ways in which the scholarly work of this group can be shared is helped in a variety of ways. By moving around Australia with the Seminar meetings, some are able to join in each place and share in the discussion that takes place. We ourselves have the opportunity to share in our own areas of vocation. We also have the opportunity of publishing papers which can be more widely available.

So What?

I believe that this group is engaged in important work. It serves the vital issues of living faithfully in Australia as Anglican Christians. It serves the renewal of our church community through our vocation as theologians. Scholarly work of this kind delivers us from repeating the mistakes of the past, and delivers us from the besetting sin of dealing with important questions on the basis of short-term utility.

This important work calls for rigorous theological consideration of important questions for Australia and for Australian Anglicans. We have looked at the issues of a theology of the laity and this time we are discussing reconciliation in church and society. Other questions which we might well consider could be issues of power and authority, or issues of institutionality. These are matters which are touched on at various points in several of the papers which we have before us at this seminar.

The work of this seminar is also difficult work. It demands the highest level of intellectual rigor in a time of rapid change. Such a period of rapid change makes it very difficult to devote time to intellectual endeavor of the highest order. Our work also demands a level of candour, courtesy and argument, because fundamental "concerns" will be uncovered. It demands significant personal openness, sensitivity and care for each other. It demands a high level of spiritual openness because it invites us to place our most cherished convictions in the balance of enquiry, and to be open to God teaching us some new ways of living. We have excellent papers before us to start our process at this seminar. What we are engaged in, is not just for our own benefit. It is of wider and quite fundamental significance in the process of the renewal of The Anglican Church of Australia. This ambition was the seed which later led to the formation of the Journal of Anglican Studies.

10

National Conferences and the Renewal of the Church[1]

WE HAVE COME TOGETHER from across this vast continent to make connections. Our challenge is to find ways of making connections and creating community both within our own church and with our fellow Australians. Our challenge is located in a society that hungers for human community. We have before us a program which helps to mark out the lineaments of that challenge, making connections within the church, with the wider community, and with the issues that we face here in Australia as Anglican Christians.

It would be very easy for us to take over the romantic aspirations of our day and imagine that our task is to find a utopian level of peace and harmony in the church and in our society. Such an ambition comes easily to a tradition of Christian faith that has assumed that it is part of the social furniture as a kind of "wall paper establishment" and a tradition which, for over three centuries, has imbibed the idea that we Anglicans stand for peaceful uniformity in both church and society.

But I want to say right up front that the very faith which we profess, the very Lord whom we serve, creates division in the human family. Jesus was not kidding when he said "whoever loves father or mother more than me is not worthy of me; and whoever loves son or daughter more than me is not worthy of me; and whoever does not take up the cross and follow me is not worthy of me" (Matt 10:37–38).

---

1. This was the opening address of the Second National Anglican Conference held at the University of New South Wales, Sydney, in 2002.

The absolute and exclusive claims of Christ create division because they put every other allegiance, every other connection, into second place. If we are to be Jesus' disciples it is still the case in the twenty first century that we must take up the cross of Christ in order to follow him.

Furthermore, within the church community the peace of uniformity is not an aspiration worthy of our attention. On the contrary the creative activity of God within the church is to produce individuality and difference rather than sameness and conformity. Paul's response to the egocentric individualism of the Corinthians was not conformist control but an affirmation of individuality. The great truth in Christianity is that these differences are creative to the extent that they are exercised as gifts from God and to the extent that those who have them demonstrate the unending love declared in the gospel.

> If I speak with the tongues of men and of angels, but have not love, I am only a resounding gong or a clanging cymbal. If I have the gift of prophecy and can fathom all mysteries and all knowledge, and if I have a faith that can move mountains, but I have not love, I am nothing. (1 Cor 13:1–2)

But this Christian love is not just any kind of love. Paul goes on to characterize that love. It is patient and kind, not envious or boastful, or arrogant or rude. Does not insist on its own way, is not irritable or resentful. It does not rejoice in wrongdoing, but rejoices in the truth. It bears all things, hopes all things, endures all things. This is what a Christian community, a church, should look like. This is what we as Christ citizens in Australia should look like.

As a church community we struggle with the differences that exist amongst us. When love, mutual respect and trust in a community are diminished it is easy for diversity and difference to turn into division and conflict. In Australian Anglicanism we have found it all too easy to retreat into our regional locations and tribal loyalties and content ourselves with a facile appearance of peace.

We in this generation have not been alone in facing this particular challenge. For two thousand years Christians have struggled with it. It is no wonder that the history of the church is the history of our unending need for forgiveness and turning again and again to the redeeming love of the crucified Lord to whom we belong.

Less than a decade after Jesus' death the early Christians were divided as to how to regard gentiles within the church. It created conflict and division. How could the manifest differences be respected but yet kept in their place in the light of the universal significance of Jesus' life and death.

The Corinthian Christians were so impressed by their own talents that they lost sight of the fact that they were part of a wider fellowship. Not only did they slip unconsciously into moral failures but also into spiritual arrogance. In frustration Paul asked them: "What do you have that you did not receive?" The mutual inter-dependence of the church applies not only to individuals within a local group, but also to groups within a greater whole.

It should not surprise us that many of the doctrinal disputes in the early church had national and cultural elements in them. Indeed, some of these doctrinal disputes were in truth driven by cultural and social forces. Doctrine can so easily provide the language for other more mundane disagreements even today.

At the time of the Reformation a commitment to the immense significance of the free and overflowing grace of God in the gospel often led to exclusiveness in other areas of life which created division and conflict. The political solution of legislated compulsory uniformity in England had more to do with the assumptions of Tudor imperialism than with the mentality of the community of the crucified. When we Anglicans were restored to political favor in 1662, we indulged in a bitter and futile program of persecution against dissent.

We in Australia have a particular form of this dividing tendency and this aspect of our history has a profound effect on our present situation. From the earliest times of European settlement local differences emerged. The separate colonies quickly developed different social and institutional characteristics. The tyranny of the physical distance soon became the tyranny of the mental and emotional distances which separated Australians. In the political and commercial arenas Australians learnt that for security and trade the different colonies had to communicate with each other and to work together. The great forces of external threat in war and the commercial realities of trade have compelled Australians to think more nationally. As a result, there emerged during the twentieth century a real sense of what it is to be Australian, a real sense of a national identity in which we all participate.

Australian Anglicans quickly found in the nineteenth century the value of communicating across the vast distances of this country. But lacking the powerful external forces of security and trade, powerful national institutions have not developed in our version of Anglicanism.

However, the problem is not so much that we have not developed powerful national church institutions. More fundamental and ultimately much more important is the fact that we have not developed a strong sense of belonging to each other in our common faith as Australian Anglicans. Rather we have overlaid our natural regional differences with religious explanations and have allowed ourselves to imagine that these religious explanations of our differences are the whole story. The effect of this is that we make it harder for ourselves to have a critical relationship to our own local cultures and at the same time we magnify in our own minds the significance of our differences so that they more easily become divisive and conflictual. This is the real evil in our nurtured diocesanism.

The distinctive feature in Australian Anglicanism is not so much the absence of powerful coercive national institutions but the absence of any creative commitment to listening to each other. That determined insularity corrodes our faith and makes us into caricatures of the gifts which we can bring to our fellow Anglicans in this land, and beyond.

We pretend to ourselves that the problem is with others. We designate the Christian community to which we belong as a denomination. It is an interesting rhetorical move for it allows the force of our gospel obligation to love each other to be turned into nothing more than a rule for the membership of some incidental social club. Or alternatively we think of others as somehow defective in their church life because they do not share our own particular perspectives, preferences or styles.

Even when fundamental issues are involved and we are tempted to think of the other as defective, even heretical, and ourselves as orthodox, our commitment to love remains with us as a gospel imperative and the first step in that love is to engage and listen.

In our Australian Anglican community the root of the distance which contradicts the gospel lies not in our local individuality but in an unwillingness to listen. John said "those who do not love a brother or sister whom they have seen, cannot love God whom they have not seen" (1 John 4:20). The question for us as Australian Anglicans is how can we say that we listen to God whom we cannot see if we do not listen to our fellow Christian whom we do see. We struggle on this point because we have been so regional, so tribal.

Even though our generation does look like a stand out case on this point we are not alone. Each generation in the past has sought ways to overcome these problems. Church Congresses from 1882 to 1924 brought Anglicans together to share ideas and insights and to encourage discipleship, but eventually they ceased to be creative and in any case were probably always a bit too clerical in orientation and interest. The General Synod from 1872 was a kind of national forum, though it soon, like other synods locally, began to look more like a parliament with parties and factions and decision strategies which appeared to have more to do with the exercising of political power and preventing activity rather than with creativity.

There have been moderately sectional means of connections through the mission and educational agencies and conferences. The first National Anglican Conference in 1997 tried to move beyond the sectional, as does this conference. Conferences are one way in which we can gather together to seek the face of our God and pray for the renewal of our faith and life.

So any contribution this conference might make to the renewal of our Christian faith and life will be conditional on our openness to listen to the Spirit of God through the gifts and individuality of our fellow Christians. In his opening address to the 1882 Church Congress bishop James Moorhouse said much the same thing. In 1882, most members of our church thought of the Church of England in Australia as the kind of spiritual and moral government of Australia. That is not our situation in 2002. We today are not government, but witnesses. A renewal of our faith and life which leads us to become a community whose diversity is creatively held together in Christian love and respect will itself be a powerful witness to a society searching for models of community.

In such a witness the way in which we disagree will be much more important than the fact that we disagree. It will not be a fault in this witness that we are marked by individuality and difference, but it will be a defeat if we are marked by an absence of love. A love which is patient and kind, not envious or boastful, or arrogant or rude, does not insist on its own way, is not irritable or resentful, does not rejoice in wrongdoing, but rejoices in the truth. It bears all things, hopes all things, endures all things.

While we may be the agents of such a witness, the community we seek will be created only by the gracious work of God amongst us. It is God who creates anew the people of God and it is the first task of the people of God to attend to the workings of the Spirit of God in that redeeming creativity. For that reason, if this conference is to play a role in the renewal of the faith and life of our church community it will do so as it helps us to attend to the living God.

May I say to you with the utmost encouragement that the degree to which this conference achieves that goal is now really in your hands.

I commend you to the God and Father of our Lord Jesus Christ. In the days that lie ahead open your heart and mind to the Spirit of God. Listen for that voice in the Bible Studies, the keynote addresses and the stories you will hear. Listen for that voice in what you yourself say to others and in what you hear from others, and as we listen together, we may yet see God work a miracle of renewal in the life of faith we share as Australian Anglicans.

11

Changing the Context of Church Schools[1]

THE LAST TIME THAT I spoke at a Conference of the National Anglican Schools Consultative Committee, I finished my remarks by saying that I had never been a school teacher and did not believe that it was my vocation. I begin these remarks by saying, that I have never been a school principal and do not believe that it is my vocation. For many years I worked not only in universities but in university colleges, and indeed for eleven years, I was the Master of a university college. Perhaps there are some analogies to be drawn, and no doubt what I have to say today has been influenced by my experience in university colleges.

The second disclaimer with which I want to begin is that this address is not about how the national Church views Anglican Schools. Given the character of Australian Anglicanism, it is entirely beyond my understanding as to how anyone could express a view about what the national Church thinks about the role of a principal in an Anglican School. My title therefore is somewhat more modest. I would like to speak about a National Perspective on Anglican Schools. I do that with the disclaimers which I have already mentioned, and in the spirit of sharing something of my own experience and thinking about Anglican institutions, and questions of leadership from my present location in the General Synod Office.

Therefore, I would like to begin by talking about the changing context of Anglican Schools and their strategic significance, then in broader strokes to mention something of what I believe is our faith situation as Australians, and the challenges facing us as Australian Anglicans.

---

1. This is an edited version of a paper given at a Conference of the National Anglican Schools Consultative Committee.

The Educational Context

In broad terms, I think there have been four stages in the development of our school situation as we presently experience it. From 1788, when the Colony of New South Wales was established until the Bourke Act in 1836, the Anglican Church had a monopoly on education. This education was not only conducted by the Anglican Church, but it was specifically Anglican in character.

The revolutionary Church Act of Governor Bourke in 1836 changed all that. It provided for government grants to each recognized church (Presbyterian, Roman Catholic, and Anglican) on a more or less pro rata basis in terms of population numbers. That pattern flowed through to the provision of schools. By this Act the religious plurality which already existed in the Colony was recognized, and the Anglican monopoly in the provision of religious services and particularly of education was destroyed.

This was the beginning of the long history of religious pluralism in Australia. In 1839, Governor Gipps tried to introduce a scheme of government schools, but he was opposed by Bishop Broughton who wanted to keep the state out of schooling. In a dramatic speech at the Bar of the Legislative Council, the Bishop said, that it was against the Constitution which was the union of church and state: "The reason for connecting the throne so inseparably with this faith, (that is to say Anglicanism) was their persuasion, that this faith was most consonant with truth and most friendly to liberty."[2]

The Governor withdrew his plans for comprehensive government schools, but the tide was running against Broughton's conception of the state. Indeed, the tide was in full flood against him, and in the course of the next decade he had to change his position radically. So it was, that in 1848 he acceded to a system of government, or national, schools which was introduced alongside the existing church systems.

In 1836, the Anglican monopoly had gone and now in 1848 the monopoly of the churches had gone and there was a dual system of state schools and church schools each overseen by a separate Schools Board.

However, after 1848 the funding for denominational schools and national schools changed. In 1866, the New South Wales Schools Act amalgamated the Denominational and National Schools Boards, under a Council of Education. The new arrangements had a built-in financial

---

2. Broughton, *Speech of the Lord Bishop*, 12.

bias in favor of the National Schools. Also, during the period 1860–80, the Roman Catholic Church became more independent minded in its approach to education, and at the same time, the tide of liberal opinion in regard to social policies in the colonies began to affect attitudes towards education. The result was a series of education Acts which cut off state aid to church schools, and the free compulsory and secular education of the Victorian Act became common throughout the country. Here, secular did not mean, not religious, but rather it meant, not controlled by the church.

Thus, in the late nineteenth century at the high point of statism in the colonies a state monopoly in education emerged. Participation of the churches was possible, but it was in the framework set by the state. As is well known the Roman Catholic Church set out to establish and run their own system for their own people. Anglicans collaborated with the new arrangements yielding their schools to the state with the exception of some of their elite schools. That is the school system in which I was educated. When I left my state high school in 1955, I was blissfully unaware that I was living through dramatic changes in the education system.

The whole theory of education was under review, the school population was increasing dramatically and the Roman Catholic school system was struggling desperately to cope with the numbers. The situation cracked in 1962 with the strike of Roman Catholic schools in Goulburn. It was at this point that Garfield Barwick, as Attorney General, assisted his Prime Minister, Robert Menzies, to provide some funds for Roman Catholic schools. It had long been thought that the establishment clause 116 of the Australian Constitution prevented governments from providing funds to churches and also to church schools. Barwick suggested that grants for science laboratories would not infringe section 116. The consequences of those initial moves are now with us, so that what we have in the present day is government funded independent schools alongside a state school system. A return to the situation we had in the middle of the nineteenth century.

It is important to reflect upon the changes that have taken place in these various stages. In 1836, the issue was the Christian character of the state. In 1848, it was about Christian participation in a plural state. In 1880, it was also about Christian participation in a plural state, but this time a state which took to itself a monopoly of public funds for education. In 1962, it was about the relaxation of that funding monopoly for

State Schools. In that sense it was about the institutional privatization of education at government expense.

The most recent phase has involved a transformation of Anglican attitudes towards education and its broader social significance. That change has gone largely unnoticed. It has significant implications for our understanding of education and its relation to society, for both private schools and for state schools.

This pluralization of education raises profound questions, which in an Anglican context we have no right to avoid. Does it mean not just the privatization of religion and values but also their ghettoization? Even if it does not necessarily mean that, is that fatal consequence now more likely than it was before?

In a way which before was not true almost everything depends on the openness and quality of Anglican Schools. If they are not open, and in some sense accessible to all, but rather aim at serving a discrete and demarcated religious group, then they are likely to create great damage to society and to Anglican Christianity in this country. I hope that will not happen. We are heirs and custodians of a religious tradition which bespeaks openness.

However one evaluates the current trends, it is manifest that the context in which Anglican Schools operate has been significantly reconfigured in the second half of the twentieth century. While funding may seem to be readily available for Anglican schools new and old, that may not always be the case. More than that, it seems to me that, in due course, just as the funding for school education has increasingly become the responsibility of the Federal Government, so the question of curriculum and the content of that education will increasingly attract the attention of that same Federal Government. In that context in secondary education, an Anglican educational identity for schools which name themselves as Anglican, becomes a matter of crucial significance for the way in which they think about their vocation.

The Church Context

At the same time as this process has been taking place, the Anglican Church itself has been undergoing great change. As those changes grow, we will be obliged to reconceptualize how we understand The Anglican Church of Australia. We are increasingly being obliged to make a distinction between the organizational institutional arrangements, which are associated with our Christian community of Australian Anglicans, and that community itself. The community of Christians who name themselves as Anglicans are a dispersed body of people scattered around this country. By community I do not mean simply the community that is visible, which for example attends General Synod, or more significantly a National Anglican Conference. Australians constitute a community of people, but you never see them assembled *in toto*. If you ask any one of us, are you an Australian? It is reasonably easy to give the answer yes. That is true whether you live in New South Wales, Victoria, Tasmania or even in Earls Court in London. My son lives in South Carolina in the United States of America. He thinks of himself as an Australian, not because he carries an Australian passport, that is simply a sign of a deeper truth. He is an Australian in the sense that he belongs to what Benedict Anderson has called, an "imagined community", a A community which exists in the imagination and mind of those who belong to it.[3]

In a similar way, Australian Anglicans belong to a community. In this sense they are a church. That community exists in all sorts of configurations and is experienced and imagined on a variety of horizons. From a base community, which might be a local house church to a wider perhaps regional or diocesan community, to a national community such as was hinted at in the 1997 National Anglican Conference in Canberra.

That community has a number of institutional and organizational arrangements which serve and promote its life. There is the diocesan synod structure, but there are also other organizations which are not necessarily linked to, or controlled by, this diocesan system. Many Anglican schools, welfare and mission agencies, have only notional or no contact with the diocesan and synodical structure. The organizational arrangements which serve the Anglican community in Australia are broader than the synod structure. In one sense structures are like parables, in that we are familiar with them but are not always clear what we mean by them.

In that context of understanding I believe that we are actually witnessing significant change in the landscape of the national church. In 1850, the bishops of the Church of England in Australasia met for a conference to discuss the state of the churches in the colonies. Subsequently diocesan constitutions and synods were created though the models did

---

3. See Anderson, *Imagined Communities*.

not follow the pattern advised by the conference. In 1872, there was a meeting of bishops and others for a General Synod. Not for another ninety years was a national constitution established and in the meantime the dioceses established their own independent characters. We should not imagine that this was simply a question of determined individualism on the part of the diocese. The diocesan character of our synodical arrangements reflects as much as anything else the social and demographic character of colonies when these institutions where being consolidated and the past local cultures were being reinforced by acquired legitimating convictions.

During the 1960s and 1970s, the General Synod set itself up much in the style of a government, with Commissions, Standing Committee, canons, rules and bills, which were called legislation, and a General Synod which used as its default guide for Standing Orders those operating in the Commonwealth Parliament. Of course, the constitution did not give the General Synod very much power, most of which was kept in the dioceses.

During the 1980s, centralizing trends in Australian government activity in education and welfare, led to the creation of networks which drew together the church agencies in those areas. NACON which recently became Anglicare, was formed during this period and a little later came the National Anglican Schools Consultative Committee.

During the 1990s, other networks began to emerge, for example networks of Youth Officers, and of Registrars. Throughout the 1990s, people began to take initiatives on their own account. Volunteer associations for agreed purposes have emerged; a community to promote the study of Australian Anglican theology, a community to promote the study of Australian Anglican history and a community to study Anglican missiology in Australia.

The great success of the National Anglican Conference in 1997 captured something of this undercurrent which had been growing for some time. That current was about a new way of connecting on the national dimension and it became visible at the National Conference. It was more about voluntary enterprise activities, and somehow it was trying to capture the elements of what it means to be Australian and what it means to be Anglican.

In his presidential address at the recent General Synod Archbishop, Rayner said that the Conference taught us "that synods are not the only, nor even the most important, vehicle for corporate life . . . creative work is most likely to happen through less formal forums at different levels."

That different impulse was also visible at the recent meeting of the General Synod in Adelaide. There was also a sense that the future requires us to address fundamental questions about our life as a church community and the inescapable challenge before us to be open to new things. It was in this context that the General Synod changed the organizational structure of the national Church when it repealed the Commissions Canon and established a new way of doing things. It is a way of doing things that is strategic, modest, aimed at the medium term and using the vehicle of Task Forces. A way which recognized, encouraged, facilitated and nurtured networks, and which put governance in the old parliamentary sense into passive mode in the background ready to be called for if needed.

Thus, I am suggesting that in the last twenty years there have been currents at work in Australian society and in the Anglican community which have only recently come to expression, and which are about a different way of being Australian Anglicans. Those currents point to changes in the disposition of the Australian Anglican Church community which have already had a radical impact on the organizational structure of our national community life.

In that process, there has been a change in the direction of outreach. A change to enterprise and to a lighter structure as in the terms of the Evangelism Task Group report to the Standing Committee in 1996, which spoke of a move from hierarchy to collaboration, from compliance to cooperation. Unity is thus in the process of being redefined in the direction of connection rather than uniformity. At the same time, in that very process, the notion of community is also being redefined and is reemerging with the accent on interdependence and relationship.

We should not imagine that these changes mean that differences between Anglicans have disappeared, rather they are being redefined. In that process these changes which I am reporting are fraught with risk because they may open the possibility that the differences between us may become more volatile. The challenge before us as a church is to find ways, in a greater spirit of openness and interaction, that will enable us to honor our own particular convictions and those of our fellow Anglicans in the conversation which is constitutive of our Australian Anglican Church community.

So far, we have only seen small beginnings to these reconfiguring changes, but they are pointers to a significant movement. It is in that context of the reconfiguration of the arrangements that exist in the Anglican church community, that Anglican church schools are emerging in a national network with significant vocational challenges, both in relation to the broader society and to the church community.

It is common these days for institutions to have mission statements. These statements seek to encapsulate what the institution is trying to achieve. Anglican schools often find it difficult to identify precisely their exact mission. That is not due to a lack of thought, or imagination, but to the very complex and often conflicting claims that are made upon a school because of the complexity of their institutional location. They owe allegiance to the church and its beliefs and values, to the government from whom they receive considerable funds often for very specifically identified purposes, and they are caught in the web of a market situation where they must compete with other schools. That competition is increasingly set in terms which are not always sympathetic with the foundation purposes and values of the school.

Even in the internal discussion the Anglican school will not always find it easy to balance these demands and constraints with commitments to fostering a Christian community in the school, to influencing the educational environment in a direction sympathetic to and supportive of Christian values and beliefs. An Anglican school cannot avoid the struggle of dealing with these competing forces.

The Institutional Context

There is a further reconfiguration taking place in our society which affects the context in which Anglican schools operate. That is the reconfiguration of institutional roles in society. One might think of the list of matters raised by Hugh Mackay in *Reinventing Australia*, in regard to work, families and gender relationships and, in his more recent book *Generations*, describes the relationship between the generations that exist in our society. In institutional life there have been changes in the way in which we can count on other people behaving. The degree to which we can be confident about how people will respond in an institutional relationship is visibly changing. In the corporate arena, the introduction of portable superannuation has led to a dramatic shortening of tenure of middle management. This changes the character of the community which inhabits those corporate structures. There is a discernible change in the way in which authority is conceived. It is in this context that notions of leadership have become a focus in institutional life generally, and not only, in the business corporation. Notions of leadership inevitably involve issues of power and power has often been found by several recent Royal Commissions to be at the root of institutional failure.

In all of these changes significant questions are raised about the transmission of values. Values used to be learned as a consequence of long and sustained relationships with other people, between parents and children, teachers and students. However, now values have to be taught in training programs. Corporations engage in team building exercises, because people are not with each other long enough for the team sense to develop naturally in the course of ordinary activities. This reconfiguration of institutional roles in our society has value implications which affect schools.

This changing context, the reconfiguration of the educational arena, the Anglican church and its institutions, particularly at the national level, and institutional roles in our society, give to Anglican schools a different strategic significance for the Anglican Church community in our country.

Anglican Schools as Interface Institutions

The first thing that needs to be noted about Anglican schools, is that they are interface institutions. They are institutions which necessarily engage people who are part of the church community with those who are not. A church school is an intentional institution, with a commitment to Anglican values and beliefs, yet it must relate to a Federal Government which is not always interested in, and sometimes has ideas which are anti-pathetic to those beliefs and values. An Anglican school must interact with students and parents who have little or no sympathy with the Anglican character of the school but join the school for other reasons, social and educational.

The Anglican school in today's Australia is an interface institution at the cutting edge of Christian faith and mission in Australia. Clearly Anglican schools have a strategic role in relation to the education of young people in a society where family life is being dramatically rearranged and where life skills and life values are being programmed rather than imbibed. The education provided in an Anglican school, intentionally committed to beliefs and values of a particular kind, becomes strategically vital in the Christian witness in this nation.

The role of the Anglican school is also strategically significant, because one of the crucial issues at stake in our society is knowledge and wisdom. Are we to be a clever country full of knowledge or a mature country marked by wisdom? A great deal depends on the education that people receive and the goals to which they are encouraged to aspire.

In my view, the school is also strategically important because it is a case model of the Christian vocation to deal with conflict and compromise, the multiplicity of values, and the plurality of plausibilities that exists in our society. The intentional school cannot but run itself into conflict in various ways, both internally and externally. The Christian virtue of appropriate compromise while maintaining a vivid and dynamic belief and vocation is a lesson that, I would guess, is presented daily in Anglican schools in this country. It is a lesson that all Christians will increasingly need to understand and to learn, because we are more and more in a mixed community in relation to values and beliefs, where we will increasingly be obliged not only to explain but to be vigorous in maintaining our beliefs and values in ways that commend those beliefs and values.

Our Faith Situation as Australians

In regard to the practice and promotion of the Christian faith, there are some particular contours to our Australian situation. These contours emerge as a consequence of historical development, some of which I have already touched on in describing the development of education in our country.

Changes took place in Australia in the first decades of the twentieth century, whereby what Paul Kelly has called "the Australian settlement," gradually took hold in our society. Anglican Christians in general found themselves as contented participants in that Australian settlement. Paul Kelly identifies a number of leading ideas in what he calls the Australian settlement. They are:

- The White Australia Policy, in order to preserve coherence in the community.
- Protection in tariff terms, in order to secure Australian industry and commercial life.
- Centralized arbitration, on the basis of what is a fair wage, largely established on the precedent of Justice Higgins' Harvester Judgement.

- State paternalism; the thought that if it is wrong or broken the government should fix it.
- Imperial benevolence in foreign affairs, whether it be Britain in the first stage or the United States in the latter years.

Paul Kelly suggests that this Australian settlement is now in disarray, as a result of weakening international ties with great powers and the globalization of much of our commercial life.

It is interesting to me to note that in more recent times, Anglicans have had to distance themselves from, or come to a new accommodation with, almost all of the questions which Paul Kelly touches on. Anglicans were the invisible partners in that long period of the Australian settlement, and the high point of their success in the population, corresponded with a high point of population growth under the Australian settlement.

However, in the last twenty years, things have been changing. The multiplicity of plausibilities, the internalization of values, a whole series of individualist and subjective impulses sometimes gathered together under the heading of post modernism, or its grandchild populism, have combined to show us that we live in uncertain times. In that context, what used to be called the absoluteness of Christianity, is not only not accepted, it seems inconceivable.

Like other Australians, we are therefore faced with many ambiguities in responding to this situation. Sometimes people respond in authoritarian terms, claiming objective authority as a way to hold the line. Others say that we must take the opportunity to enable people to make their choice. So, Christianity becomes one of a number of boutique offerings in the market place of leisure options.

Neither of these responses is adequate to the Christian faith and the presence of the living God in this or other generations. Another way needs to be found whereby we can with due confidence not only live out the Christian life but commend it to others. It is in that context of the faith situation in Australia that significant challenges face Australian Anglicans generally and Anglican schools specifically.

This analysis leads me to think that there are three fundamental challenges facing us as Australian Anglicans. I leave aside here the organizational issues. They are important but not fundamental. These challenges have to do with how we can live and commend the faith in our Australian context. I put them in terms of questions.

- How can we live and act with due confidence about our faith in Christ in a confused world?

- How can we be and become a Christian community within which there is real difference of gift and vocation and real bonding in the body of Christ, in a society which is so radically plural and which has such little understanding of the nature of an interactive and interdependent community?

- How can we engage with our fellow Australians who have moved discernibly into a compartmentalized mentality and lifestyle?

In some form or other Anglican schools are at the sharp edge of all of these challenges.

I am grateful to the National Anglican Schools Consultative Committee for regularly inviting me to speak at your annual conferences on subjects for which I do not have answers, but which raise for me in my place, challenges and hopes, beliefs and disappointments. I think I can thank you for putting me through this Lenten experience. I am certain that I can salute our Anglican schools as fellow pilgrims in exciting times.

12

Some Directions in the Anglican Church of Australia for Examining Chaplains[1]

IN THIS CONFERENCE THE question of where we are going is of particular importance in terms of the contributions that are made to the life of the Anglican church community by clergy, since this is a conference of people who exercise significant influence on the selection and training of clergy. The particular aspect of the question of where we are going also relates specifically to the position of this conference, which has previously been sponsored by the Ministry and Training Commission of the General Synod. The General Synod abolished that commission in February 1998 as part of a package of changes to enable a more effective engagement with the wider Australian society.

It was envisaged that those involved in the Ministry and Training Commission would be encouraged to engage with the challenges of Examining Chaplains more broadly and with more initiative. Members of this conference therefore have a vital interest in the broad question of where the Anglican Church of Australia is going and the vision that lies behind the new arrangements.

If we step back a little from our immediate concern with the church and set our thinking in the broader context of changes in Australia, we will have a better vantage point from which to see the context in which our Christian witness and the ministry of our church is set.

As a nation we have been experiencing a period of significant institutional and cultural change. Hugh Mackay speaks of a plague of anxiety

---

1. This paper was originally given at a meeting of the Examining Chaplains Association held in Melbourne.

and Paul Kelly of the end of certainty. These anxieties and uncertainties, have been documented for us by writers, such as Paul Kelly, Hugh Mackay, Paul Sheehan and Greg Melleuish. However, there are particular themes which apply to Anglicans and which accentuate the position which these writers outline. I say this because our Anglican history in the past two hundred years has not prepared us well for the last twenty years. Let me portray the story as I see it in broad-brush strokes.

Anglicanism came to this country in 1788 It was part of a government structure in a command society. While the first chaplain, Richard Johnson, may not have exercised much command authority, his successors certainly did, and in due course the archdeacon was assumed to be a member of the Executive Council of Government. In 1836, this Anglican hegemony was divided amongst what the Governor, Richard Bourke, called the three main pillars of Christianity, Presbyterianism, Roman Catholicism and The Church of England. They each received state benefits as well as state privileges.

At the same time as Anglicans lost their monopoly on the privileges of their exclusive church state relationship, they also lost their monopoly on one of their principal instruments for the propagation of their faith, namely their schools. The public culture of the colony had been dominated by the strong presence of Christian public values, which had been largely dressed in Anglican clothes. During the course of the 1840s and 1850s these values were increasingly eclipsed by what came to be called a democratic spirit. During the latter part of the nineteenth century, Anglicans lost their monopoly on state aid, indeed lost state aid for their churches altogether. Their place in education was mostly taken over by the state and during the course of the twentieth century they became players on the sidelines.

During the first part of the twentieth century, because of an accommodation between conservative political forces and the conservative establishment mentality of Anglicanism, there was a sense in which the Anglican Church remained a socially prominent institution. The association of Roman Catholicism with the Labor Party, and the strategy of Roman Catholic education in preparing people for the public service combined in the first half of the twentieth century to produce an entirely different situation, especially in New South Wales.

This period characterized by Paul Kelly as the Australian Settlement, was sustained by what he calls five pillars:

1. The White Australia Policy
2. Tariff Protection
3. Centralized Arbitration of the labor market
4. State paternalism
5. Imperial benevolence

Kelly's argument, colored somewhat by his own commitment to globalized capitalism, is that all of these five pillars have diminished in the last twenty years to the point of insignificance. He portrays the challenge for Australia as being a contest between international rationalists and sentimental traditionalists. Of course, it is a highly colored account, but nonetheless one which points to significant changes which have had implications for the position of Anglicans. By and large Anglicans identified with the Australian Settlement, and the recent changes described by Kelly have left Anglicans significantly at sea and on the back foot in terms of their relationship to Australian society generally, and to government policy in particular.

The changed relationship with society for Anglicans has highlighted the internal differences within the Anglican community, and has left them confused about their identity as Anglicans, and more particularly as Australian Anglicans. The pathologies of the big angst are certain to be present amongst Anglicans as they are amongst Australians generally, and the temptations are clearly there.

- The temptation to escape.
- The temptation of social amnesia and thus of hope.
- The temptation of self-absorption, and avoidance of engagement with the wider culture.
- A preoccupation with internal church affairs.
- The temptation to think that unity demands uniformity.

These regressions to the peculiarities of the past remained as temptations for Australian Anglicans in the 1990s.

In the last two hundred years, the story of Anglicans in Australia, and the difficulties, which they presently confront, raises a number of critical issues. The three most important issues in the present situation for Anglicans are those of:

- Confidence, as that capacity to resonate persuasively with the experience of our fellow Australians in sharing our Christian faith.
- Community as that capacity to grow in inter dependent diversity.
- Engagement so that we represent both individually and as a community of Christian people.
- A respectful visionary approach to the future of Australian society.

These things are all critical issues for the future of Anglicanism in the Australian environment. Of course, in a certain sense these are secondary issues, because the fundamental question which faces us all is how we are to live as God's people, individually and together as a community of Christians, in the society in which God has placed us.

I recently took part in a parish consultation as part of the process of seeking a new minister for our parish. In the discussion the facilitator encouraged the group to identify those things which it believed it did well. Various items were identified. The group was then asked to identify those things which could be done better. A number of items were mentioned, amongst them the capacity to reach out to the local community. The facilitator pointed out that the group had declared itself to be accessible and welcoming. Why then was there a difficulty in reaching out to the community? One response was that while we feel comfortable in what we do within our church community, we are not certain that what we believe and do here will work or make sense out there. It was a quite telling observation, more particularly since the acid test for any Christian community is the degree to which the faith of the members of that community works "out there."

It is in this context that I want to highlight some tendencies that face us in our institutionality as a community of Anglicans.

Changes in the Anglican Church of Australia

The institutions which serve the Anglican Community in Australia are not all located in, or necessarily related to, the synod structure. There are many things that happen that are part of that Anglican community's life and mission that are facilitated by institutions that are not associated with and often not even connected with the synod structure. Of the missionary agencies, only the Anglican Board of Mission Australia has an official connection with the synod structure. SAMS, CMS and BCA do not, and many of the welfare agencies are quite separately structured, either from General Synod or the dioceses. Many Anglican schools are similarly independent institutions. Communication agencies, *Church Scene* as it was, and other communication agencies that exist to serve the Anglican community are not necessarily connected to the synod structure.

The truth is that a great range of institutions serve the Anglican community, some connected with the synodical organization and some not.

A number of cultural and institutional currents are running in Australia as a whole which affect the relationships between these various institutions. Local community organizations are being drawn by Federal government funding arrangements into broader national connections. The Federal government prefers to deal with national organizations. Principally these relate to welfare and educational organizations. Independent welfare organizations around the country are beginning to come under the auspices of a network called Anglicare. These welfare agencies have adopted public imagery in the form of a common name which probably makes them appear more coherent than perhaps they really are. However, Anglicare Australia represents an enormous step in national identity for our welfare agencies. Diocesan organizations which belong to Anglicare now have a dual connection. One which is regional, that is to say diocesan, and one which is national. The national connection is created by forces shaped by finance and Federal Government policy.

A similar tendency can be seen with Anglican schools, though there is a significant division between the more recently established independent low fee system schools, and the older more traditional high fee schools. No doubt in due course this division will have to be resolved, but in a schooling system, the same kinds of federalizing tendencies are driving church schools into national liaisons.

These two examples arise directly in the first instance out of federal government policy and finance considerations. As Australia becomes a tighter political and cultural entity other areas will become significant as well.

This can also be seen in the way in which certain kinds of services, particularly financial and communication lead to national liaisons of one kind or another. The provision of insurance for example, has been the subject of a number of national collaborative endeavors, facilitated through the General Synod Office, and they represent collaboration driven by national tendencies in the insurance industry. The same is true of commercial arrangements to purchase cars and telecommunications services negotiated through the General Synod Office for the use of all Anglican entities.

We are therefore in a period of some fluidity and transition in regard to patterns of relationships between the various institutions which serve the Anglican community in Australia. I also observe that many neighboring dioceses are beginning to find a basis for collaboration. Those collaborations do not necessarily come through provincial synods, or even diocesan synods. They are about working relationships between people who are involved in the same kinds of responsibilities.

The Synodical Picture

When we turn to the situation of synods similar changes might be expected. Australia contributed significantly to the emergence of diocesan synods in the nineteenth century. The democratic spirit that was strident in the colonies at the time and the popular ownership of the Church of England combined to shape synods as single chamber gatherings that included lay and clerical representatives together. That popular ownership of the church reflects the lay control of the English Christendom through the Royal Supremacy, though whether that thought motivated those involved in the Australian colonies at the time is not clear.

Synod structures emerged separately in the independent colonies. The dioceses came together in 1872 for a conference which turned itself into a General Synod but it carried little jurisdictional authority in the constituent dioceses. At the turn of the century a nation forming spirit produced a Commonwealth of Australia and a constitution. The churches participated in the preparatory discussions seeking recognition and church independence, but did not capture the nation forming spirit in their own ecclesiastical life. A national church constitution did not come until 1962 by which time local diocesan culture had become entrenched and the new constitution provided incorporation and clergy disciplinary appellate functions but little else by way of jurisdictional authority. Thus, for historical reasons the Anglican Church of Australia is highly decentralized. It is thus in some sharp contrast to the Church of England which retains strong national and centralized church structures. This structural character means that any movement for the renewal of the life of the church community has to work not within but in relation to this silo structure.

Some changes in the processes of the General Synod were introduced in 1998 in order to facilitate more cooperative ways of working together and to encourage engagement across the "silo" differences between dioceses. These changes arose from a report to the Standing Committee on how conflict resolution methods might be introduced in the synod arrangements. The proposals went to the General Synod in 1998 and were enthusiastically supported by synod members.

The initial form was to introduce small group discussion of key substantial or contentious matters. This was achieved by resolving the synod into committee for the process to be conducted without the formal constraints of standing orders, which were based on parliamentary procedures. Debate for the chosen issue was introduced by a lead speaker from each side with a brief to introduce what they saw as the issues at stake in the motion and their own arguments on the motion. This was followed by a question time prior to breaking into groups for discussion. Groups were formed on the floor of synod by turning chairs around. This meant people from different dioceses were in the same group, which itself was possible because the seating arrangement were changed to break up block seating of diocesan representatives. There was then an open reporting and question time before the committee returned to a formal synod process for the formal debate on the motion.

This whole process was developed at the 2001 General Synod and incorporated into the Standing Orders of the Synod. A number of dioceses around the country changed their own arrangements in the light of the success of these moves.

However, these are not the only changes which have taken place in the General Synod arena in the last few years. The 1998 General Synod in Adelaide also completely changed the structural arrangements for a great deal of the work that is done under the aegis of the General Synod when it passed the Strategic Issues, Task Forces and Other Bodies Canon.

Strategic Issues and Flexible Arrangements

In 1998, the General Synod Strategic Issues canon provided for the abolition of all the existing commissions and replaced them with some housekeeping advisory groups, and a commitment to dealing with strategic issues facing the church in its interactions with the wider society. This was a dramatic positional change for the General Synod. It was very seriously debated at the synod. Some members opposed the change but it was quite clear in the decisive vote that the synod as a whole wished to adopt the changes embodied in this bill.

What Then Is the Purpose of These New Arrangements and What Exactly Are They?

The changes were presented to the General Synod as a way of giving expression to a significant revolution in the structure of the General Synod arrangements. These changes point to the fact that we need to engage with the key issues facing our church more directly given the rapid and extensive changes that have taken place in Australian society over recent decades. The canon envisages structures that will be more flexible and responsive to this changed environment. This is so that we may better serve our church's ministry and mission. These changes, it was said, will enable the church to take initiatives rather than simply being reactive, and will enable us to live and work strategically so that we might be a people who are effective in mission and engagement in modern Australia. This is a medium and long-term strategic approach. It is designed to move our church more into an interactive mission mode with the pluralistic and secularizing society which is our context.

The actual terms of the appointment of all of the bodies under this canon are defined by the canon. All panels and task forces created under this canon will focus their efforts primarily on outreach, the promotion of the gospel, and ensuring the engagement of the Anglican Church with the culture in which we live. Furthermore, the canon requires the General Secretary to seek applications from people wishing to be considered as members of the Strategic Issues Advisory Panel and Task Forces, taking into account the following membership criteria.

- Those with a passion for people to come to faith.
- Those who are likely to be the next generation of leaders.
- Those with a passion for a just society.
- Those with appropriate gifts and skills to contribute.
- Those who reflect the composition of Australian society.

The New Arrangements Are Reasonably Straightforward

A Strategic Issues Advisory Panel discerns the significant trends in Australian society and culture in order to assist Anglicans to live faithfully and proclaim Christ effectively. This Strategic Issues Advisory Panel makes recommendations to the Standing Committee on the formation, terms of reference and the membership of Task Forces to enable us to respond creatively to these issues. It is then the responsibility of the Standing Committee to consider the recommendations, and to establish such Task Forces to deal with these issues in order to achieve a specific purpose in any area of the mission of the church.

It is quite clear from this structure, that the Standing Committee have the central responsibility for appointing Task Forces. The thrust of the new operation is that task forces are appointed for specific purposes, and for specific times. They will be appointed to advance in a creative way the effectiveness of the mission of the church. Those task forces will be accountable to the Standing Committee and will be action orientated. They will be designed to establish initiatives, and to contribute to the way in which Anglicans are able to live faithfully in Australian society.

The canon also established a number of Reference Panels in the areas of doctrine, ministry, liturgy, and church law. The panels were established in order to respond to questions put to them by the Standing Committee, the Primate, or the General Synod. There was limited capacity for initiative by the panels in regard to shaping the questions they were to deal with. Essentially these panels were there for reference purposes. They are described as expert reference panels.

The canon also establishes a system of networks. It authorizes the Standing Committee to facilitate the formation and recognition of a network of people engaged in a discrete area of ministry. Networks that are to be facilitated or recognized by the Standing Committee must satisfy the following guidelines:

The function of the network shall be:

- To share information and ideas among those with common concerns.
- To facilitate joint action by the members of the Network from within their own shared resources.
- To communicate with Standing Committee on issues of significance.

Membership of the network should be effectively open to all Anglican institutions or Anglicans who are involved in the area of ministry designated by the network. A network recognized by the Standing Committee may describe itself as a recognized network of The Anglican Church of Australia General Synod.

The Standing Committee has now recognized a number of networks, having previously considered submissions and a report on their constitutions. The networks were of the mission agencies, the welfare agencies in the form of Anglicare Australia, youth officers, diocesan registrars, childrens' ministry workers and the Australian Anglican Diaconal Association.

A number of other changes in the way in which things take place in the General Synod arena have also been established.

Engaging Australia Project

The Standing Committee has set aside the non-assessment income on its balance sheet into a reserve fund and after the protection of the capital of that fund, has allocated the income available to support projects that will assist the church in its engagement with Australian society.

The terms for the use of these funds are as follows:

a. That the Reserve Fund's income over and above amounts needed to preserve its real capital value be applied to projects concerned with the interface between church and society.

b. Projects must be geared to make a creative contribution to effective engagement and representation of the Christian faith in Australian society by the Anglican Church, and should be concerned with the shaping forces of that society.

c. Projects can embrace a wide range of fields including social analysis, journalism, theology, electronic media or the arts, but funding is not available for projects that could otherwise be supported through existing activities of General Synod Commissions, Boards and Committees. Submissions for grants have been invited in advertisements in diocesan newspapers and the April Standing Committee have received recommendations and projects funded.

Working Groups

These groups deal with short term specific tasks which are defined by the General Synod when setting up the Working Group, or these may be set up by the Standing Committee in order to deal with a particular question. They deal with specific issues such as:

1. Clergy Discipline
2. Ordained Ministry
3. Women Bishops
4. Standing Committee Review
5. Primacy—its role in the future
6. Ecumenical Strategies

Review of the Standing Committee

At the request of the General Synod the Standing Committee has established a review of its own activities and membership. This has been occasioned by the changing role that the Standing Committee is fulfilling in these changed circumstances, and has meant submitting the Standing Committee to the same kind of scrutiny that the other areas of the General Synod have begun to undergo. Under the recent changes, Standing Committee, of course, is now being obliged to consider more substantial questions in regard to the mission situation of Australian Anglicans, than has previously been the case.

General Synod Process

At the 1998 Synod, the processes were significantly and quite dramatically changed. The way in which certain key matters were handled incorporated small group discussion which involved synod members in the same groups that were used for morning bible study. Worship was incorporated into the actual agenda of the Synod in the hall.

All of these changes represent quite a dramatic shift in the direction and the orientation of the work that is going on in the General Synod arena. Those changes reflect the different circumstance in which we find ourselves and the challenges which those changed circumstances present to us as Anglicans.

National Anglican Conferences

The General Synod and the Standing Committee have recognized the great impact of the National Anglican Conference, which was held in Canberra in 1997. The Primate in his Presidential Address at the 1998 General Synod, said he could not recall a more exciting event in the life our national Church. The General Synod and the Standing Committee resolved that a further conference be held in 2002. That conference duly took place at the University of NSW in Sydney. The first conference made a profit of fifty thousand dollars, the second conference a loss of twenty thousand dollars, leaving a balance of thirty thousand dollars to seed fund a third national conference. The Standing Committee accepted the offer of the then archbishop of Melbourne, Peter Watson, for Melbourne to host a third conference in 2005. That third conference has yet to take place.

Networks

Now I want to go back to the new canon and the role of the networks. The networks are an attempt to incorporate into the new arrangements something of the dynamic which was touched upon at the National Anglican Conference. It was clear that many people made contact with others who were involved in similar areas of ministry and found that contact to be both encouraging and informative. The networks are not part of any direct activity on the part of the General Synod or the Standing Committee. They are a recognition that there are many people around the country engaged in the same kinds of activities for whom contact with others in their particular area has proved to be both stimulating and encouraging.

This canon enables such networks to be recognized and to be affirmed in what they are doing. It also gives the networks the opportunity to report to the Standing Committee on matters which they regard as being important in the life of the church community. The networks provide for a learning environment. They create an environment where members of the networks listen, stimulate each other, and advance their capacity to fulfil their ministry in their own particular circumstances.

In that sense the networks provide a healthy context for confidence, for interdependent diversity and for the encouragement of respectful visionary approaches for our life as Anglicans in this country.

These networks recognize the benefit of such connection and they involve not control, but recognition, support and affirmation. They touch a dynamic and a nerve, which is operating in our church community, and will become extremely important sources of vitality for the life of Anglicans in Australia. In that sense, I believe that the networks may well prove to be a sleeper in the canon, and they will prove to be of immense significance in the coming decades in the life of our church. This group of Examining Chaplains represents a very important role in the life of our church, and I hope that you will embrace the new national affirmation of your work and become a recognized National Network of the Anglican Church of Australia.

So What?

What can we conclude from all of these changes? First of all, in the General Synod arena a new direction and new structures mean that a new spirit is at work in what we are trying to achieve. The new canon provides for a structure that is outward looking. I believe that without that orientation we are wasting our time, we are retreating from our own place in history and shutting our ears to clear imperatives from our own Anglican faith tradition. However, in the end what we are looking for is not simply reorganization. What we are in fact looking for is the renewal of faith, for individuals and for our Anglican community. Thus, while I salute and support the changes that are taking place, in the end the most important question facing us is how we each walk with Christ and our neighbors.

13

Purpose and Dynamics of General Synod

CHANGES MADE IN THE procedures at General Synod began a process of rediscovery which could lead to the synod being a vital part of the renewal of the life of faith of the Anglican Church of Australia. We are yet to see if this early promise is to prosper. In order to make that assessment we need to bear in mind the purposes for which synods exist, the powers of the General Synod and the kinds of steps that have been taken in the General Synod to change its processes.

The Purpose of Synods

Historically the idea of having synods goes back to the early gatherings reported in The New Testament documents. An example of such a gathering is the so-called Council of Jerusalem described in Acts 15. Here the early Church tried to deal with a disagreement amongst some of its members which affected relationships between the group in Jerusalem and that in Antioch. Representatives came together from each of these communities and the issue was openly debated and a decision arrived at. From the earliest times when there has been disagreement and controversy Christians have gathered together to make decisions about those divisions. More locally Christians have also gathered together to make decisions about the life of their community.

This habit arises from a theological conception of the Church in its totality as the body of Christ. This community of people contains within it a variety of gifts which contribute to the general good of the community. It was articulated early by Paul in 1 Corinthians 12. Paul there describes the different contributions which members of the Corinthian Church make to their assembly. Some are apostles, some prophets, some teach, some interpret, some are administrators or have other gifts, but they come, says Paul, "from the same spirit." He suggests an image of a body with its different parts operating in a coordinated fashion.

However, he goes on to describe a better way to approach relationships in the church. He repeats his references to the gifts but declares that without love these gifts are nothing. Having asserted the fundamental principle of the community life of the Corinthians he then goes on to describe the moral characteristics of this love.

> Love is patient; love is kind; love is not envious or boastful or arrogant or rude. It does not insist on its own way; it is not irritable or resentful; it does not rejoice in wrongdoing, but rejoices in the truth. It bears all things, believes all things, hopes all things, endures all things. (1 Cor 13:4–7)

This is clearly not an organizational system, but rather a process principle, of relating in the community according to the gospel character of love.

Historical processes of delegation within the life of the Church and the development of institutional arrangements in changing circumstances led in due course to role differentiation within the community. That differentiation turned in some areas to demarcation. In the case of the emergence of an ordered ministry, a distinction began to emerge between those in ministry and others, what today has come to be the distinction between clerical and lay.

These demarcations were strongly invested from both sides of this distinction. Parson's freehold emerged from developments which took place early in the eighth century in western Europe in a situation where clergy were appointed by landholders for the benefit of the landholder's tenants. This meant that the clergy were given the same kind of remunerative privileges as other tenants, namely land which could be worked or used. Like other tenants, clergy could be dismissed from these tenures. On the other hand bishops wanted to have access to the clergy on the landlord's land for pastoral oversight and discipline. Out of that conflict, in which the lay leadership in the community (the landholders) had a dominant role, arose the principle that clergy could hold their land, their tenure, for life. This deal brokered by bishops involved also the responsibility of clergy to visit their bishop annually to report on their activities.

Between the twelfth and fourteenth centuries the conciliar reaction to claims of a centralizing papacy were met by arguments as to the character of the Church and the powerful influence that lay princes particularly might properly have in decision making in the Church. The so called Galican and English liberties from papal control established in the thirteenth and fourteenth centuries arise from a similar claim to the influence and jurisdiction of the godly prince in his own principality. Even in the sixteenth century in the Reformation legislation in England the royal supremacy which placed the king as the head of the Church was a strong declaration of the control of the Church at law by the principle lay person in the Church, namely the monarch. Even the appointment to parishes in the Church of England between the seventeenth and twentieth century was mostly in the hands of lay people who held the patronage of the parishes.

In Australia in the middle of the nineteenth century the emergence of synods happened at a time of rising democratic sentiment and political moves to establish local representative government. The bishops of Australasia met in 1850 to discuss church problems. The minutes of the conference, which were distributed in the dioceses, recommended a synod of bishop and clergy with a parallel convention of laity. This recommendation was not followed in any diocese. Rather all adopted a single chamber synod containing clergy and laity and all issues were debated together. The Australian experience led the way in other Anglican churches around the world and this pattern is common throughout world wide Anglicanism.

These Anglican patterns are quite different from Roman Catholic practices. It is one of the great differences between Anglicanism and Roman Catholicism that the Anglican experience has produced a governance tradition which draws in the whole church in the categories of lay and ordained whereas the governance model in Roman Catholicism has been retained on the basis of the Episcopal monarchy of the Bishop of Rome.

The constitutional position in the Anglican Church of Australia reflects this Anglican history. The constitution describes a basis for Anglicans to order certain aspects of their affairs so that there is sufficient coherence in the community and an adequate basis for the provision of an ordered ministry of word and sacraments. There is no provision in the constitution for the discipline of lay people, only the ordained, which rather highlights the purpose of the constitution to define how the church community is to be served by its officers. The church referred to in the constitution is the institutional form which is created by and subject to the constitution.

The Powers of General Synod

Section 26 of the constitution heads Chapter 5 which deals with the powers of the General Synod. Section 26 reads as follows:

> Subject to the terms of this constitution Synod may make canons, rules and resolutions relating to the order and good Government of this church including canons in respect of ritual, ceremonial and discipline and make statements as to the faith of this Church and declare its view on any matter affecting this Church or affecting spiritual, moral or social welfare, and may take such steps as may be necessary or expedient in furtherance of union with other communions.

This clause is followed by a series of elaborate clauses describing the manner in which canons and rules are to be passed particularly paying attention to canons which affect certain categories of activities such as ritual, ceremonial, discipline and finance. However, the three points to be noted out of Section 26 are that:

1. Synods may make canons, rules and resolutions relating to the order and good government of this Church.
2. May make statements as to the faith of this Church.
3. May declare its views on any matter affecting this Church or affecting spiritual, moral or social welfare.

The constitution then goes on to spend a good deal of time describing the procedures to be used for the making of canons that is to say decisions about the institutional operations of the life of the Church. Not a great deal is said in the constitution about the procedures for making statements as to the faith of the Church or for declaring its views on matters affecting spiritual and social matters in the constitution itself. However, such details given in Rule V. Clause 4 of the constitution gives the General Synod plenary power "to make statements as to the faith, ritual, ceremonial or discipline of this Church" provided they are consistent with the Fundamental Declarations in the constitution.

A great deal of attention has been focused upon what have come to be called the legal or legislative aspects of the powers of the General Synod. In part, because of the emphasis in the details of the subsequent clauses of Chapter 5 of the constitution, but also because the constitution, is itself the schedule of an act passed by each of the state parliaments and the Commonwealth Parliament of Australia. The legal powers of the General Synod have been the subject of much debate and apprehension. The debate has been affected by the idea that the constitution of the Church was enforceable by the Courts of the land. Of course, that had long been the case in England where the Church of England was established and where there was a separate jurisdiction of ecclesiastical law which provided for the disciplinary aspects of the English Church canons. Even so beyond that, because the Church was established by law, its arrangements were not only subject to the law but protected by that law. In one sense this is the so called Constantinian conception of the Church and it has been part of the inheritance of Australian Anglicanism from The Church of England. The difference between England and Australia in this matter is that the Constantinian elements have been totally abolished in Australia.

In Australia that established position collapsed very early in the nineteenth century. But the question remained in the minds of many as to whether or not the constitution, or aspects of various diocesan constitutions, would be enforced by the courts of the land because the constitution existed as a schedule to a piece of legislation. In other words, it was argued the constitution was a piece of subsidiary legislation and therefore would be enforced by the courts. That is the precise question which was tested in New South Wales in the legal case Scandrett versus Dowling. That issue arose because Bishop Dowling of Canberra and Goulburn declared he would ordain a number of women as priests.

At that time the General Synod had not declared its view on this matter and it was widely regarded as not allowed under existing canons or the constitution of The Anglican Church of Australia. Bishop Dowling took the view that in his role as Bishop he had the authority within himself to make such a decision. Scandrett and others appealed to the New South Wales Supreme Court and after a series of hearings at different levels the court ruled that the constitution did not have such a force of subsidiary legislation as would justify the court in enforcing the terms of the constitution or any canons which had been passed under the constitution of the diocese of Canberra and Goulburn.

In the majority judgement extensive material was presented which argued that where property was concerned then the observation of the terms of the trusts by which that Church property was held would be a basis for courts making decisions about the content and operation of canons in the Church. Since, however, that question had not been raised in this case the court found against Scandrett and his friends.

There have been different interpretations of this case. In an address to the Anglican Church League in Sydney in July, 1992 Mr. Neil Cameron argued that the "first and most important implication (of the Scandrett Dowling judgment) is that the 1961 constitution does not have the effect which it hitherto was believed to have—either by operation of the 1961 Act or by consensual compact. The 1961 constitution and the canons and rules made under it are binding only in respect of the property of the church." He then went on to point out that since under the General Synod's Constitution a canon of the General Synod does not have any force or effect in a diocese unless the diocese adopts that canon. In New South Wales, he said, the 1917 Church Act gives the dioceses in New South Wales considerable powers to vary trusts and therefore they may do their own thing. He concluded that "the General Synod is and has always been little more than an expensive debating society so far as dioceses in New South Wales are concerned."[1] Of course, while the 1917 Church Act gave considerable powers to dioceses to vary trusts those powers were not unlimited and were ultimately subject to the authority of the Attorney General of the state.

In June 1993, the Canon Law Commission presented a paper on Scandrett versus Dowling which took a quite different point of view from Mr. Cameron. It specifically rejected the notion that the General Synod was simply an expensive debating society. The Canon Law Commission drew attention to the fact that the court was only asked to decide on the issue in terms of whether the constitution was delegated legislation and secondly whether there existed a contract between the parties in the Church. The Court divided on the second question and one judgement expressed the views that in general the rules of the Church were enforceable in contract but not all of them. They also noted Mahoney JA gave his preliminary view in his judgement that only the General Synod was empowered to make a rule that extended beyond the limits of a diocese.

---

1. Cameron, *Scandrett v. Dowling*, quoted from Ballantine Jones, *Inside Sydney*, 66

They summarized their view that the position after Scandrett versus Dowling was much the same as it was before:

1. The Attorney General may at the relation of a member of the Church sue to police a Church trust.
2. Probably the court may interfere in a Church dispute if the plaintiff's membership of the Church or personal rights are affected.
3. The court may possibly interfere if there is no other available avenue to solve a dispute.
4. The Church's internal tribunals may deal with disputes within their jurisdiction.

The commission concluded its document by saying "that apart from the legal rights of people it must not be forgotten that people expect that if clergy have sworn oaths at their ordination or (lay officers have made a promise) to observe the rules of the Church, their word will be their bond."

Clearly the judgment did not settle very much. Certainly, it did not overrule the issue of property as being a point of entry for the law into the affairs of the Church nor did it overrule the point that Church property trusts, despite some powers given in New South Wales to dioceses in that state, cannot be changed at will. It is not possible to turn trusts given for the benefit of the Anglican Church even in a diocese in New South Wales into something which is altogether different. The crown law officers are responsible for supervising such matters.

A similar case went before the Supreme Court of Western Australia as a result of proposed action by the Archbishop of Perth. In that case the matter failed quickly, largely because the plaintiffs did not argue their case, and they sought the action at the very last moment. The Archbishop went ahead and ordained some women as priests before the General Synod had agreed to such action. For an archbishop to anticipate the conclusion of a debate at an approaching General Synod is to say the least unusual and reasonably unhelpful to the processes of the church which one might reasonably expect a senior cleric to support.

In part because of these disputes in recent history and because of the way in which the General Synod has spent a good deal of time on canons and rules, many people have come to think of the General Synod as primarily concerned with legislation and that the appropriate image for the General Synod is that of a parliament. According to this image, the power of the General Synod is to be judged according to whether its decisions can be legally enforced. The implication of this is that the power of the General Synod is to be thought of in legal terms and anything beyond that is of no consequence. That perception is almost entirely erroneous and is certainly debilitating to the life of the church. Of course, there is a place for clarifying the legal basis by which property is held and by which the Church conducts its affairs. But the reality which lies behind this legal element is actually much more important and more profound in terms of the life of the community.

Section 26 gives the General Synod power to make statements as to the faith of this Church or to declare its view on matters affecting spiritual, moral or social welfare. The constitution does not spell out precisely how the Synod should do this, though Rule V passed by the General Synod lays down a procedure for making such a statement. Matters dealing with the order and good government of the church will, even if only indirectly, imply something about the faith of this church. However, whether by resolution, canon or rule, things to do with the faith of the church, or with spiritual, social or moral welfare will not be restricted to matters concerning trust property, however broadly defined. In moving beyond the reach of church property the General Synod has two kinds of powers at least, political and spiritual or moral power.

Any community existing over time and of any size will inevitably develop "politics," and in our cultural environment these are likely to turn into party politics. That has existed in the General Synod from the earliest days. As time has gone by, and especially in the second half of the twentieth century and the early decades of the twenty first century, the trend has become more pronounced. Some of those party politics look a little more like "tribal politics" but that has to do more with the persistence of regionalism in Australian Anglicanism than anything else. The issue is not whether there is a political aspect to the General Synod. The issue is what kind of politics, since politics is simply a way of speaking about the way large communities form into subgroups for certain kinds of united action and for the purposes of making decisions where large numbers of people are involved.

One useful test for the quality of such politics, as will inevitably exist in the General Synod, is the degree to which there is candor and honesty in dealings with each other and respect for those who differ. The records of the General Synod since 1872 in its more informal phases and its more constitutionally based phase since 1962 are replete with these kinds of politics and they have not always been a disgrace to the church. Politics becomes a very important way by which we are able in a large community of people to make decisions. But I am not the only person to observe that there have been politics of the more popular kind in parliamentary life where it has been more difficult to say that there has been candor and respect and where the "party" or regional differences have sometimes appeared more important than the issue upon which they are deployed. The challenge in the General Synod, as in the church community generally, is how people conduct themselves.

The Possible Spiritual and Moral Power of the General Synod

However, there is in my view another aspect of the power of the General Synod which has not been much considered, namely the spiritual and moral power of the General Synod. After all the Church's institutional arrangements, of which the General Synod is but one, exist to serve the community as that community seeks to fulfil its Christian vocation in Australia.

Effective spiritual and moral power exercised by the General Synod will arise as a consequence of a number of factors:

1. The relevance of the issues considered by the General Synod to the vocation of Anglicans in Australia.
2. The manner in which these issues are treated.
3. The quality of the processes and the relationships within the General Synod amongst those involved.
4. The degree to which the event of the General Synod manifestly points to God as the author and sustainer of the vocations of Anglicans in Australia.

We do very little on this front to our very great loss. It is in this sense in my view that the General Synod can be properly thought of as a worshiping event, almost a kind of prayer meeting, a sacrament, certainly a sign of the transcendent.

The General Synod represents the present point of an historical tradition that has become a significant theme in the Anglican heritage, namely that the whole Church is responsible for the life of the Church.

Furthermore, that life is set within the horizon of the kingdom of God and the vocation of Anglicans individually and together to live Christianly in the world in which God has placed them. The General Synod exists to sustain and to support that vocation by, as the constitution puts it, making rules for the good order of the life of the Church, making statements about the nature of our faith and declaring its view on matters affecting the Church or affecting spiritual, moral or social welfare. What gives spiritual and moral power to these things arises from the spiritual and moral quality of the activities of the General Synod. What diminishes such spiritual and moral power is the descent into purely party politics played for the sake of the party, or the diocese, and its interests.

Recent Changes in the Process of General Synod

Significant changes were made at the Adelaide meeting of the General Synod in 1998 as to the processes of the General Synod. The origins of these changes lie in the disputes in 1992 about the ordination of women as priests and residual dissatisfaction about the processes at that time. As well, the National Anglican Conference in 1997 offered a different way of Anglicans being together as a community nationally. The use of conflict resolution methods and the resources of the Conflict Resolution Network were used in preparations for the 1998 synod in Adelaide.

The changes in Adelaide were promoted from the Standing Committee and involved a number of important changes.

Worship was moved from the chapel outside the normal meeting time of the General Synod into the General Synod hall and set within the framework of the meeting of the synod.

Small groups of people from different dioceses were used for the worship at the beginning of each morning in the synod hall and also those same groups were used later in the day for the discussion of selected contentious issues which were on the agenda of the synod meeting.

The selected subjects were introduced from two aspects by two speakers at the beginning of the debate. These introductory speakers approached the question from two different points of view. Before the Synod they had identified together what issues were at stake in the matter. That list of issues was used for discussion in small groups. After the two introductory speeches and a time for questions the synod broke into small groups for the discussion of the issues identified. The small groups were formed so that they contained members from different dioceses.

Contentious issues were identified beforehand by The Standing Committee and the speakers were to meet before the General Synod assembled for a briefing on the method involved. The subjects dealt with in this way were:

1. Future issues facing the Church.
2. Indigenous representation in General Synod.
3. "The Bringing Them Home Report" (a Royal Commission report on the children taken from their families and placed in government and church institutions) and the Churches Responses.
4. The Strategic Issues and Other Bodies Canon.

The effect in the General Synod was quite considerable. Connections were established between members which had not previously easily been made. People had the opportunity in small groups in face-to-face discussion to identify their views with people with whom they strongly disagreed. Some of those connections between synod members continued long after the meeting of the General Synod. Indeed, some connections turned into friendships. All the subjects considered in this way by the General Synod, were adopted in one form or another. Indigenous membership of the General Synod was agreed to and the constitutional change came into effect. The Strategic Issues and Other Bodies Canon was passed by the General Synod and has come into operation as a canon. It dramatically affects the way the General Synod operates in between its meetings.

The resolution on women bishops has continued and The Standing Committee established a working group under the co-chairmanship of the two women who had presented the issue at the General Synod in Adelaide. Their report went before the Brisbane meeting of General Synod but was withdrawn by the promoters in the face of perceived determined opposition. The Future Issues Resolution was passed by the General Synod but has subsequently died and nothing has been done about it.

The new processes which were introduced at the Adelaide Synod were very popular among the Synod members. A response form which was filled out by 95 percent of the members of the synod showed that they overwhelmingly approved of the changes and asked for more. That more has been worked on by the Standing Committee and modest steps forward in the process will be put in place in the Brisbane meeting of the General Synod. These changes have been incorporated into the Standing Orders of the synod.

The effect however of this process has reached beyond the General Synod and the General Synod institutions. There was a clearer perception within the church community that the General Synod could be something more than simply a debating chamber with the worst kinds of party politics and that it was possible to discuss contentious issue in a more constructive fashion. Some dioceses have taken up the pattern marked out in the General Synod and adopted some similar processes in their own arenas.

At issue in these processes is the nature of the synod as an assembly of representatives of people who share a common faith. They meet together to seek God's will for the way in which this community should be served. A large community such as the Anglican Church of Australia will always have within it differences and conflict. The issue at stake in the General Synod processes which were introduced in Adelaide in 1998 directly relates to the way in which we behave with each other in resolving and managing conflict and differences. In a plural environment that is a very important issue of witness.

The Brisbane Proposals

The Brisbane proposals continue the Adelaide process. Worship will be incorporated into the meeting of the General Synod and there will be a guest speaker at the bible studies each morning. The subjects which will be considered in the group process had yet to be finalized but the Standing Committee had resolved that there will be a balance between social and domestic church matters. The discussion process will be maintained in the synod form and the protocols for participation were being refined and developed.

Does this however go far enough? Not really in my view. Probably the time has now come to look at other things in the program of the General Synod. If the principle of serving the church community and its vocation is to be given sustained priority and if the General Synod is to be itself a clearer witness to our corporate seeking for the will of God, then it seems to me that there are some other things that should be considered. I think that at least three things are worth considering in this whole process.

First, what sorts of associated activities could be arranged to take place before and after the meeting of the General Synod? Such gatherings would bring the General Synod meeting into a wider context of Church activity. If the General Synod were surrounded by meetings of different groups of Church people concerned with particular aspects of the life of the Church and those people had more immediate contact with the members of the General Synod in the framework of a meeting of the General Synod then it seems to me the total event would be enhanced. On this point I acknowledge the example of the General Convention of The Episcopal Church.

Secondly, it seems to me the time is long overdue for us to be taking positive steps to nurture women in leadership positions in the General Synod. We have had a good deal of debate about the technical position of women in the orders of ministry, but the General Synod still remains a distinctly masculine event in a church the majority of whose active membership is female. Apart from that simple numerical point there is a wealth of talent amongst the women in our church whose absence deprives the church of much benefit and blessing. Their absence reflects a moral fault line in our community and is a handicap that we cannot really afford. Furthermore the disproportionate number of men elected by dioceses to the General Synod reflects a very unsatisfactory attitude to women in the cultures of the dioceses.

Thirdly, it seems to me that we would benefit from elements within the meeting of the General Synod where stories of faith and creativity are shared. There are many such stories in the life of this church and they are to be found already in the Projects File of good ideas shared amongst dioceses, which is circulated by the General Synod Office. They are to be found also in the projects which are supported with seed funds by the Engaging Australia Project. Such sharing of stories of faith and creativity would enhance the sense at the meeting of General Synod of the vital character of the faith of this Church expressed across this land. It would also honor the moral, spiritual and social issues with which this Church community is now already creatively engaging. Giving these things some public place in the event of the General Synod would be a significant enhancement of the total event.

The General Synod is a contemporary expression of a long history in Anglicanism of the theological truth that the Church in its totality is responsible for its life and affairs and that while different categories of people may have delegated responsibilities, we are together as a whole the Anglican community, the Anglican Church of Australia. The Synodical pattern gives expression to that truth. Furthermore, in representing the church community the General Synod represents a community in which there are many creative and inspiring activities being pursued in order to support the vocation of Anglicans in Australia.

The recent changes in the process at the General Synod have begun a path of rediscovery which could lead to the synod being a vital part of the renewal of the life of faith of the Anglican Church of Australia. We are yet to see if this early promise is to prosper. The degree to which it is likely to prosper is largely in the hands of the members of the General Synod and the influence upon them of those people in the church community whom they are called to represent at this event.

14

Conflict, Constitution, and Community

Cultural Change and Gender in the Anglican Church of Australia[1]

AFTER A PUBLIC PLEBISCITE that produced a 60 percent majority in favour of same-sex marriage, the Commonwealth Parliament of Australia changed the Marriage Act to exclude any reference to gender from the provisions for marriage. The Act protected the rights of religious minorities not to conduct marriages under the act that were against their beliefs. In 2019, the diocese of Wangaratta passed a regulation to allow the liturgical blessing of a same-sex couple who had been married under the revised civil Marriage Act. This was referred to the Appellate Tribunal (AT) of the Anglican Church of Australia (ACA) to decide whether this regulation was consistent with the constitution of the Church. The Tribunal decided in November 2020 that it was not inconsistent with the constitution. Thus did the gender revolution in western culture reach the institutions of the ACA in the darkness of the year of COVID.

This paper is designed to clarify the structure and institutional place of the judgment of the AT, to refer very briefly to some of the immediate responses to it and offer a possible way to respond to what is at stake in this for the Anglican Church of Australia (ACA). It was written in

---

1. An earlier form of this paper was distributed to the bishops in the church in February 2021 as a contribution to the wider debate on blessing same-sex marriages conducted under the revised Commonwealth Marriage Act. See Kaye, "What Is at Stake?"

the months following the delivery on November 11, 2020, of the judgment of the Appellate Tribunal of the ACA on a move by the diocese of Wangaratta to provide for a service of blessing for same-sex couples who had been married under the recently revised Marriage Act of the Commonwealth of Australia.

The judgement was widely criticized and the constitution often misunderstood. This episode offers a very good example of the way the Anglican Church of Australia is organized and how it conducts its affairs. It also illustrates the particular relationship between the community of church members and the constitution and its institutions and how church discipline applies to the clergy, but not the laity. It is also interesting in that the matter is ongoing and its outcome is far from certain.

At the same time, it serves to highlight the institutional character of the ACA within the spectrum of Anglican ecclesial patterns around the world. Anglican Ecclesiology has been much considered in recent decades. The Anglican Churches of the Anglican Communion have many things in common, but there are also significant differences about who decides what, where authority lies and how it is exercised, and the relation between clergy and laity in the structured life of the church. For example, the constitution of The Episcopal Church in the USA establishes its connection with the "One, Holy, Catholic, and Apostolic Church" via membership of the Anglican Communion and by upholding and propagating "the Historic Faith and Order set forth in its Book of Common Prayer,"[2] as amended and adopted by the Episcopal Church. The New Zealand church establishes such a connection by seeing itself as a branch of the United Church of England and Ireland as set out in a constitution first established in 1857. It also incorporates its prayer book into the constitution.[3]

The Australian model is often misunderstood. In fact, there are numerous ways for any national configuration of an Anglican church. Within the terminology of the Anglican Communion there is some confusion between a Province, traditionally a combination of several dioceses with a provincial organization and a Metropolitan Archbishop, on the one hand, and on the other a National church made up of a number of Provinces. The configuration of these national churches varies quite significantly. Some national churches are significantly centralized as in

---

2. General Convention of the Episcopal Church, *Constitution and Canons*, Preamble.

3. See Anglican Church, "Canons and Statutes."

the Church of England, or largely centralized in the case of The Episcopal Church. On the other hand the Anglican Church of Australia is very distinctly decentralized. In all of these cases local history has played an important role in the pattern that has survived to the present.

This essay offers an illustration of the Australian model at work on a contemporary contentious issue within the church, namely, the blessing of a same-sex marriage effected under the revised Commonwealth Marriage Act (2017). This Wangaratta case reveals some interesting and significant elements in the configuration of the ACA that may be of interest in the broader study of Anglican ecclesiology.

The Story So Far

In 1955, in the final stages of the debate of the new constitution for the Church of England in Australia, Broughton Knox from Sydney attempted "to have the Book of Common Prayer and the Articles moved from the Ruling Principles in the constitution into the unalterable Fundamental Declarations chapter."[4] Broughton had just returned from Oxford where he had completed a doctoral thesis on the doctrine of Justification in the Reign of Henry VIII. In 1954, he was appointed by his brother in law, Marcus Loane, to be Vice Principal and to lecture on doctrine and the Prayer Book at Moore College, Sydney. His biographer, Marcia Cameron, reports. "Without question, Broughton's own theological position had been forged by his encounter with the English Reformation."[5] He failed in 1955 at the General Synod but continued to press this change on two occasions at the Sydney synod in 1957.[6] Nonetheless the Sydney synod easily passed the constitution without any change with clear majorities including from the clergy.

The place of the Fundamental Declarations was contentious because it went to the heart of what was essential and unchangeable in the new constitution. Broughton and his younger colleague at Moore College, Donald Robinson, both thought that the only way to maintain the reformed evangelical position as that of the Church in Australia was to embed the reformation documents in the unchangeable Fundamental

---

4. Davis, *Australian Anglicans*, 156.

5. Cameron, *Enigmatic Life*, 124.

6. The frenetic work done by Knox in his opposition to the new constitution is described in Cameron, *Enigmatic Life*, 163–73. She notes that after the 1957 Sydney synod he was admitted to hospital for what she describes as a breakdown.

Declarations. In England of course, the reformation legislation was never unchangeable. The 1662 version was an act of the British parliament which in fact changed earlier Acts and itself was changed over time, as indeed have plenty of legislation on ecclesiastical matters.

Undoubtedly individuals, lay, clerical and episcopal, will hold differing opinions on a lot of things, some of which they will hold dear and regard as crucial in their Christianity and their membership of the ACA. Indeed it is very possible that some held to their memberships of the ACA on the basis of a misunderstanding of the constitution. However, this debate is not about the personal views of individuals. It is about the decision of a diocese that is an institution operating under the constitution of the ACA. The question is therefore about the meaning of the constitution and the canons made under that constitution. That debate has raised the question of the role and meaning of the Fundamental Declarations in the Anglican Church of Australia. The idea of "fundamentals" has a relevant history in Anglicanism. I hope to show later that the fundamentals tradition is addressed to what is necessary for a church to be Christian. It is not concerned with what an individual Christian might believe when they are part of a "particular" or "national" church. This fundamentals tradition is thus relevant to the question of the Fundamental Declarations in the constitution of the ACA.

Differences of conviction about relations between the sexes have been widely agitated in the Anglican Communion. Some parishes and dioceses have broken away from their churches. The Global Anglican Future Conference (GAFCON) has actively sought to offer support for dissenters in existing Anglican Provinces and has been active in opposing what they see as any loosening of the traditional moral teaching and practices of Anglican churches. Alternative jurisdictions have been established in a number of countries, most notably in the United States. There is a GAFCON branch in Australia, whose Chair is Richard Condie, the bishop of Tasmania. This group made a submission to the Appellate Tribunal. The Anglican Communion has been preoccupied with these issues and has struggled to deal with the alternative organizations that have been established. In the United States an alternative ecclesiastical province has been created. The presenting issue has been the institutional recognition in the church of same-sex relationships in marriage, and ordination.

Actual decisions by the ACA on gender relationships have been somewhat limited. This has been in part due to the loose federal structure of the church, of which more later. The ordination of women was finally agreed by the General Synod in 1992 but has not been accepted in a number of dioceses. Ordination of women as bishops was deemed not inconsistent with the constitution and canons in 2007 and a number of women have been so ordained. There has been a running debate about male headship reflected in the alternative marriage services in A Prayer Book for Australia (APBA) which was approved in 1995 and in which one service retains a promise of obedience from the bride and the other does not. Same-sex marriage was made legal in Australia in 2017 by an Act of the Commonwealth Parliament. There have not been any steps to take up the opportunity provided by the new civil law for the church to provide marriage services for same-sex couples. In the ACA the accepted view of marriage as a heterosexual relationship remains unchanged.

The present matter from the diocese of Wangaratta is the first time the issue of same-sex marriage has come up institutionally in the church, not as an example of a same-sex church marriage, but as the blessing of a marriage between two people already married under the revised Commonwealth Marriage Act. The Wangaratta move was seen as highly controversial and asserted by some to be inconsistent with the constitution of the church. It was referred to the Appellate Tribunal (AT) for an opinion on that question. On November 11, 2020 the AT handed down its response to this reference stating that the Wangaratta regulation was not inconsistent with the constitution.[7]

Then There Were Dioceses

The constitution for the ACA came into force in 1962 after long and difficult debate. In part this was because from 1847, when the dioceses of Australia began to be established, they developed their own social, cultural, institutional and ecclesiastical character. This was shaped and influenced by the same kind of diversity in the separate colonies generally. When Victoria and South Australia were added to the colonies of New South Wales and Tasmania, the Imperial government established the governor of NSW as the Governor General of Australia with a view to the creation of a national government structure. However, funds were not provided and the scheme came to nothing. Separatism became consolidated in

---

7. The relevant documents are all available on the website of the General Synod: http://www.anglican.org.au/.

both church and state. This context had significant implications for the church when it came to separating from the Church of England.

The Church of England in England was still part of the state when the British Government founded colonies in Australia. The Royal Supremacy still existed, though subject to the increasing power of parliament. The Church of England moved in stages from being the State Church to being an Established Church. Steps to provide for any independent ecclesial self-government structures did not come until the twentieth century and even then, there were still some close connections with state power. Elements of the English Christendom linger on into the twenty first century. Even to this day an English bishop must wait upon the Queen and make an act of fealty to her before he or she can take up episcopal ministry. Despite the dramatic political changes in Australia from 1836, the bishops at their 1850 conference thought they were still bound hand and foot by the Royal Supremacy.

When the Australian Anglicans were faced with creating their diocesan structures from 1847, they did not have much help from the then existing English model. From 1850 they were all quite separated from the state and in the colonies the Royal Supremacy had gone with the coming of local representative government. In the second half of the nineteenth century local interests in the states and dioceses were burgeoning.

These background issues help us to understand why the diocese was becoming the focus and essential unit of the church. As a consequence, in the debates that led to the formation of the present constitution the interests at play were those of the dioceses. The first General Synod met in 1872 with representatives from each diocese. A constitution was agreed and adopted in 1876. But it was a loose affair and was hindered by the continuing legal connection with English law and the decisions of English ecclesiastical and civil authorities.[8] That did not mean it did nothing. It provided a gathering in which common problems were shared and on occasion also meant having a united front in dealing with the English authorities, not least the Archbishop of Canterbury.

Fundamentals and Church Identity

The first and unchangeable part of the constitution of the ACA is called the Fundamental Declarations, though it was initially called just

---

8. See Withycombe, "Imperial Nexus."

Declarations. "Fundamental" was introduced in 1951, probably under the influence of the language of Archbishop Geoffrey Fisher who had visited Australia in 1948 and corresponded with the Constitution Committee following his visit. He had also sent them some "suggestions" about a way forward with the constitution. The Fundamentals tradition in Anglicanism is quite important in constitutional debates and has a long tradition in Anglican theology.[9]

In 1988, Stephen Sykes opened an important essay in which he provided a brief account of the use of Fundamentals in the Church of England in these words.

> Within Anglicanism there is a long tradition of direct appeal to the "fundamentals of Christianity," or to the "fundamental articles of the faith." ... [T]here are good reasons why the contrast between fundamentals and non-fundamentals found a ready home among Anglicans, and has been in use in various ways to the present day.[10]

The identification of "fundamentals" has a significant history, especially following the divisions between the Protestant churches of the Reformation and the Roman Catholic Church. At issue in these arguments was the ecclesial standing and character of the Church of England. The Reformation Acts assert that the Church of England was a truly Christian church and that it was an independent church not subject to the jurisdiction of Rome. Relations between the Church of England and the Church of Rome had a long history going back to the earliest days of Christianity in England. When Pope Gregory the Great sent Augustine to evangelize the English in the sixth century he encouraged him to use local practices to build the English church and made no requirement to follow Roman practices. The expansive reform movement of Pope Gregory VII in the eleventh century ran into King William I and any jurisdiction for the Pope was completely rebuffed. The saga had its ups and downs but lay Royal Supremacy continued and under Henry VIII reached full and overweening proportions.

The ecclesial and theological fracturing of Europe in the sixteenth century presented a serious ecumenical challenge. Many, but not all, of

---

9. I am indebted to the excellent 1990 PhD thesis of Stephen Pickard: "The Purpose of Stating the Faith: An Historical and Systematic Inquiry into the Tradition of Fundamental Articles with Special Reference to Anglicanism."

10. Sykes, "Fundamentals," 232.

these national churches had connections with the state. How to conduct a conversation about the character and standing of the new churches was not straightforward. In this context the notion of "fundamentals" became a useful category especially for the Church of England which retained some of the forms of the Roman church such as three orders of ministry.

Edward Stillingfleet, a prominent theologian, Dean of St. Paul's and Bishop of Worcester, regularly used the category "fundamentals." In a long work in 1665 just three years after the 1662 Book of Common Prayer, he addressed a Roman Catholic writer who had demanded that the Church of England should have a list of doctrines that were essential to believe for being within the church and thus for salvation. In chapter IV, "The Protestant Doctrine of Fundamentals Vindicated," Stillingfleet argued at length that for the Church of England the "doctrine of Christ" is that doctrine that is necessary for salvation. It is what has been accepted in all ages and is found in the creeds.

> But by what peculiar Arts you can thence draw, that something else is necessary to be believed in order to Salvation besides what hath been owned as Fundamentals in all ages, I am yet to learn.[11]

This does not mean that Stillingfleet thought that this was all that is believed in the Church of England. He is committed to the formularies as recently established by law in 1662. For the purposes of an ecumenical debate, in this case with a Roman Catholic, the Christian identity of the Church of England is its commitment to the "fundamentals in all ages." This is a more expansive category and in practical terms provides a point of connection with other churches who are organized differently and with different doctrinal particulars. The Fundamentals are what makes the Church of England a Christian church.

For Stillingfleet, the doctrinal commitments of his "particular national" church were the formularies promulgated after the Restoration. This particular pattern of uniformity goes back to Edward VI[12] and the documents are important instruments of that national and ecclesiastical uniformity. Their authority comes from the crown in parliament. All elements were obligatory for the church whose membership was coterminous with the subjects of the crown. Each national church could be

---

11. Stillingfleet, *Rational Account*, 3.5.626.

12. The longer history of this lay/clerical form of government, that is to say the English Christendom, goes back into the origins the English nation. See Kaye, *Rise and Fall*.

differently configured. These were formularies for a particular or national church, in this case the Church of England in England.

Stillingfleet's Roman Catholic opponent argued on the basis of the declarations of the Council of Trent that their propositions were all necessary for a church to be a true church, to be Christian. It is a universal claim. There cannot be particular or national churches that legitimately differ from this. This is the claim of universal primacy. It was a vital issue at the time. With the plurality of churches so manifestly present, the first thing you want to know is whether this is a Christian church. The English found an appeal to fundamentals of the kind referred to by Stillingworth to be very useful.

However, it should be noted that the fundamentals are not a brief statement of doctrines. Rather they are historical claims. Stillingfleet's form of words is a little different from those used in Section 1 of the ACA constitution but the essential meaning is the same. Stillingfleet has "necessary to be believed in order to Salvation . . . what hath been owned as Fundamentals in all ages." The ACA constitution Section 1 has the ACA as part of "the One Holy Catholic and Apostolic Church of Christ, holds the Christian Faith as professed by the Church of Christ from primitive times and in particular set forth in the creeds known as the Nicene and the Apostles' Creed."

Neither of these formulations lifts the material out of the particularities of history. Both trace it back to the earliest times and to Jesus Christ. This is not a set of particular doctrines or practices. It is a claim to beliefs and practices that have their origin in Jesus Christ and the apostolic period and thereafter what has been commonly held by Christians. This sits alongside those beliefs and practices that might pertain in a "particular" or national church. Thus, when Section 1 of the constitution of the ACA declares that it "holds the Christian Faith as professed by the Church of Christ from primitive times" it lays claim to be first and foremost and fundamentally a Christian church. This is the model of the "fundamentals" seen in Stillingfleet and points up the appeal to the early church by the English reformers. What is constant through this is the faith which, in Stillingfleet's terms, is "necessary to be believed in order to Salvation" or in the terms of the ACA constitution a faith that includes "the obligation to hold the faith." It is the faith that identifies you as a Christian.

In any debate between churches that are not constitutionally or legally connected, the use of "fundamentals" can have an important role in asserting, or demonstrating, the Christian character of that church.

This was precisely the situation at the formation of a constitution that would finally make the Church of England in Australia independent legally from the Church of England in England. Clarifying this situation was the key issue in the "nexus" report,[13] and central to the framers of the constitution of the ACA.

When separate churches in far flung English colonies, became in any sense independent politically, the assumed relationship of the Church of England with the sovereign power forced a reconsideration as to how such churches might frame their identity. This first occurred quite abruptly after the war of independence in the new separated United States of America and, more gradually and without a war, in the middle of the nineteenth century in Australia. It was the underlying key issue at the 1850 bishops' conference in Sydney namely, local provincial jurisdiction along with some particular continuing theological and ecclesial identity.

The Nexus report in 1905 made it clear that there remained a legal connection between the Church of England in Australia and the Church of England in England. A constitution creating a legal entity was necessary to deal with that remaining obstacle to create a "particular or national" church in Australia. First, it was a Christian church in Section 1, then in Section 2 identifies some items which have to do with the character of this church as a "particular" or "national church."

Forming the ACA Constitution

The present Constitution began life in a serious way in the first decade of the twentieth century and went through five constitutional drafts each with significant differences (1926, 1932, 1939, 1946, 1955). The approach to these drafts was full of tensions and generally based on each diocese trying to defend its position. In the reasons for her dissenting view in the AT, Ms. Davidson gives some detail of this in relation to the role of Archbishop Mowll of Sydney, in supporting a constitution. He knew there were strong voices in the dioceses against the constitution but he deployed his full support for it, notably in the name of relations with the welfare of the wider church. She quotes Mowll's appeal:

> I would be failing in my responsibility as the Diocesan if I did not take every precaution necessary to safeguard the tradition of the Diocese. . . . We must therefore, approach this matter,

13. Church of England in Australia, *Legal Nexus*.

having in mind the welfare of the wider Church in Australia, of which we are the mother Diocese, and at the same time, with the determination that the point of view this Diocese represents should be both recognized and safeguarded.[14]

Ms. Davidson also refers to the role of T. C. Hammond who changed his mind about the constitution and advised Mowll that it should be supported. A crucial concern at this point was to defend the diocese against the use of mass vestments because they were seen to carry objectionable theological views. He concluded that recent changes in England declaring that these vestments did not carry any theological meaning meant that it would be better to rely on a local constitution that could be influenced in the present debates rather than an uncertain English church. This proposed change in the English canons had been made clear by the Archbishop of Canterbury (Geoffrey Fisher) when he visited Australia in 1948.[15] This was a significant visit in the development of the constitution. When he arrived, he found the Australians despairing of getting any agreement from the dioceses on the contents of a constitution. His energetic contributions stimulated a renewed effort with a different approach.

At the heart of the constitution is how this tradition of Christian faith, formed in the local particulars of England and its church, should be expressed in a quite different constitutional and cultural context and in a quite different history of church development. That continuity and change puzzle inevitably focused on Part I of the constitution. In the 1926 and 1946 drafts the BCP and Thirty Nine Articles were included in the Fundamentals, but in 1951 they were moved out of the Fundamentals into the Guiding Principles. It seems to me to be highly likely that this change was made as a result of Fisher's contributions during his visit and in his later correspondence. In his "suggestions" he wrote of the Fundamentals (the term was only later changed to Fundamental Declarations) that they were

> in a Part by themselves to show that they differ in character and purpose altogether from the second part which contains not what the Church essentially is, but how it governs itself.[16]

The language of "Fundamentals" here reflects the language of the earlier English debates. It is an important distinction that Fisher makes.

14. Anglican Church of Australia, "Appellate Tribunal," 48–51.
15. Davis, *Australian Anglicans*, 134.
16. Davis, *Australian Anglicans*, 138.

The Fundamentals are what makes a church a Christian church. The other matters are the distinguishing characteristics of a particular national church. That highlights the significance of the title of the second part of the constitution—these are Ruling Principles.

The Fundamental Declarations has three sections. The first declares the faith of the church in the language of the fundamentals tradition. The language of section 1 is used in a context where a break in the legal connection with the Church of England in England is being established. Nevertheless it asserts a fundamental Christian faith continuity. In that sense it is similar to the ecumenical debates of the seventeenth century which were between churches located in different legal jurisdictions. At the time when the constitution was established the Anglican Church of Australia was clearly in a different and separate legal jurisdiction from the Church of England. The constitution was agreed and enacted in part to establish an institutional and legal separation from the Church of England. That had been the significance of the Nexus Opinion which motivated the move to agree a constitution for the Anglican Church in Australia.

Section 2 of the Fundamental Declarations refers to scripture in terms that resonates with Article VI in the Thirty Nine Articles, but it does not replicate the exact terms of that article. Both statements make it clear that scripture is both sufficient and the ultimate standard for faith, that is the faith that is necessary for salvation. Section 3 refers to more generally traditional material that resonates with the broad historical background of the Church of England. This Section states the intentions of the church and does not include any specific theological rationale for them.

Chapter II, The Ruling Principles, provides the reference point for the forms that are to guide this "particular or national" church. They retain the historical documents of the Restoration but assert that the church "has plenary authority at its own discretion to make statements as to the faith ritual ceremonial or discipline of this church and to order or revise such statements forms . . . provided they are . . . consistent with the Fundamental Declarations."[17]

When Broughton Knox from Sydney unsuccessfully attempted "to have the Book of Common Prayer and the Articles moved into the

---

17. Anglican Church of Australia, "Constitution," II.4.

unalterable Fundamental Declarations chapter"[18] he was addressing this question. The reference to the Reformation documents stayed in the Ruling Principles. They contained material from the "particular" or "national" Church of England. Of course, the Church of England material referred to here is not unchangeable in the Church of England itself. Indeed, it had been changed on a number of occasions. To install such material in the Fundamental Declarations of the new constitution would have been to fossilize the ACA in a way that was not even the case in the Church of England in England.

Given the origins of the constitution and the strong and established independence of the dioceses in Australia, the constitution represents a series of compromises. On occasion it seemed like an ecumenical endeavor but in the end a national conclusion of sorts was reached. Of course, the dioceses retained extensive authority and independence. As a consequence, the ACA is really a loose federation of dioceses and the constitution sets out the terms of the union between the dioceses. When the constitution refers to the church it is referring to the institutional entity as set out in the constitution.

Appellate Tribunal as Constitutional Arbiter on Interpretation of Constitution

In the constitution the AT acts as a final court of appeal from diocesan and provincial clergy disciplinary tribunals and also as a court of interpretation of the constitution. It has only acted once in the first capacity but more often and more recently in the second capacity. Its task in this second capacity is essentially to answer an institutional question according to the terms of the constitution. No one's personal theological opinions are on trial here, least of all the members of the AT or individual members of the Wangaratta synod.

The question before the Appellate Tribunal was an institutional one: "is the Regulation passed by the synod of Wangaratta consistent with the constitution."

---

18. Davis, *Australian Anglicans*, 156. The extensive quotations that follow are drawn from the text of this judgement of the Appellate Tribunal and are identified by the paragraph number in that judgement.

The Structure of the Constitution

The constitution is in two parts. Part I contains the Fundamental Declarations (1–3) which describe the identity and unchangeable commitments of the church and the Ruling Principles (4–6) which identify the ecclesiastical pedigree of the ACA and provide for some specific actions. Part II concerns the Government of the Church.

Part 1

Chapter 1: Fundamental Declarations

I have argued above that the tradition of "fundamentals" in Anglican theology provides a valuable framework for interpreting the first Section of the Fundamental Declarations of the constitution. Furthermore, that background amplifies the conclusions reached by successive judgments of the AT.

Chapter 1 of the constitution, Fundamental Declarations, identifies the Christian faith to which the church is unchangeably committed. It asserts that this church is "a part of the One Holy Catholic and Apostolic Church of Christ, holds the Christian Faith as professed by the Church of Christ from primitive times" and in particular as set out in the Nicene and Apostles creeds. This is an absolutely basic historical proposition. It means this is a Christian church tracing its point of reference to the earliest times and to Christ. Section 2 further declares that it receives scripture as the ultimate rule and standard of faith. It identifies what you might need for salvation, but not necessarily all that you might want to know or even believe as a Christian trying to live a Christian life. The third declaration is what the church will do; it will obey the commands of Christ, teach his doctrine, administer his sacraments of Baptism and Holy Communion, follow and uphold his discipline, and preserve the three orders of bishops, priests and deacons. These items are stated in fairly general terms and no theological rationale or interpretation of them is included. These are simply said to be the things this church will do, not why or how they might be done. The AT judgement deals with each of these Sections in turn.

According to Section 66 of the constitution, this chapter cannot be changed under any circumstances.

Chapter 2: Ruling Principles

The Ruling Principles (Sections 4–6) indicate how the church is to be guided in its governmental decision-making and refers to the historical pedigree of the church in the Church of England. They identify three documents, the Book of Common Prayer, the Ordinal for ordaining bishops priests and deacons, and the Thirty Nine Articles. These were key documents of the Church of England in 1788 when the Church of England arrived in the colony and derive from the Reformation period and the legislation at the time of the Restoration. The constitution specifically declares (Section 72) that in questions arising as to the faith, ritual ceremonial or discipline of this Church or as to the authority and duties of clergy "nothing in this constitution shall prevent reference being made to the history of the Church of England in England to the same extent as such reference might have been made for the purpose of the Church of England in the dioceses of Australia and Tasmania immediately before the day on which this constitution takes effect." The effect of this is to include the experience of the Church of England in Australia during the period when the Royal Supremacy had died and the dioceses established their own constitutions.

The particular historical character of these documents and the pedigree they refer to is clear in Section 6 which says that this church will remain in communion with the Church of England and churches in communion with that church so long as that "is consistent with the Fundamental Declarations contained in this Constitution." Thus if the Church of England were to abandon episcopal ministerial order, as had occurred in England once, then the ACA would not be in communion with that church.

Unlike the Fundamental Declarations, these Ruling Principles can be amended, though only with substantial requirements of agreement. (Section 67(c). The second paragraph of Section 4 deals with some practical matters about variations in liturgical use. Apart from this paragraph action taken under these Ruling Principles must in all respects be consistent with the Fundamental Declarations.

This foundational material makes it abundantly clear that it is the constitution that defines the institutional and legal form of The Anglican Church of Australia. The constitution took many years to settle and was strongly argued. It embodies compromises for the participating dioceses, and is not an attempt to formulate a perfect or complete form of Christian faith or of the church. Rather it is a negotiated document for the circumstances of the time that elaborates a way of securing the "fundamentals" and providing for a way of working together as a church within the tradition of faith formed in the history of the Church of England according to the Ruling Principles.

From the point of view of the constitution, the ACA is a loose federation of dioceses. That not only arises from the vested interests of the dioceses in the formulation of the constitution, but also from the very general character of the material in Chapter 1. That Section has the effect of leaving a great deal to be worked out when new questions about church life arise in the future.

Part 2: The Government of the Church

The first chapter in this part concerns bishops and asserts the foundational importance of the diocese.

> A diocese shall in accordance with the historic custom of the One Holy Catholic and Apostolic Church continue to be the unit of organization of this Church and shall be the see of a bishop.

Chapters then go on to deal with the General Synod, the provinces and provincial synods, the dioceses and diocesan synods, the tribunals, the corporate trustees, the alteration of this constitution, and its operation.

Under the constitution, canons of the General Synod that affect ritual, ceremonial or good order and government, have no force in a diocese until they are adopted by that diocese. Thus, for example, the most recent Prayer Book passed by the General Synod is adopted and used in some dioceses but not in others. Similarly, the General Synod canon authorizing the ordination of women only applies in those dioceses that have adopted it.

This element in the constitution guarantees the independence of the dioceses. It shows that in effect the Anglican Church of Australia is a relatively loose federation of very independent dioceses. While this arrangement causes difficulties, it has contributed to the fact that so far, the ACA has been able to avoid any significant constitutional split.

When coming to the theological evaluation of this arrangement it is significant that the church in this constitution is not the community of

Anglicans in Australia. It is the institutions that are described in the constitution. However, any ecclesiology of Anglicanism in Australia needs to be aware of this distinction, not only in terms of identifying the body of believers who might be referred to as the Anglican church in Australia, but also in terms of the categories that might appropriately be applied to the institutions created under this constitution. This is not the same as the community of Anglicans across the country. Like all large communities its members are hardly ever present to each other in any significant numbers. Most communities to which we belong are not always immediately present to us. We see them occasionally. In a study of expatriate migrant groups Benedict Anderson developed a notion of "imagined communities" to describe communities that people felt strongly part of but which were only in part and on occasion visible to those belonging.[19] The community of Australian Anglicans is somewhat like an "imagined community" as identified by Benedict Anderson.

Of course, all the office holders in the institution are also at the same time members of the community, but as officers of the institutional church they exist to serve the community. That is the context in which to understand the significance of the fact that the constitution provides jurisdictional arrangements only for clergy but not for lay members of the church. Laity do have an institutional role in the government of the church as members of the General Synod and in the membership of some tribunals. Laity are also deeply involved in governance within dioceses though the governance of dioceses is not specified in the constitution.

The institutions envisaged in the following Sections of the constitution are really matters of how to get certain things done, principally the provision to the Anglicans in Australia of a disciplined ministry of word and sacrament and such other activities that from time to time are put in place by the General Synod.

With this general background and the shape of the constitution we can look more directly at the Wangaratta move.

The Wangaratta Move and the Appellate Tribunal

Highly controversial and deeply felt issues have come to the surface now because in 2019 the diocese of Wangaratta synod agreed a regulation that provided for a Blessing of Persons Married According to the

---

19. Anderson, *Imagined Communities*.

(Commonwealth) Marriage Act 1961 (which had been revised in 2017 to include same-sex marriages). The regulation appealed to the General Synod Canon Concerning Services 1992 as the basis of their action. This 1992 General Synod canon had been previously adopted by many dioceses including Wangaratta, Sydney and others.

Accordingly, the Appellate Tribunal was asked:

1. Whether the regulation Blessing of Persons Married According to the Marriage Act 1961 Regulations 2019 made by the Synod of the diocese of Wangaratta is consistent with the Fundamental Declarations and Ruling Principles in the Constitution of the Anglican Church of Australia?

2. Whether the regulation is validly made pursuant to the Canon Concerning Services 1992?

The first question concerns the first two chapters of the constitution—the unalterable Fundamental Declarations, and the Ruling Principles.

The Appellate Tribunal is the final court of appeal under the constitution for church law and the current tribunal contains very senior legal and ecclesiastical people.[20] Its decision by a five to one majority was that

> Wangaratta Diocese's proposed service for the blessing of persons married in accordance with the Marriage Act does not entail the solemnization of marriage; is authorized by the Canon Concerning Services 1992; and is not inconsistent with the Fundamental Declarations and Ruling Principles of the Constitution of the Church.

The Appellate Tribunal Reasons (1 November 2020)

The Task of the Appellate Tribunal Is Constitutional and Legal

The reasons given by the Tribunal are closely argued and essentially legal in character. In that respect they follow a clear order as they deal with the issues involved in this reference. What follows here is a reasonably close summary with some comments. Parentheses refer to the clauses in the text of AT Reasons.

---

20. See Anglican Church of Australia, "Appellate Tribunal."

In the opening section they deal with introductory matters about the role of the AT and the general context of the reference. The AT was not set up to settle general doctrinal matters, much less factional disputes within the church. The AT is bound by the constitution.

In testing the crucial Section 5(3) in the Canon Concerning Services that services under the regulation must not be contrary to or a departure from "the doctrine of this Church" the AT is bound to treat this phrase strictly according to its meaning within the terms of the constitution. As a consequence, in the very strict and particular context of the question posed to the AT in its role as interpreter of the constitution, the meaning of the phrase "doctrine of the church" means exactly what the constitution says it means.

This is a very particular point and it needs to be clarified at the start because in general parlance, especially in a church, doctrine is clearly used in other ways. Various topics in theology are regularly spoken of in terms of a "doctrine of . . ." Even a brief inspection of a general theological handbook or library catalogue is evidence of this. The AT had to define doctrine as used in the constitution and in brief terms they conclude that there it means the "Church's teaching on the faith which is necessary to salvation."

The question before the AT clearly relates to issues of marriage and in particular same-sex marriages since they are encompassed in the revised Commonwealth Marriage law in Australia. The AT briefly reviews salient issues in this background.

This preliminary material is very important because its sets out the terms of operation in the Reasons that follow. They are not asked to settle some general theological dispute; they are obliged to work within the terms of the constitution in answering their question. The meaning of doctrine in its constitutional setting must be determined by the terms of the constitution itself, even if that may be confusing for a general reader. This is a legal answer to a legal question about the constitution and the Wangaratta Regulation.

Having set out these parameters for their work the AT proceeds directly with the issues at hand.

The Canon concerning Services 1992 and the Wangaratta Blessing Service (E) (39–134)

The General Synod Canon of 1992 was properly and unanimously passed by the General Synod and adopted by many dioceses including Sydney and Wangaratta. The Wangaratta Regulation was passed appropriately by the synod of the diocese. Attention is drawn to Section 5(3) and the wide discretion given to the minister within the constraint of the "doctrine of this church."

The issue of marriage was central to submissions in this case and the Tribunal therefore examines elements in the history of marriage law and practice in the Church of England from 1662–1962, being the period from the BCP up to the commencement of the Constitution of the ACA. This record of the practices and doctrines of marriage in the Church of England shows wide variety and often seemingly absolute authorities for practices that were changed by decisions of the church. The AT makes this observation in order to make a point about how to regard what is said to be a theological account of marriage and the manifest alterability of current practices.

> The untidy history of the Church's grappling with the messages of Holy Scripture as regards liturgies and laws relating to marriage should caution against declaring that any aspect of "the doctrine of marriage" is clear beyond argument, eternally rooted in Scripture, and beyond reformation by the Church in light of deeper understanding of the teachings of Jesus Christ and of Holy Scripture. (126)

Of course, this does not mean that there are not important principles at work in the way the church has approached marriage or that there are not serious warrants for these practices. Clearly there are. It just means that the details of these practices are not unalterable in any constitutional sense in either the ACA or the Church of England. The AT makes it clear that the Wangaratta service of blessing is not a marriage service and is not under consideration.

The Wangaratta Blessing Service Is Not "Contrary to or a Departure from the Doctrine of This Church" (134–81)

The AT is addressing a basic constitutional question for this case—what is the definition of "Doctrine." At the same time, they set out reasons to show that there is a clear tradition of interpretation on this matter. They provide extensive material to demonstrate the meaning of Doctrine in the constitution and also in previous judgements of the AT.

Clearly any word can have a range of meanings within its semantic field. This is particularly so with words that are commonly used and even more so when different usages of a word appear in debates on strongly held matters. Doctrine is such a word. However, the question before the Tribunal concerns the meaning in the constitution of the ACA. Not surprisingly the Tribunal carefully spells out what doctrine means "within the four corners of the constitution." They say that the meaning of doctrine in this constitutional sense "is closely defined in 74(1). Unless the context of subject matter otherwise dictates, it means 'the teaching of this Church on any question of faith'" (143).

The judgement then tracks through the previous judgements of the AT in order to demonstrate that this interpretation is not new or unusual but rather in line with previous judgements of the tribunal.

In its 1987 *Report Re the Ordination of Women to the Office of Deacon Canon 1985*, the Tribunal (Archbishop Robinson dissenting) held that the said 1985 Canon was not inconsistent with the Fundamental Declarations or the Ruling Principles in the *Constitution*. There follows material from some of the separate reasons in this case. The material quoted by the Tribunal is extensive. It is sufficient here to quote Mr. Handley QC, who at the time was Chancellor of the Diocese of Sydney. He took a broad historical view in relating Section 1 of the constitution and the definition in 74(1):

> Notwithstanding the importance of the issues before us, the strongly held views on all sides, and the fundamental nature of the theological and biblical arguments which have been raised, in my opinion the questions involved are not part of the Christian faith professed by the Church, they are not dealt with in the Creeds, and do not directly involve matters necessary for salvation. This question before us therefore does not involve any principle of "doctrine" as that expression is used in the Constitution. (150)

In the same judgement Archbishop Rayner related 74(1) to Section 2 on the description of canonical scripture (ultimate rule and standard of faith) and also Article 6 of the Thirty Nine Articles (contains all things necessary for salvation):

> "Doctrine" must therefore be understood in the Constitution as the Church's teaching on the faith which is necessary to salvation. That faith is grounded in scripture and set forth in the creeds; and the Church's doctrine or teaching on that faith may be explicated and developed, provided it is always subject to the test of scripture.

The AT then turns to the 1991 case. There the Tribunal repeated its view of 1987 when they were again asked a number of questions on the ordination of women which provided the basis for the 1992 canon authorizing the ordination of women.

The current Tribunal declared that it would not lightly depart from its earlier decisions on matters of constitutional import (158). They repeat this point after considering some of the submissions made to them.

> We are not disposed to depart from the settled meaning of "doctrine" in the Constitution. Nothing has been put to us to justify such a step. The additional remarks in the following paragraphs add further explanation for the conclusion to which this Section of the Opinion proceeds. (166)

> In our view, the matters in the present reference do not involve issues of faith or doctrine properly so called any more than the dispute over female ordination. The contending views about "blessing" same-sex marriages are strongly held. But, with respect to some of the recent rhetoric, and the actions taken abroad by some bishops of this Church, the blessing of same-sex marriages does not [necessarily] involve denial of God or repudiation of the Creeds or rejection of the authority of Holy Scripture or apostasy on the part of bishops or synods prepared to support such measures. The history of the Church's approach to many of the teachings about marriage in the BCP confirms that none of the BCP teachings about marriage are "teachings of the faith which is necessary to salvation," to use the formulation of Archbishop Rayner and Justice Cox. Nor do they engage matters dealt with in the Creeds or directly involve matters necessary for salvation, to use Mr Handley's words (assuming to the sake of argument any conceptually different approach on his part). (180)

The Tribunal concludes that "doctrine" must therefore be understood in the Constitution as the Church's teaching on the faith which is necessary to salvation. Furthermore, according to earlier judgements of the Tribunal, this is the previously settled meaning. It is neither narrow nor novel.

Given this framework the Tribunal declares that there is no constitutional inconsistency with the Wangaratta canon. In a concluding summation they deal with the principle in the Christian faith as professed from primitive times, Holy scripture and the injunction to obey Christ's commands and teaching his doctrine. They specifically respond to the reports of the Board of Assessors and the Bishops who had been asked some specific questions by the tribunal. The tribunal gives details of their response to these reports, though they note that these bodies were asked specific questions according to the procedure laid out in the canons.

The Christian Faith as Professed from Primitive Times (185–92)

The argument so far has dealt with doctrine elements of Chapter I of the constitution, Fundamental Declarations Section 1. This Section considers a very helpful history of marriage presented to them in a submission from Sydney but point out that these issues are not in the category of a teaching on a question of faith in the sense of what is necessary for salvation.

> To show that the Church's teaching/doctrine about heterosexual, monogamous marriage has been ancient and durable certainly assists aspects of the case advanced by Wangaratta's opponents. But it does not turn the selected aspect of the doctrine of marriage into "the Christian Faith as professed . . . and in particular as set forth in" the Creeds. (192)

Holy Scriptures (193–230)

In relation to the second Section in the Fundamental Declarations on the reception of scripture the AT again points out that there is more in scripture than can be regarded as necessary for salvation. For those wishing to promote a constitutional view about homosexuality they need to do so in the context of the doctrine of the faith that is necessary for salvation (188).

It is very important to notice the terms of the AT response to scriptural arguments about marriage and in principle other things. It is a category definition and really repeats material presented earlier in relation to marriage.

> Holy Scriptures contain doctrines and a whole lot more. Their messages about marriage and homosexuality are contested but they cannot be ignored on that account. But the Appellate Tribunal is not the place to make definitive rulings on such matters unless essential to do so in the exercise of its constitutional functions. (202)

Two very important things are asserted here. First, scriptural material on marriage and homosexuality cannot be ignored simply because its meaning is contested. That would be an extraordinary proposition in a Christian church, let alone the Anglican Church of Australia. Secondly, this really shows that these are subjects that require serious interaction and argument. They are arguments that belong under Part II of the constitution. That demarcation is stated by the AT in relation to what they are at liberty to deal with. The AT has constitutional functions and unless those functions specifically include consideration of disputed interpretations of scripture such matters are not their concern. If not theirs then whose? Clearly those who have been referred to earlier in this judgment, the laity and clergy of the ACA, or the General Synod. In other words, the body of the church in its life today.

Obeying Christ's Commands (240–53)

The AT points to contrasting views about what are the commands of Christ in the AT case of 1991 dealing with the ordination of women represented by Bishops Holland and Robinson.

They quote favorably a long section of Archbishop Rayner's reasons on this point in the course of which he states a view adopted by the AT.

> What have been taken in the New Testament itself and in the subsequent history of the Church to be commands of Christ have frequently represented the application of Christ's broad commands to particular people and particular situations. (242)

That AT rejects arguments in some submissions deriving a "doctrine" from a teaching about marriage.

> Nearly all of the submissions in this Reference proceed mainly from Christ's teaching about divorce, inferring or discerning a "doctrine" of marriage said to be directly stemming from a "command" of Christ to the effect that no marriage should be solemnised or recognised that is not between a man and a woman.... Insofar as these invoke the "Christ's doctrine" rather than the "Christ's command" arm of s 3 of the Constitution, all of these submissions proceed as if the constitutional definition of "doctrine" has no role to play. It is not open to the Tribunal to approach the constitutional issue in this manner. (245)

They conclude that they are not persuaded there is any "command of Christ" directly referable to this case.

By Way of Summary

The arguments and the material in these reasons are extensive and the legal reasoning tight and restrained. They basically flow from their decision to follow previous decisions of the AT in defining the Doctrine of this Church in tightly constitutional terms, "within the four corners of the constitution." They see that to be their constitutional responsibility. Essentially the argument is set by the reference to "the doctrine of this church" in section 5(3) of the 1992 General Synod Canon Concerning Services of 1992. The Reasons are taken up with what is the doctrine of this church in the constitution and clarifying that over against other uses of the word. Clarifying confusion about this matter takes up quite an amount of space in these Reasons.

This definition of the doctrine of the church resonates closely with the tradition in Anglican theology of "fundamentals" expounded earlier. Section 1 of the Fundamental Declarations reflects that mode of understanding. But that very context also points to the specific theological commitments and practices that rightly belong with "particular" or, in the terms of the seventeenth-century, national churches. The Fundamental Declarations contain an extra two Sections beyond the first doctrine Section and the AT Reasons negotiate these Sections in the latter part of their argument. But these extra two Sections are more in the nature of statements of intent which define the commitments of this particular church.

The Ruling Principles turn to the principles that are to guide the ecclesial processes of the church under this constitution. Here the historical pedigree of the Church of England comes to the fore, but it is not immutable. The first Section in the Ruling Principles declares that the church retains these Restoration documents but then asserts that the church has plenary authority to do certain key things provided they are "consistent with the Fundamental Declarations." The final test is the Fundamental Declarations and restated in each Section of the Ruling Principles.

It seems to me that the way Geoffrey Fisher characterized the special place of the Fundamental Declarations in the constitution is quite apt.

> In a Part by themselves to show that they differ in character and purpose altogether from the second part which contains not what the Church essentially is, but how it governs itself.[21]

Initial Responses and Some Issues

This Opinion from the Appellate Tribunal has been much anticipated. Within the church it deals with a highly contentious subject, not just about attitudes to sexuality and marriage, but also the theological norms of the Anglican Church of Australia and the structure and operation of its constitution. The bishop of Wangaratta issued a short statement at the time of the release of the AT judgement saying the diocese had been affirmed by the judgement and could now go ahead. The Primate, Archbishop Geoff Smith, described the judgement as "an important contribution to the ongoing conversation within the Church." He pointed out that the judgement "did not authorize any Anglican clergy to officiate at weddings other than those between a man and a woman."

Other immediate contributors were less sanguine: "judicial innovation"; "trajectory was disintegration"; "unity would be paper thin"; because the AT judgement "undermines the teaching of scripture it dishonours God." The advice to the AT from the Board of Assessors said it was clear that the teaching of the Bible was that the sexual union of two persons of the same-sex was sin, and furthermore that persistence in such sin will incur the harshest of condemnations in scripture. In fact, "sexual union" was undefined in the Board of Assessors advice to the AT and glossed over in many of the submissions. Neither did the advice, nor the submissions, address the possibility that the newly conferred status of legal marriage might impact upon this.

---

21. Davis, *Australian Anglicans*, 138.

The AT warned that resolution or statements from bodies not subject to the constraint and freedoms of the constitution of the ACA need to be viewed with caution. That need is only amplified by the fact that the AT has now provided clarity about the "doctrine" focus of the constitution of the ACA. No doubt this is early days in responding to this judgement. Strong feelings are at play in this matter and they are not just about same-sex marriage. Also involved are political considerations about the long-standing traditions of different dioceses which do not very often have to engage directly with each other.

They also touch on the place of the Anglican Church of Australia in the broader world of global Anglicanism. These gender issues have been convulsing the Anglican Communion for at least the last thirty years. Part of the swirl of factors in that "convulsion" has been cultural diversity and the historical memories of individual Provinces. Also included in this wider scene is the GAFCON movement, not least in this instance, because of the significant roles of the diocese of Sydney in the beginning and maintenance of that movement. That is of course, the legitimate choice of the diocese, but for the purposes of the ongoing conversation within the ACA it brings the influence of those other relationships into the frame on both sides of this debate.

This debate before the ACA concerns the meaning and operation of the constitution because that is the basis of the union between the dioceses, that is the legal basis of this church's existence. For its own integrity the coming debate in the ACA will need to stay focused on the actual issues within this church.

As these debates roll on, some key issues will probably emerge and, in part, they are addressed in this AT judgement. I say in part because the AT makes it clear that their task is not to settle theological debates in the church. Their task it to answer questions put to them under the constitution of the ACA. Their task is an interpretative one that is both legal and constitutional.

On a number of occasions, the AT underlined this point. Early in their reasons they say:

> As long as constitutional boundaries are respected and existing laws obeyed, it will be up to the clergy and laity of the ACA to determine the Church's interaction with same-sex attracted people and their families. (38)

And towards the end they state more expansively.

> The issue of approving the solemnization of a same-sex marriage is not before the Tribunal. And, as will be apparent from our reasons, the Tribunal has not had to address the "merits" of blessing services or even the theology of blessing same-sex "coupling" beyond the inquiry as to whether it entails a relevant teaching on a question of faith. All we have done is to declare that the Synod of the Diocese of Wangaratta has not acted contrary to the *Constitution* nor contrary to the scope of authority given by the General Synod in 1992. All of the issues in this Reference are of a legal nature. No questions of fact or credibility are involved. Indeed, the reasons published above show that the matter has turned upon constitutional principles already decided by the Tribunal in the past. (277)

Some have criticized the meaning of doctrine in the judgement as narrow, an innovation, or unworkable. The AT in its reasons goes to some length to point out the consistency between their reasoning and previous judgements in section E and elsewhere.

Many of the participants in this debate focused on moral issues they saw as crucial to the matter. Many thought doctrine to be something akin to teaching. The tribunal regularly referred to the constitutional meaning of doctrine, or, one might say, the way the word doctrine is used in this constitution. What the constitution means is of course the task of the Tribunal. This judgment makes a clear definition of doctrine in the constitution as those things necessary to believe for salvation. This is "the Christian Faith" of the first Section of the constitution. The Tribunal shows that it is following previous judgements and reasons of the Tribunal. They declare that they do not intend changing the earlier interpretation given by the tribunal. They give detailed evidence in support from previous judgements to demonstrate this tradition of interpretation.

I have tried above to show that this approach to the doctrine of the faith of a church is known in Anglican history. It is particularly apparent in the debates with Roman Catholics in the seventeenth century using the notion of "fundamentals." Indeed, as illustrated above in Edward Stillingfleet's use of almost exactly the form of expression as appears in the Tribunal's reasons.

For the purposes of assessing this judgment I think time will reveal that what we have here is tight legal reasoning in relation to a legal question about the current terms of the constitution of the ACA and the regulation of the diocese of Wangaratta. That is quite a lot, but it surely is not enough. The AT judgement simply clarifies some terms and the framework of the debate that now falls to the laity and the clergy of the ACA to engage with the ethical issues.

The Task in Front of Us

The judgement and how we got to it raise some very serious questions on which people have different opinions strongly held. Those divisions cannot be simply ignored. Excellent though the individual essays of the Doctrine Commission are, they take us only so far and much of the discussion proceeds on the basis of a meaning of "doctrine" quite removed from its constitutional use as now set out by the AT. The Introduction by the Chair of the Commission (Bishop Jonathan Holland) points out what the General Synod asked them to do and how they carried out this request. He also sets out what he thinks might be points of "common ground" that seemed to emerge in the discussion. One essay did devote itself to how we might approach this conflict.[22]

These essays provide very useful material for the task that lies before us. In broad terms that task is how we are to respond to the constitutionally legitimate actions of the Wangaratta synod. In other words what can be done under the constitution to enable quite significant differences between dioceses to be properly dealt with.

During the formation of the constitution there were serious issues represented by the diocese of Sydney as to how their particular evangelical tradition at that time could be preserved. That challenge was argued in terms of the continuity of the Australian Church with the Church of England. That issue then focused on the liturgical use of the mass vestments which were seen as striking at the heart of the principles of the English Reformation teaching on salvation. This was indeed a critical matter both in itself and especially at that time. Its importance at the time was magnified by the intimate relation between ecclesiastical and lay elements in the governance of England. Religion inevitably had a political connotation to it. It is worth noting that the oaths of office affirmed by Philip as Governor of the new colony of New South Wales in 1788 contained a categorical denial of the doctrine of transubstantiation. With the passing of that Christendom model in the colony the political heat went out of this issue but not out of the theological conflict. It became more clearly an intra church issue focused on liturgical practice. The heat of

---

22. Pickard, "Disagreement and Christian Unity."

that debate has diminished in the Church of England where established church characteristics remained and evangelicals there have come to see that they could live with vestments in their church on the basis that by official declaration they had no theological significance.

The present conflict, however, is a matter of central ethical significance and relates directly to the representation of Christian faith in the wider community. It is not a question about relations between the ACA and another church. It is about the relation between the ACA and the host society and its law on marriage. Furthermore, it has to do with liturgy and what clergy can do. It is thus directly relevant to the function of the constitution.

As with any debate about a moral question in the ACA the role of scripture has had an important role in this discussion. It has been present in submissions, responses, public comment and of course in the essays of the Doctrine Commission. The AT engages with this topic only in brief terms in relation to references in the constitution relevant to the question at hand.

In the wider Anglican community in churches across the nation same-sex marriage is a very present question. The cultural wave of change that brought this question to us is the same across the whole country and thus in every diocese. That is not a reason for every diocese doing the same thing, but it is an argument for sharing resources and insights. Respectful and charitable difference between dioceses is quite a different matter from determined independence, or insisting that everyone else agrees with my or our opinion.

This question is also quite important in the church in the sense that it is a touchstone for how we as Christians, and as a Christian community, seek guidance from the God whom we worship and the Christ we profess. Within that it is also an issue of "by what authority" do we do these things, whatever policy we wish to advocate. In this context the character of scripture and its role in decision making, or personal guidance for Christians, is quite fundamental. Behind any claim that scripture says something lie fundamental questions about the character of scripture, how scripture works and how its authority is perceived. The terminology of Section 2 of the Fundamental Declarations seems to suggest that the authority of scripture is for all things necessary for salvation, but clearly there is more involved here.

In other words, in this difference of convictions, we need to go beyond our respective views. We will need to engage with each other's underlying assumptions and warrants. That requires patient listening and high levels of openness and trust. Such a process is in essence a form of theological work. As we examine these issues more deeply and in company with those who take a different approach, we will open up the possibility of better understanding and thereby see what is really at stake. In that way we might be better able to see ahead and what we might be able to do within the reasonably capacious terms of the federal union of the dioceses that provides the framework of our institutional church life in the ACA.

However, especially in the ACA, we need help in actually engaging with those with whom we disagree. History has not prepared us well for this challenge. Our loose federal structure has not forced us together very much and we have lived out of the past of our local independence. The present cultural challenge is much greater for us because of this history. Towards the end of the last century a meeting of the heads of the Anglican Theological Colleges met for the first time ever. A few of these principals attended the annual bishops' conference and reported on their meeting. When asked if they planned to meet again, they said no. One of their number declared he could not see any value in such a meeting. It was a cameo of the cultural divide that exists in the Anglican Church of Australia.

On the other hand, that history has left us with an organizational structure that enables very considerable local diocesan freedom of action within a loose federal institutional connection. That also means that we have the possibility of a wide degree of diversity between the dioceses.

One of the benefits of the AT judgement is that it draws attention to the very limited category of the fundamentals in Section 1 of chapter I, and also the absence of any rationale for the activity commitments in Sections 2 and 3 of chapter I in the constitution. The AT judgment has also drawn attention to the breadth of possibility allowed by the 1992 Canon on Services.

I drew attention earlier to a distinction between institution and community. The constitution describes the institution called the Anglican Church of Australia and describes how that institution operates and what it is committed to. That institution is not an end in itself, rather it exists to serve the very real "imagined community" of Anglicans in Australia.

That, in part, is why the constitution provides jurisdictional arrangements only for the officers of the institution, that is to say, the clergy.

Their obligations to the communities around the country are set out in the formularies and canons of the General Synod and of the dioceses. That is one of the reasons why matters of "ritual, ceremonial or discipline" are given such priority in the formation of canons. The task of the officers of the institution is to provide a disciplined ministry of word and sacrament. The constitution provides for an important role for lay people in the General Synod. They constitute a distinct House alongside those of bishops and clergy.

Relations within this community are more personal than the requirements for the officers of the institution. They are also more challenging for the lives of Christians as they sustain their faith and live as witnesses of Christ in the broader society. It is in the daily lives of these Anglican Christians that the cultural challenges are existentially encountered. The clergy have a stake in this matter because of their institutional obligations. But lay members of the church are the front line witnesses in the community and they also have a great deal at stake here. Their voice will need to be heard.

Almost as important in my view is how we reach any resolution on this question. I do not mean that the question is how to find some kind of compromise to incorporate into our institutional life. That may be necessary, a good thing or neither of those. A compromise is not an end, though it might become a step towards an end. The end needs to be some kind of resolution that can lead on to a future that honors the fundamentals of the faith to which the constitution points, whatever that future might be. It also needs to be a resolution that honors the daily lives of Anglicans in their witness to our fellow Australians. Resolution in both these senses requires an agreed commitment to the future in some form or another.[23]

What Is at Stake for Australian Anglicans

The root question here in my view is our calling as Anglican Christians to live in such a way that we are worthy witnesses to the Christ we profess. Of course, that is our constant vocation, but the present situation offers a particular and quite specific context for that calling. Here we have an institution, the Anglican Church of Australia, that exists to serve a specific

---

23. In this respect I am very sympathetic to the essay by Stephen Pickard in the Doctrine Commission collection. Pickard, "Disagreement and Christian Unity."

community of Christians. The host society is legally sympathetic in broad terms to the Christian life we seek. It is a little different with the culture within which we live. It is more pervasively and subtly challenging to personal Christian life and witness. It is the wave of cultural change, mostly in the western world, that has shaped the gender issues before us.

When approaching a question like same-sex marriage in church it is immediately obvious that this is an institutionally framed question. The individual Christian does not conduct weddings. Clergy as officers of the church do that. Furthermore, they do it as recognized representatives of the state in the terms of the current Marriage Act. By conducting the service, they in fact perform a legally effective act. This reflects something of the English tradition brought with the first colonists. In that respect it is a hangover from the past. It was not always so, nor indeed is it so everywhere now. Nor is it inconceivable that it might be changed here. Were it to be changed the question would be differently framed but the essential question would still be whether same-sex marriages are deemed to be Christianly defensible for the church in its institutionally framed corporate life.

It seems to me that we need some unravelling of the terms of this conversation. Is there such a thing as a Christian marriage? The New Testament material tends to be comment, with theological supporting arguments, on aspects of married life that the early Christians faced. This is true of most of the material in the New Testament documents on social relationships. While later Christians might consider formulating their thoughts around the question "what is a Christian marriage" that in itself is neither necessarily a reasonable use of the New Testament material nor in itself an obvious way to formulate the question generally.

Quo Vadis?

I think this is much too serious a matter to be dealt with at short notice. Postponing the meeting of the next General Synod for twelve months provided a rich opportunity to undertake this challenge with some expectation of reaching a worthwhile resolution. The church is faced with a really serious issue and history has not enabled us to deal well or quickly with it. The way forward will take time and patience all round.

Referring this question to the AT has simply asked about the legal and constitutional issues involved. There are many things, some more important than others, that are within the constitutional ambit. That is what the Guiding Principles are about. Those things are decided by the relevant bodies under the constitution. Any resolution of this current challenge lies outside the AT, as the AT itself has clearly indicated. Serious engagement with each other's arguments is necessary to open up the underlying issues. Neither "scripture says," nor "new relationships need to be embraced for love of those involved" are adequate on their own as an argument. Nor does simply declaring without any accompanying argument that the AT judgement is wrong in law and in theology. Reasons and argument are what we need. Not bald assertions. For the sake of the future of our witness in this country, we need to provide for a better and more seriously engaged process. The nature of the question and its presence in our society and within the church, means that any longer term process would need to be shaped in a way that assures all involved that the question will be dealt with and not just deferred or walked away from.

The General Synod has developed some ways of dealing with highly contentious matters. There is provision for a different kind of debate in the Standing Orders that enables small group discussion, introduced with speeches that focus on the issues at stake. Sometimes the synod has taken a two-step approach with a preliminary debate at one synod moving towards a decision at a following synod. These processes have proved to be helpful in the past.

However, this conflict is upon us and more serious arrangements need to be sought in order to confront it adequately.

There are widely developed methods of dealing with conflict resolution. Good advice is available as to how such principles might be applied in this situation. The skills for this kind of exercise will be needed in any group given responsibility in this task. Some informed theological presence is by no means the only skill needed and given the public and social character of this matter lay, that is to say other professional and personal experience and competences than clerical, will be needed. The question here is not just difference of opinion, but deep disagreement between people. It is not just an intellectual difference. It is a conflict with a long history of cultural and social elements. It is a prime case for serious conflict resolution approaches. Such a process would take more time and require a great deal of effort for those involved. But then this is seen by many to be a really important matter for the church. If it is really as important as is said then a serious commitment to dealing with it is surely required.

The Appellate Tribunal has delivered a judgement as to the constitutionality of the Wangaratta Resolution for blessing marriages made under the revised Commonwealth Marriage Act. No doubt there will be a lot of public and private discussion and argument about this. For my part I think the judgement will hold up under any criticism. It seems to me to be quite clear that the Fundamental Declarations are the ultimate point of reference constitutionally. It also seems to me that it is misguided to think that the Fundamental Declarations are the only guidance available to the church in making decisions about this matter. The Ruling Principles provide a wealth of material for ways of approaching particular questions. The church has plenary authority to make those decisions under the broad umbrella of the Fundamentals. There is plenty of room under that umbrella.

There is a great work to be done here. The General Synod cannot do it directly, nor indeed the Standing Committee. But they can and surely must put in place the resources and plans for this task to be engaged effectively. There is a lot at stake for the Anglican Church of Australia. We do have the resources in the church community to enterprise what needs to be attempted. The most important challenge is how we, as Anglicans, can show what it is to be a Christian community by the way that we do these things and the way we treat each other and our fellow Australians.

Bibliography

Anderson, Benedict. *Imagined Communities: Reflections on the Origin and Spread of Nationalism*. London: Verso, 2006.
Anglican Church in Aotearoa, New Zealand, and Polynesia. "Canons and Statutes." https://www.anglican.org.nz/Resources/Canons.
Anglican Church in North America. "Constitutions and Canons." https://anglicanchurch.net/wp-content/uploads/2021/10/ACNA-Constitution-and-Canons-June-2019.pdf.
Anglican Church of Australia. "Appellate Tribunal." https://anglican.org.au/governance/tribunals/appellate-tribunal-current-matters/.
———. "The Constitution of the Anglican Church of Australia." https://anglican.org.au/wp-content/uploads/2019/12/Constitution-update-011219-for-web.pdf.
The Anglican Communion. "The Primates' Meeting, February 2005 Communiqué." https://www.anglicancommunion.org/media/68387/communique-_english.pdf.
Anglican Consultative Council. *The Communion We Share: Anglican Consultative Council XI, Scotland*. Harrisburg: Morehouse, 2000.
———. *Mission in a Broken World: Report of ACC-8, Wales 1990*. London: Anglican Consultative Council, 1990.
———. "Resolutions." https://www.anglicancommunion.org/structures/instruments-of-communion/acc/acc-12/resolutions.aspx#s44.
———. "Resolutions 14 - ACC." https://www.anglicancommunion.org/media/66941/resolutions-acc-14.pdf.
Anglican Consultative Council, and Inter-Anglican Theological and Doctrinal Commission. *For the Sake of the Kingdom: God's Church and the New Creation*. Cincinnati: Forward Movement, 1986.
Avis, Paul. *Anglicanism and the Christian Church*. Edinburgh: T. & T. Clark, 1989.
Ballantine Jones, Bruce. *Inside Sydney: An Insider's View of the Changes and Politics in the Anglican Diocese of Sydney, 1966–2013*. Self-published, 2016.
Barlow, William. *The Summe of the Conference before the Kings Majesty*. London, 1604.
Barth, Karl. *Church Dogmatics*. Vol. 1.1, *The Doctrine of the Word of God*. Edinburgh: T. & T. Clark, 1975.
Bauer, Walter. *Rechtglaubigkeit und Ketzerei im ältesten Christentum* [Orthodoxy and Heresy in Earliest Christianity]. Tubingen: Mohr Siebeck, 1934.
Bayne, Stephen Fielding. *Mutual Responsibility and Interdependence in the Body of Christ, with Related Background Documents*. Edited with Introduction and Concluding Chapter by Stephen F. Bayne. London: SPCK, 1963.

Bede. *The Ecclesiastical History of the English People; The Greater Chronicle; Bede's Letter to Egbert.* Edited by Judith McClure and Roger Collins. Oxford: Oxford University Press, 1994.

Broughton, W. G. *A Charge Delivered to the Clergy of New South Wales, in the Diocese of Australia, at the Visitation Held in the Church of St. James, Sydney, on Wednesday, October the 6th, 1841.* Sydney: Tegg, 1841.

———. *Speech of the Lord Bishop of Australia in the Legislative Council upon the Resolution for Establishing a System of General Education.* Sydney: Tegg, 1839.

Brown, Callum G. *The Death of Christian Britain: Understanding Secularisation, 1800–2000.* 2nd ed. London: Routledge, 2009.

Brown, Peter. *The Rise of Western Christendom: Triumph and Diversity, AD 200–1000.* Oxford: Blackwell, 1996.

———. *The Rise of Western Christendom: Triumph and Diversity, AD 200–1000.* 10th anniversary rev. ed. Malden, MA: Wiley-Blackwell, 2013.

Butterfield, Herbert. *The Whig Interpretation of History.* New York: Norton, 1965.

Cameron, Marcia Helen. *An Enigmatic Life: David Broughton Knox, Father of Contemporary Sydney Anglicanism.* Brunswick East: Acorn, 2006.

Cameron, N. M. *Scandrett v. Dowling: Aftermath.* Papers of the Standing Committee of the Diocese of Sydney, August 7, 1992.

Campenhausen, Hans von. *Ecclesiastical Authority and Spiritual Power in the Church of the First Three Centuries.* London: Black, 1969.

Cantor, Norman F. *Church, Kingship, and Lay Investiture in England, 1089–1135.* Princeton: Princeton University Press, 1958.

Carey, Hilary M. *God's Empire: Religion and Colonialism in the British World, c. 1801–1908.* Cambridge: Cambridge University Press, 2010.

Chandler, Alfred D. *The Visible Hand: The Managerial Revolution in American Business.* Cambridge, MA: Belknap, 1977.

Chandler, Alfred D., and Herman Daems. *Managerial Hierarchies: Comparative Perspectives on the Rise of the Modern Industrial Enterprise.* Cambridge: Harvard University Press, 1980.

Chiwanga, Simon. "Beyond the Monarch/Chief: Reconsidering Episcopacy in Africa." In *Beyond Colonial Anglicanism: The Anglican Communion in the Twenty-First Century,* edited by I. T. Douglas and K. Pui-lan, 297–317. New York: Church Publishing, 2001.

Church of England. *Book of Common Prayer.* https://www.churchofengland.org/prayer-and-worship/worship-texts-and-resources/book-common-prayer.

———. *Saepius Officio: Answer of the Archbishops of England to the Apostolic Letter of Pope Leo XIII on English Ordinations: Addressed to the Whole Body of Bishops of the Catholic Church.* London: Longmans, Green, and Co., 1897.

Church of England in Australia. *Legal Nexus: Case with Opinion from Counsel in England and in the Commonwealth.* Sydney, 1912.

Congregation for the Doctrine of the Faith. *Profession of Faith.* https://www.vatican.va/roman_curia/congregations/cfaith/documents/rc_con_cfaith_doc_1998_professio-fidei_en.html.

Cowdrey, H. E. J. *Lanfranc: Scholar, Monk, and Archbishop.* Oxford: Oxford University Press, 2003.

———. *Pope Gregory VII, 1073–1085.* Oxford: Clarendon, 1998.

———. *Popes and Church Reform in the 11th Century.* Aldershot: Ashgate, 2000.

Cranmer, Thomas. *A Defence of the True and Catholic Doctrine of the Sacrament of the Body and Blood of Our Saviour Christ, with a Confutation of Sundry Errors concerning the Same, Grounded and Stablished upon God's Holy Word, and Approved by the Consent of the Most Ancient Doctors of the Church*. London, 1550.

———. "A Fruitful Exhortation to the Reading and Knowledge of Holy Scripture." In *Certain Sermons or Homilies Appointed to Be Read in Churches in the Time of Queen Elizabeth of Famous Memory*, edited by the Church of England, 1–10. London: SPCK, 1864.

Cross, Claire. *Church and People, 1450–1660: The Triumph of the Laity in the English Church*. London: Fontana, 1976.

Cross, Peter R. *The Influence of Recent Ecumenical Dialogue on the Anglican Theology of the Historic Episcopate: The Church of England and the Free Churches, 1920–1982*. Rome: Pontifica Univeristas Gregoriana, 1983.

Dalrymple, William, and Olivia Fraser. *The Anarchy: The Relentless Rise of the East India Company*. New York: Bloomsbury, 2019.

Davis, John. *Australian Anglicans and Their Constitution*. Canberra: Acorn, 1993.

Donfried, Karl P. *The Romans Debate*. Rev. ed. Edinburgh: T. & T. Clark, 1991.

Douglas, David C., and G. W. Greenaway, eds. *English Historical Documents*. Vol. 2, *1042–1189*. London: Eyre and Spottiswood, 1953.

Douglas, I. T. *Fling Out the Banner! The National Church Ideal and the Foreign Mission of the Episcopal Church*. New York: Church Hymnal, 1996.

Douglas, I. T., and Kwok Pui-lan, eds. *Beyond Colonial Anglicanism: The Anglican Communion in the Twenty-First Century*. New York: Church Publishing, 2001.

Dulles, Avery. *The Catholicity of the Church*. Oxford: Clarendon, 1985.

Dunn, James D. G. *Jews and Christians: The Parting of the Ways, A.D. 70 to 135: The Second Durham-Tübingen Research Symposium on Earliest Christianity and Judaism (Durham, September 1989)*. Grand Rapids: Eerdmans, 1999.

———. *Unity and Diversity in the New Testament*. London: SCM, 1977.

The Episcopal Church. *Constitution and Canons*. New York: Church Publishing, 2006.

———. *The Constitution and Canons Together with the Rules of Order*. New York: Office of the General Convention, 2019.

Eusebius. *Church History, Life of Constantine*. In vol. 2 of *Nicene and Post-Nicene Fathers, Series 2*, edited by Philip Schaff and Henry Wace. Grand Rapids: Christian Classics Ethereal Library, 1995.

———. *The History of the Church: From Christ to Constantine*. Translated by G. A. Williamson. Baltimore: Penguin, 1965.

Evans, Christopher Francis. *Is 'Holy Scripture' Christian? And Other Questions*. London: SCM, 1971.

Fahey, Michael A. "The Catholicity of the Church in the New Testament and in the Early Patristic Period." *The Jurist* 52 (1992) 44–70.

Ferguson, Niall. *The Square and the Tower: Networks, Hierarchies, and the Struggle for Global Power*. London: Penguin, 2017.

Figgis J. N. *Hopes for English Religion*. London: Longmans, 1919.

Gallagher, Edmon L., and John D. Meade. *The Biblical Canon Lists from Early Christianity: Texts and Analysis*. Oxford: Oxford University Press, 2019.

Gamble, Henry Y. "The New Testament Canon: Recent Research and the *Status Questionis*." In *The Canon Debate*, edited by L. McDonald and J. Sanders, 267–94. Peabody, MA: Hendrickson, 2002.

Gellner, E. *Nations and Nationalism.* Oxford: Blackwell, 1983.
The General Convention of the Episcopal Church. *Constitution and Canons.* https://extranet.generalconvention.org/staff/files/download/23914.
Goodin, Robert E. *The Theory of Institutional Design.* Cambridge: Cambridge University Press, 1996.
Greer, Rowan A. *Anglican Approaches to Scripture: From the Reformation to the Present.* New York: Crossroad, 2006.
Hahneman, G. M. "The Muratorian Fragment and the Origins of the New Testament Canon." In *The Canon Debate,* edited by Lee Martin McDonald and James A. Sanders, 405–15. Peabody, MA: Hendrickson, 2002.
Harnack, Adolf von. *Bible Reading in the Early Church.* Translated by J. R. Wilkinson. London: Williams & Norgate, 1912.
———. *The Origin of the New Testament and the Most Important Consequences of the New Creation.* London: Williams & Norgate, 1925.
Hassett, Miranda Katherine. *Anglican Communion in Crisis: How Episcopal Dissidents and Their African Allies Are Reshaping Anglicanism.* Princeton: Princeton University Press, 2007.
Hastings, Adrian. *The Construction of Nationhood: Ethnicity, Religion and Nationalism.* Cambridge: Cambridge University Press, 1997.
Hatch, Edwin. *The Organization of the Early Christian Churches.* London: Longmans Green, 1892.
Hauerwas, Stanley. *With the Grain of the Universe: The Church's Witness and Natural Theology: Being the Gifford Lectures Delivered at the University of St. Andrews in 2001.* Grand Rapids: Brazos, 2001.
Heck, Gene W. *Charlemagne, Muhammad, and the Arab Roots of Capitalism.* Studien zur Geschichte und Kultur des islamischen Orients 18. Berlin: de Gruyter, 2006.
Herrin, Judith. *The Formation of Christendom.* Princeton: Princeton University Press, 1989.
Hilliard, David. "The Religious Crisis of the 1960s: The Experience of the Australian Churches." *Journal of Religious History* 21.2 (1997) 209–27.
Hobsbawm, E. J. *Nations and Nationalism Since 1780.* Cambridge: Cambridge University Press, 1990.
Hooker, Richard. *The Folger Library of the Works of Richard Hooker.* Edited by W. Speed Hill. 7 vols. Cambridge: Harvard University Press, 1977–98.
———. *Of the Laws of Ecclesiastical Polity: A Critical Edition with Modern Spelling.* Edited by Arthur Stephen McGrade. 3 vols. Oxford: Oxford University Press, 2013.
Inter-Anglican Theological and Doctrinal Commission. *Communion, Conflict, and Hope.* London: Anglican Communion Office, 2008.
———. "Meetings Communiqués and Documents." https://www.anglicancommunion.org/media/107645/IATDC-Inter-Anglican-Theological-and-Doctrinal-Commission.pdf.
———. *The Virginia Report: The Report of the Inter-Anglican Theological and Doctrinal Commission.* London: Anglican Consultative Council, 1997.
Irenaeus. *Against Heresies.* In vol. 1 of *The Ante-Nicene Fathers: Translations of the Writings of the Fathers Down to A D. 325,* edited by Alexander Roberts and James Donaldson. Grand Rapids: Eerdmans, 1950.

BIBLIOGRAPHY 191

Jenkins, Philip. *The Lost History of Christianity: The Thousand-Year Golden Age of the Church in the Middle East, Africa, and Asia—And How It Died*. New York: HarperOne, 2008.

John Paul II, Pope. *Ad tuendam fidem*. https://www.vatican.va/content/john-paul-ii/en/motu_proprio/documents/hf_jp-ii_motu-proprio_30061998_ad-tuendam-fidem.html.

Kaye, Bruce N. "Anglicanism's Uncertain Apostolicity." *Journal of Anglican Studies* 10.2 (2012) 135–46.

———. "Catholicity and a Vocation for the Anglican Communion." *Anglican Theological Review* 102.1 (2020) 71–95.

———. *Colonial Religion: Conflict and Change in Church and State*. Adelaide: ATF, 2020.

———. *Conflict and the Practice of Christian Faith: The Anglican Experiment*. Eugene, OR: Cascade, 2009.

———. "D. F. Strauss and the European Theological Tradition: 'Der Ischariotismus unsere Tag'?" *Journal of Religious History* 17 (1992) 172–93.

———. "How Can We Speak of 'Canonical Scripture' Today?" *Journal of Anglican Studies* 11.1 (2013) 1–14.

———. *An Introduction to World Anglicanism*. Introduction to Religion. Cambridge: Cambridge University Press, 2008.

———. "The Laity in Church Governance according to Bishop Broughton." *Journal of Religious History* 20.1 (1996) 78–92.

———. "Lightfoot and Baur on Early Christianity." *Novum Testamentum* 26 (1984) 193–224.

———. "Orthodox Anglicans and Catholicity." *Journals of Anglican Studies* 9.2 (2011) 125–33.

———. "Plurality and Identity in the Modern World." *Journal of Anglican Studies* 9.1 (2011) 1–8.

———. "Reality and Form in Catholicity." *Journal of Anglican Studies* 10.1 (2012) 3–12.

———. "Recent Roman Catholic New Testament Research." *Churchman* 84 (1975) 246–56.

———. *The Rise and Fall of the English Christendom: Theocracy, Christology, Order, and Power*. London: Routledge, 2018.

———. "The Role of Eschatology in Recent Anglican Ecclesiology: A Study of Three International Doctrine Commission Reports." *Sewanee Theological Review* 56.3 (2013) 262–72.

———. "The Sidelining of the Anglican Consultative Council in a Time of Turmoil." In *To the Church, To the World: Essays in Honour of the Right Reverend John C. Paterson*, edited by John Fairbrother, 67–74. Auckland: Vaughan Park Anglican Retreat Centre, 2010.

———. "The Strange Birth of Anglican Synods in Australia and the 1850 Bishop's Conference." *Journal of Religious History* 27.2 (2003) 177–97.

———. "'To the Romans and Others' Revisited." *Novum Testamentum* 18 (1976) 37–77.

———. *Web of Meaning: The Role of Origins in Christian Faith*. Sydney: Aquila, 2000.

———. "What Is at Stake in the Wangaratta Move: Getting to the Fundamentals." https://www.academia.edu/attachments/65866346/download_file?s=portfolio.

Kaye, Bruce N., and G. R. Trelaor. "J. B. Lightfoot and New Testament Interpretation: An Unpublished Manuscript of 1885." *Durham University Journal* 21.2 (1990) 161–75.

———. "J. B. Lightfoot on Strauss and Christian Origins: An Unpublished Manuscript." *Durham University Journal* 59.2 (1987) 165–200.

Kelly, J. N. D. *Early Christian Creeds*. 3rd ed. New York: McKay, 1972.

Kelly, Paul. *The End of Certainty: The Story of the 1980s*. St. Leonards: Allen & Unwin, 1992.

Kelsey, David H. *The Uses of Scripture in Recent Theology*. Philadelphia: Fortress, 1975.

Kreider, Alan, ed. *The Origins of Christendom in the West*. Edinburgh: T. & T. Clark, 2001.

Lake, Kirsopp, ed and trans. *The Apostolic Fathers*. Cambridge: Harvard University Press, 1965.

Leithart, Peter J. *Defending Constantine: The Twilight of an Empire and the Dawn of Christendom*. Downers Grove, IL: IVP Academic, 2010.

Leo XIII, Pope. *Apostolicae curae*. https://www.newadvent.org/library/docs_le13ac.htm.

———. *Providentissimus Deus*. https://www.vatican.va/content/leo-xiii/en/encyclicals/documents/hf_l-xiii_enc_18111893_providentissimus-deus.html.

Lightfoot, J. B. *The Apostolic Fathers, Part II: S. Ignatius, S. Polycarp: Revised Texts with Introductions, Notes, Dissertations, and Translations*. London: Macmillan, 1885.

———. *St. Paul's Epistle to the Galatians: A Revised Text with Introduction, Notes, and Dissertations*. London: Macmillan, 1881.

———. *St. Paul's Epistle to the Philippians: A Revised Text with Introduction, Notes, and Dissertations*. London: Macmillan, 1868.

Limerick, David. "The Shape of the New Organization: Implications for Human Resource Management." *Asia Pacific Journal of Human Relations* 30 (1992) 38–52.

Limerick, David, et al. *Managing the New Organisation: Collaboration and Sustainability in the Postcorporate World*. Crows Nest: Allen & Unwin, 2002.

Lopez, Mark. *The Origins of Multiculturalism in Australian Politics, 1945–1975*. Carlton: Melbourne University Press, 2000.

Lühmann, Niklas. *Social Systems*. Translated by John Bednarz Jr., with Dirk Baecker. Stanford: Stanford University Press, 1995.

Mackay, Hugh. *Generations*. Sydney: Pan Macmillan, 1997.

———. *Reinventing Australia*. Pymble: Angus and Robertson, 1993.

Markus, R. A. *The End of Ancient Christianity*. Cambridge: Cambridge University Press, 1990.

McDonald, Lee Martin, and James A. Sanders. *The Canon Debate*. Peabody, MA: Hendrickson, 2002.

McLeod, Hugh. *The Religious Crisis of the 1960s*. Oxford: Oxford University Press, 2007.

Metzger, Bruce M. *The Canon of the New Testament: Its Origin, Development, and Significance*. Oxford: Oxford University Press, 1987.

Mitchell, Basil. *How to Play Theological Ping-Pong: And Other Essays on Faith and Reason*. Edited by William J. Abraham and Robert W. Prevost. Grand Rapids: Eerdmans, 1991.

Moffett, Samuel Hugh. *A History of Christianity in Asia*. Vol. 1, *Beginnings to 1500*. Maryknoll, NY: Orbis, 1992.

Moorman, John Richard Humpidge. *A History of the Church in England*. 3rd ed. London: A. and C. Black, 1973.
Moule, C. F. D. *The Birth of the New Testament*. Harper's New Testament Commentaries. New York: Harper & Row, 1962.
Münz, Peter. *The Origin of the Carolingian Empire*. Leicester: Leicester University Press, 1960.
Nicholls, David. *The Pluralist State*. London: Macmillan, 1975.
Nineham, D. E. *The Use and Abuse of the Bible: A Study of the Bible in an Age of Rapid Cultural Change*. London: Macmillan, 1976.
Paul VI, Pope. *Lumen gentium*. https://www.vatican.va/archive/hist_councils/ii_vatican_council/documents/vat-ii_const_19641121_lumen-gentium_en.html.
Phillips, Andrew, and J. C. Sharman. *Outsourcing Empire: How Company-States Made the Modern World*. Princeton: Princeton University Press, 2020.
Pickard, Stephen K. "Disagreement and Christian Unity: Re-evaluating the Situation." In *Marriage, Same-Sex Marriage, and the Anglican Church of Australia*, edited by Jonathan Holland, 241–66. Mulgrave: Broughton, 2019.
——. "The Purpose of Stating the Faith: An Historical and Systematic Inquiry into the Tradition of Fundamental Articles with Special Reference to Anglicanism." PhD diss., Durham University, 1990.
——. *Theological Foundations for Collaborative Ministry*. Burlington, VT: Ashgate, 2009.
Pius XII, Pope. *Divino afflante Spiritu*. https://www.vatican.va/content/pius-xii/en/encyclicals/documents/hf_p-xii_enc_30091943_divino-afflante-spiritu.html.
Poguntke, Thomas, and Paul Webb, eds. *The Presidentialization of Politics: A Comparative Study of Modern Democracies*. Oxford: Oxford University Press, 2004.
Primates Meeting Communique. "Anglican Communion News Service." https://web.archive.org/web/20091024161739/http://anglicancommunion.org/acns/news.cfm/2009/2/5/ACNS4574.
Radner, Ephraim, and Philip Turner. *The Fate of Communion: The Agony of Anglicanism and the Future of a Global Church*. Grand Rapids: Eerdmans, 2006.
Reicke, Bo. "Unity and Diversity in New Testament Theology." In *Good News in History: Essays in Honor of Bo Reicke*, edited by Ed L. Miller, 173–92. Atlanta: Scholars, 1993.
Rieger, Joerg. *Christ & Empire: From Paul to Postcolonial Times*. Minneapolis: Fortress, 2007.
Ross, Alexander. *A Still More Excellent Way: Authority and Polity in the Anglican Communion*. London: SCM, 2020.
Rothe, Richard. *Die Anfange der Christlichen Kirche und Ihrer Verfassung: Ein Geschichtlicher Versuch*. Wittenberg, 1837.
Saul, John Ralston. *The Collapse of Globalism and the Reinvention of the World*. London: Atlantic, 2005.
Schleiermacher, Friedrich. *The Christian Faith*. Edited by H. R. Mackintosh and J. S. Stewart. Edinburgh: T. & T. Clark, 1928.
Schweitzer, Albert. *The Mysticism of Paul the Apostle*. Translated by William Montgomery. New York: Macmillan, 1956.
Shaw, G. P. *Patriarch and Patriot: William Grant Broughton, 1788–1853*. Melbourne: Melbourne University Press, 1978.

"A Statement by the Primates of the Anglican Communion meeting in Lambeth Palace." *ACNS*, October 16, 2013. https://www.anglicannews.org/news/2003/10/a-statement-by-the-primates-of-the-anglican-communion-meeting-in-lambeth-palace.aspx.

Stillingfleet, Edward. *A Rational Account of the Grounds of Protestant Religion Being a Vindication of the Lord Archbishop of Canterbury's Relation of a Conference*. London: White, 1665.

Strong, Rowan. "An Antipodean Establishment: Institutional Anglicanism in Australia, 1788–c.1934." *Journal of Anglican Studies* 1.1 (2003) 61–90.

Sykes, S. W. "The Fundamentals of Christianity." In *The Study of Anglicanism*, edited by S. W. Sykes and John Booty, 231–44. London: SPCK, 1988.

Tertullian. *Apology*. https://www.newadvent.org/fathers/0301.htm.

Thomas, John Heywood. Review of *How to Play Theological Ping-Pong*, by Basil Mitchell. Religious Studies 28.3 (1992) 431–32.

Treloar, Geoffrey R. *Lightfoot the Historian: The Nature and Role of History in the Life and Thought of J. B. Lightfoot (1828–1889) as Churchman and Scholar*. Wissenschaftliche Untersuchungen zum Neuen Testament 2. Tübingen: Mohr Siebeck, 1998.

Vaughn, Sally N. *Archbishop Anselm: Bec Missionary, Canterbury Primate, Patriarch of Another World*. Farnham: Ashgate, 2012.

Ward, Kevin. *A History of Global Anglicanism*. Cambridge: Cambridge University Press, 2006.

Westcott, Brooke Foss. *A General Survey of the History of the Canon of the New Testament during the First Four Centuries*. London: Macmillan and Co., 1855.

Williams, Rowan. "Archbishop's Letter to Anglican Primates." http://rowanwilliams.archbishopofcanterbury.org/canterbury/data/files/resources/2268/Advent-letter-Abp-Primates-291111.pdf.

———. "Defining Heresy." In *The Origins of Christendom in the West*, edited by Alan Kreider, 313–36. Edinburgh: T. & T. Clark, 2001.

Witherington, Ben, III, and Darlene Hyatt. *Paul's Letter to the Romans: A Socio-Rhetorical Commentary*. Grand Rapids: Eerdmans, 2004.

Withycombe, Robert S. M. "Imperial Nexus and National Anglican Identity: The Australian 1911–12 Legal Nexus Opinions Revisited." *Journal of Anglican Studies* 2.1 (2004) 62–80.

Wong, Kam Ming. "Catholicity and Globality." *Theology Today* 66 (2010) 459–75.

Zahn, Theodor. *Geschichte des Neutestamentlichen Kanons*. Erlangen: Deichert, 1888.

Zink, Jesse. "Changing World, Changing Church: Stephen Bayne and 'Mutual Responsibility and Interdependence.'" *Anglican Theological Review* 93.2 (2011) 243–62.

Name/Subject Index

absoluteness, xx
ACNA (Anglican Church in North
    America), 20
activist groups, 19
Aidan (bishop of Lindisfarne), 58
Alcuin, 36
analogia entis, Barth's strictures
    on, 81
"Ancient Christianity," end of, 37
Anderson, Benedict, 18–19, 116,
    167
    Imagined Communities, 87
Anglican Board of Mission
    Australia, 127
Anglican Church in Nigeria,
    constitution, 20
Anglican Church in North America
    (ACNA), 20
Anglican Church League, 142
Anglican Church of Australia
    Australian opinions on, 86–87
    changes, 115, 127–29
    as community, 87
    constitution, xvii, 20, 129, 139,
        140–45, 156, 161–62
    constitution formation, 160–63
    constitution Ruling Principles,
        162, 165–66, 175
    constitution structure, 164
    cultural change and gender,
        151–85
    decentralization, 153
    Fundamental Declarations,
        153–54, 156–60, 161–62,
        164, 176, 185

    in global Anglicanism, 177
    government, 166–67
    institutional and legal form, 87,
        165
    monopoly on education, 113
Anglican churches
    differences, 152
    organizational structure, 21
    outside English state, 19
Anglican Communion of Churches,
    3, 39, 72, 104
    character of, 4
    doctrine commissions, 73
    organizations of, 11
Anglican Communion Trust, 6
Anglican Consultative Council
    (ACC), 11, 73–74
    1990, Wales, 7
    1999, Dundee, Scotland, 6
    2005, Nottingham UK, 7
    2009, Kingston Jamaica, 12–13
    constitution, 7
    marginalization, 8
    sidelining, 3–14
    Standing Committee, 13
Anglican Covenant, 12
Anglican ecclesiology, 102
    role of eschatology, 71–82
Anglican Mission in America, 7
Anglican Project, 72–83
Anglican Province, 60n15
Anglican Province of the Indian
    Ocean, 16

195

Anglican schools. *See also* church schools
    federalizing tendencies, 128
    mission, 119
    openness and quality of, 115
Anglican Theological Colleges, meeting of heads of, 181
Anglican theology, in church renewal, 98–105
Anglican tradition, apostolicity of, 53
Anglicanism, xvii, xix–xx
    antecedents, 38–39
    catholic in, 32
    church state relations, 125
    contribution, 101–2
    governance tradition, 139
    history, 72
    identity as, 126
    institutional church life, 58
    institutionality in, 54
    rupture, 62
    synodical decision making, 103
Anglicans in England, 23
Anglicare, 90, 117, 128
Anselm (archbishop of Canterbury), 58
anxiety, 89
apostolic succession of order, in Church of England, 46
apostolicity
    in Anglicanism, 42–55
    received theory on, 43–44
Appellate Tribunal (AT), xvii, 155
    as constitutional arbiter, 163
    initial responses and some issues, 176–79
    and same-sex couple regulations, 151
    task of, 168–69, 177
    and Wangaretta Move, 167–68
arbitration, 121
Archbishop of Canterbury, 3, 8, 161
    Anselm, 58
    Carey as, 4
    Commission on Unity and Women in the Episcopate, 8
    as focus of unity, 11
    role of, 10
archdeacon, 125
Augustine, 157
Australia
    change in 1980s and 1990s, 89
    Commonwealth, 129
    community dynamics, 88–89
    historical contribution, 104
    national identity, 108
Australia Day, as "Invasion Day," 86
Australian and New Zealand Association of Theological Schools (ANZATS), 98
Australian Anglican Theology study group, 104–5
Australian Anglicans
    challenges, 97
    as community, 94, 96, 167
    distinctive feature, 109
    dynamics, 90–91
    ecclesial context, 99–101
    identity, 99
    personal connection with others, 100
    regionalism of, 144
    sense of belonging as, 109
Australian church community, challenges, 91
Australian Constitution, establishment clause, 114
Australian Council of Churches, 101
Australian Royal Commission into Institutional Responses to Child Sexual Abuse, 54
Australian Settlement, 88, 121–22, 125–26
authority, 103
Avis, Paul, 43–44

Banyo Theological College, 98
baptism, 27, 63
Barwick, Garfield, 114
Bauer, Walter, 66–67
    Orthodoxy and Heresy in Earliest Christianity, 25–26
Baur, F. C., 25, 66
belonging

NAME/SUBJECT INDEX 197

to community, 87
need for criteria, 27
sense of, 109
Belonging Together, 5
Benedict XVI (pope), 52–53
Bible. *See* New Testament; scripture
Biblische Zeitschrift, 44
bishops, 34, 50, 138
position of earliest, 51
women as, 8, 147, 155
Blessing of Persons Married According to the (Commonwealth) Marriage Act 1961, 167–68
body of Christ, 137–38
Book of Common Prayer (1662), xiii, 2, 27, 32, 165
on ceremonies, 54
ordination services, 21n18
Preface, 54
Bourke, Richard, 125
Bourke Act (1836), 113
Bracht, Werner, 45
Bringing Them Home Report, 147
Britain, 15
British Empire
conception of, 16
decolonization process, 72
Broughton, William Grant, 48–49, 52, 113
Brown, Peter, 35
Browning, George, 92
Bultmann, Rudolf, 25
Burundi, genocide (1994), 6
business corporation, 19

Cameron, Marcia, 153
Cameron, Neil, 142
canon, 62, 67
1998 revision, 52–53
changing, 47
emergence of, 63
procedures for making, 140
scholarship on, 64
study of history, 68
Canon Law Commission, 142–43
canon of scripture, 43, 56–70

Canon on Services (1992), 181
Carey, George, 4, 6
Carey, Hilary, 17
catalogues, 64
cathedrals, 103
catholic, 31
in Anglicanism, 32
in early church creeds, 33
"catholic" network of recognition, 28
catholicity, 40, 77
reality and form, 32–41
Catholicos, 34
ceremonies, xiii–xiv
Book of Common Prayer (1662) on, 54
Chalcedon, Council of, 35
Chandler, Alfred, Jr., 19
change, xiv
in early 20th century, 121–22
chaplains, 124–36
Charlemagne, 35, 36
Christendom
under Charlemagne, 36
Constantinian, 65, 68
decline of, 57
dissolution of model, xiii
ecclesiastical elements, xvii
Latin, 30
slow death of English, 58
Christian communities, 41
institutions in, xix
Christian ethical decisions, in early church, 69
Christian identity, 24
Christian marriage, 183
Christian mission, 29
Christian "norm," 29
Christianity
Arian and Nestorian disputes, 35
disruptive character in, 28
Christology, 69
Chronicle of Edessa, 34
church, 76
authority and power problems, xiii
brokenness and communion, 78

church (*continued*)
    connection to civil power, xiii
    Constantinian conception, 141
    doctrinal disputes in early, 108
    history, 107
    as pilgrimage, 77
    reconceiving as people of God, 85–88
    relationships in, 138
Church Act (1917), 142
church and state, 113
    in England, 102
church communities, colonization by Constantinian Empire, 70
Church Congress (1882), 110
church congresses, 109–10
Church in Australia, landscape, 85–97
Church of England, 19, 30, 141
    apostolic foundations of ministerial order, 49
    apostolic succession of order in, 46
    apostolicity of, 51
    British government and, 156
    communion with, 165
    key documents, 165
    Reformation Acts on, 157
    relationship of colonial churches to, 160
    separation of churches from, xvii
    state benefits, 125
church schools, 112–23
    church context, 115–19
    educational context, 113–15
    funding for denominational, 113
    institutional context, 119–20
    as interface institutions, 120–21
church state relations, 52
    separation of church and state, 57
churches
    in Canada, 10
    institutional life, 58
    relationship of colonial to Church of England, 160
    in Roman Empire, 57
civil power, connection to church, xiii
clergy, 181–82
    role differentiation in church, 138
colonization of church communities by Constantinian Empire, 70
commands of Christ, 174–75
Commonwealth Parliament of Australia, 151
communication
    and community, 16
    value of, 108
communion
    and church brokenness, 78
    with Trinity, 76–77
Communion, Conflict, and Hope (2008), 73, 76–78, 81
    differences with other reports, 78–80
community, 107
    Anglicans as, 116
    Australian Anglicanism as, 94
    and communication, 16
    continuity, xviii–xix
    imagined, 87, 88, 107, 167, 181
    outreach to, 127
complex issues, 24
compromise, 182
    need to understand, 121
Condie, Richard, 154
confidence, 127
    lack of, 99
conflict, xviii, 66
    in the church, 77
    in early Christian communities, 66
    within New Testament, 25
    between provinces, 3
conflict resolution, 130, 184
Conflict Resolution Network, 146
conformity, 107
Congregation for the Doctrine of the Faith, 47
Constantine, xiii, xvii, 65
    preparation of scripture copies, 64
Constantinian Christendom, 65, 68

NAME/SUBJECT INDEX   199

Constantinople, 35
Constitution of Australia,
    establishment clause, 114
continuity, institutions and, 80
Corinth, Christians in, 108
corruption, 70
Council of Chalcedon, 35
Council of Jerusalem, 137
Council of Nicaea, xvii
covenant design group, 11
Cranmer, Archbishop, 61
Cyprian, 51, 102
Cyril of Jerusalem, 33

Dadyeshua, 34
Davidson, Ms., 160–61
deacons, 50
decolonization process, 74
delegation, 138
denomination, 109
differences, 109
Diocese of Canberra, Liturgical
    Group, 95
Diocese of New Westminster, 6, 8, 9
Diocese of Sydney, 87, 179
Diocese of Wangaratta, xv–xvii, 151,
    155
dioceses, 155–56
    constitutions, 116–17
    decisions, 154
    diversity, 181
    government strength, 83
    importance of, 166
    independence, xvii, 166
    organizations in Anglicare, 128
"discretion space," 13
diversity, 66
    in early Christian communities,
    66
    within New Testament, 25, 26
    in society, 17–18
doctrinal disputes in early church,
    108
doctrine, meaning of, 178
Doctrine Commission, 179
"doctrine of the church," 169

Eames, Robin, 5
Eames Commission, 4, 8, 75
Eastern churches, independence, 34
ecclesiastical arrangements, xiv
economy, globalization, 89
ecumenical affairs, 101–4
Edessa, 34
education. *See also* church schools
    Anglican attitudes toward, 115
    state monopoly in late 19 c., 114
Edward VI, ordinal of, 46
EFAC (Evangelical Fellowship in the
    Anglican Communion), 20
Elizabeth I, 32
empire, Christianity adoption as
    religion, 30
Encyclical Letter *Divino afflante
    Spiritu* of Pius XII, 44–45
Encyclical Letter of 1895
    Providentissimus Deus of
    Pope Leo XIII, 44
engagement, 127
Engaging Australia Project, 133
    seed funds by, 149
England, 15
Englert, Francois, 43
English canons, proposed change,
    161
English Christianity, xiii, 156
English church, national
    consolidation, 38
English crown, supremacy in
    church, 60
episcopacy, 102
Episcopal Church, General
    Convention, 149
Episcopal Church (USA), 9, 17
    constitution, 30
    General Convention, 8
Episcopalians, 19–20
Ernest, Ian, 16
eschatology, role in Anglican
    ecclesiology, 71–82
ethnicities vs. nation, 16
Eucharist, 27
European Council for Nuclear
    Research (CERN), 42
Eusebius, 35, 64, 65, 66

NAME/SUBJECT INDEX

Eutyches, xix
Evangelical Fellowship in the
    Anglican Communion
    (EFAC), 20
Evangelism Task Group report
    (1996), 118
Evans, Christopher, 58
    Is 'Holy Scripture' Christian? And
        Other Questions, 56, 68
Executive Council of Government,
    125

faith, 23, 94, 136
    of Australians, 121–23
    and Christian identity, 159
    of the church, 162
    General Synod power to make
        statements on, 144
    as professed from primitive
        times, 173
    sharing, 149
faithfulness, 40
fealty, 38
Federal government, 128
Figgis, John Neville, 18
Fisher, Geoffrey (archbishop), 157,
    161, 176
For the Sake of the Kingdom (1987),
    73, 81
    differences with other reports,
        78–80
France, nation-state, 16
Fraser government, 89
Fundamental Declarations, 153–54,
    156–60, 161–62, 164, 176,
    185
Future Issues Resolution, 147

GAFCON (Global Anglican Future
    Conference), 11, 154
Galbraith, J. K., 96
Gamble, Henry, 64
gay couples, liturgical blessing for, 8
gender relations, 2, 8
    absence of issues, 6

General Synod, 17, 110
    in 1872, 156
    Canon of 1992, 170
    canons, 166
    changes in process, 146–48
    and church community, 150
    constitution, 142
    contentious matters, 184
    governmental style, 117
    Ministry and Training
        Commission, 124
    as a parliament, 143–44
    powers, 140–45
    process, 134–36
    process changes in 1998, 130
    purpose and dynamics, 137–50
    spiritual or moral power, 144,
        145–46
    Standing Committee, 92, 132,
        134
    Strategic Issues canon, 130–31
    Working Groups, 134
General Synod (Adelaide, 1998),
    118, 131, 146
General Synod (Brisbane), 148–50
General Synod Canon Concerning
    Services of 1992, 175
General Synod Office, 92
    strategies, 95–96
    study groups, 100–101
    study groups' significance,
        104–5
gentiles, early Christians and, 107
Gipps, Governor, 113
Global Anglican Future Conference
    (GAFCON), 11, 154
globalization, 72
Gnostics
    as aliens, 28
    tendency to reject teaching, 27
goals, 136
God, Kingdom promise, 73
Goodhew, Harry, 93
gospels
    differences between, 66
    as sovereign truth, 74
government, and municipal
    decisions, 86

grace of God, 40, 108
"Great Church," 33
Great Schism (1054), 32
Gregory the Great (pope), 37, 157
Gregory VII (pope), 37, 38, 157

haeresis, 27
Hahneman, Geoffrey, 64
Hammond, T. C., 161
Hampton Court Conference, 103
Handley, Kenneth (Chancellor of Diocese of Sydney), 171
hard sciences, 43
Harnack, Adolf von, 63, 65
Harvester Judgement, 121
Hastings, Adrian, 19, 21, 72
  The Construction of Nationhood, 15–16
Henry I, 58
Henry II, 58
heresy, 28
  ecclesial connotations, 31
  orthodoxy and, 26
hermeneutics, xv
Higgins, Justice, 121
Higgs, Peter, 43
Higgs Boson, 42
Hobson, William, 48
Holland, Jonathan (bishop), 174, 179
Holy Spirit, 26
homosexuality, 4
  constitutional view of, 173
  place in Church's public life, 7
  scripture on, 174
Hong Kong, 8
Hooker, Richard, xix, 39
hope, 78
Hort, Fenton John Anthony, 62
House of Bishops of the Church in Rwanda, 7
humility, 40, 41

identity
  as Anglicans, 24, 126
  and plurality, 15–22

Ignatius, 51
  letter to the Smyrneans, 33
imagined communities, 87, 88, 107, 167, 181
incarnation, 26
Indigenous Australians, land rights for, 86
individualism, radical, 89
individuality, 107
Ingham, Michael, 6
Innocent III (pope), 38
institutional creep, 54, 55
institutional positions, xiv
institutional relationship, change in response, 119
institutionality, in Anglicanism, 54
institutionalization, 29
institutions, xv, 69–70
  antipathy in 1960s, 62
  challenges, 94
  change, 13
  in Christian communities, xix
  growth in early Christianity, 64
  mission statements, 119
  revulsion against, 56
  social structure influences, 30
  Virginia Report on structures, 80
Instruments of Communion, 12
"Instruments of Unity," 20, 75
insurance, 128
Inter-Anglican Theological and Doctrinal Commission (IATDC), 3, 4
  Communion, Conflict, and Hope, 40
  For the Sake of the Gospel, 40
Inter-Trade and Industry Mission, 90
"Invasion Day," Australia Day as, 86
Irenaeus, 51, 63
Isaac, 34

James (disciple), xviii
James I, 103
Jenkins, Philip, 35

Jesus, xv, 22, 27, 106–7
    announcement of kingdom of God, 28
    commands of, 174–75
    historical connection with, 51
    humanity or divinity, xix
    as New Testament focus, 67
John (disciple), xviii
John Paul II (pope), 47
Johnson, Richard, 125
Journal of Anglican Studies, 84, 105
Judaism, Tannaitic, 27

Kelly, J. N. D., 33
Kelly, Paul, 121–22, 125–26
    The End of Certainty, 88–89
Kelsey, David, 67
Kingdom of Christ, 49
Kingdom of God, 81
    Jesus' announcement of, 28
Knox, Broughton, 153, 162–63
Kolini of Rwanda (archbishop), 7

Labor Party, Roman Catholicism and, 125
laity, 182
    in church decision making, 103
    concept of, 98–99
    role differentiation in church, 138
    role in church government, 167
The Lambeth Commission on Communion, 8
Lambeth Conference (1988), 4
Lambeth Conference (1998), 1, 3–4, 74
land for clergy, 138
Lanfranc (archbishop), 38, 58
Latin Christendom, 30
Lawson, Henry, "A Song of the Republic," 85–86
leadership, 120
Leo (pope), 36
Leo XIII (pope), 45, 46, 52
    Apostolicae curae, 47
    Encyclical Letter of 1895 *Providentissimus Deus*, 44, 59
Lightfoot, J. B., 33, 49–53, 62, 63, 66
    Phillippians commentary, 80–81
Limerick, David, 19
listening, 94, 109
Listening Groups, 92
Liturgical Group of the diocese of Canberra, 95
Loane, Marcus, 153
long 1960s, 65, 67, 68
Lord's Supper, 63
love, 22, 40, 41, 107, 109, 110, 138

Mackay, Hugh, 124
    Generations, 119
    Reinventing Australia, 89, 119
MacLagan, William, *Saepius Officio*, 46–47
Markus, Robert, 37
marriage, 169
    Christian, 183
    history of Roman Catholic interpretation, 173
    same-sex, 155, 169, 178, 180
    scripture on, 174
Marriage Act (2017), xv, 151, 153
martyrdom, 27
Marutha, 34
Mauritius, 16–17
McLeod, Hugh, 59, 62, 67
    The Religious Crisis of the 1960s, 56–57
Mediterranean, Arab invasions, 35
Melbourne, 87
mission statements of institutions, 119
missionaries to U.S., 7
Mitchell, Basil George, 23, 31
    How to Play Theological Ping-Pong, 23–24
monasteries, 103
monopoly on state aid, 125
Moorhouse, James, 110
Moses Tay of South East Asia (archbishop), 7

Moule, C. F. D., *The Birth of the New Testament*, 69
Mowll, Howard (archbishop of Sydney), 160
multiculturalism, 18
municipal decisions, government and, 86
Münz, Peter, 36
Muratorian fragment, 33, 66
Murphy, Chuck, 7

NACON (National Anglican Caring Organizations Network), 90, 117
nation vs, ethnicities, 16
National Anglican Church, constitution, 1962, 88
National Anglican Conference (Canberra, 1997), 85, 91–95, 100, 110, 116, 117, 135, 146
National Anglican Conference (Sydney, 2002), 135
National Anglican Schools Consultative Committee, 117
National Anglican Theology Seminar, 98
national churches, 152
national conferences, and renewal, 106–11
National Council of Churches in Australia, 101
nationalism, modernist view, 15
Nestorius, xix
networks, 135–36
 canon establishing, 132–33
New Hampshire, Bishop of, 8
New South Wales, 48, 52, 113, 125, 179
 Scandrett vs. Dowling, 141
New South Wales School Act, 113–14
New Testament
 "catholic" and, 25
 Church office in, 45
 conflicts and diversity within, 25
 German scholars, 53
 gospel differences, 66
 Jesus as focus, 67
 letters of Paul, 25
 role as text of authority, 26
 scholarship, 67
 studies, 25
New Westminster, Diocese of, 6, 8, 9
New Zealand, 48
New Zealand church, 152
Nexus Opinion on Fundamental Declarations, 162
Nexus report (1905), 160
Nicaea, council of, 65
Nicholls, David, *The Pluralist State*, 18
Nigeria, Anglican Church constitution, 20
Nineham, Dennis, 67
nineteen sixties, 65, 67, 68
 crisis, 62
non-government organizations, 19

Of Ceremonies statement, xiii–xiv
Olympic Games, Melbourne (1956), 86
ordained ministry, 43
orders of ministry, 102
Ordinal, 165
ordinal of Edward VI, 46
ordination of women, 5, 8, 109, 141–43, 146
 General Synod on, 155
The Origins of Christendom in the West, 26–29
orthodox Anglicans, and catholicity, 23–41
orthodoxy, 31
 heresy and, 26
Oswald (king of Northumberland), 58
outreach, change in direction, 118
Oxford revival, 52

Parson's freehold, 138
party politics, 144

Paul, 63, 107, 108
  letters of, 25
peaceable kingdom, 41
persecution, 108
Perth, archbishop, 143
Pickard, Stephen, 44
Pius XII, Encyclical Letter *Divino afflante Spiritu*, 44–45, 60
plurality, and identity, 15–22
Poguntke, Thomas, 13
political realm, power and authority in, xvii
Pontifical Biblical Institute, 44
pope, as Peter's successor, 38
power, xix, 29, 64, 103
  ambiguity of, xviii
  humility and service vs., xviii
  imperial notions of, 65
prayer book (1995), 85
A Prayer Book for Australia (APBA), 90, 155
Presbyterianism, state benefits, 125
presbyters, 50
priesthood, universal, 50
priests
  Roman recognition of Anglican orders, 46
  women as, 4
Primates
  2003 statement, 8
  protest of autonomy, 10
Primates Meeting, 1, 5
  2003 Brazil, 8
  2007, 11
  2009, 11, 13
  Joint Standing Committee, 11
Protestant scholars, 60
Province Nine, 17
provinces, 152
  autonomy, 14
  conflicts between, 3
  constitution and canons, 60–61
public debate, 90
  on theological matters, 24

Queen's University (Belfast, Ireland), 15

radical individualism, 89
Ramsey, Ian, 23
Ratzinger, Cardinal, 47, 52–53. *See also* Benedict XVI (pope)
Rayner, Keith (archbishop), 92, 117, 172, 174
received theory on apostolicity, 43–44
Reference Panels, 132
Reformation, 108
  in England, and catholic, 32
  English legislation, 139
  reference to documents, 163
Reformation Acts, 157
regula fidei, 28
Reicke, Bo, 67, 70
relationships, 15, 70
  in church, 138
  institutionalization of, 57
religious pluralism, 113
renewal, 96–97
  Anglican theology in, 98–105
  national conferences and, 106–11
Report Re the Ordination of Women to the Office of Deacon Canon 1985, 171
Reserve Fund, 133
Restoration, unity of government, xiii
Reunion (island), 17
Righter, Bishop, 4
  acquittal of charge for ordaining homosexual, 5
Robinson, Bishop, 174
Robinson, Donald, 153
Robinson, Gene, 8
Robinson, John, *Honest to God*, 62
Rodgers, John, 7
Roman Catholic Church, 59
  approach to education, 114
  governance model, 139
  as member of NCCA, 101
  state benefits, 125
Roman Catholic scholars, 60
Roman Empire, adoption of Christianity, 64
Rothe, Richard, 50

Royal Commission on Institutional Responses to Child Abuse, xviii
Royal Supremacy, 102, 103, 156
Ruling Principles, 162, 165–66, 175
Runcie, Robert, 4, 7
Rwanda, genocide in 1994, 6

sacraments, 29–30
  Christological framework for, xix
same-sex couples, 151
  blessing for, 8, 153
same-sex marriage, 155, 169, 180
  Tribunal and, 178
same-sex relations, 1
Scandrett vs. Dowling, 141
scripture, 173–74. *See also* New Testament
  as canon, 43, 56–70
  canon development, 26, 29–30
  "catholic" and New Testament, 33
  character of, 180
  Cranmer on, 61
  Fundamental Declarations on, 162
  history of interpretation, xv, 44
  reliability of, 25–26
  role of, 61, 180
  as ultimate authority, 53, 164
Second Vatican Council (1962-65), 57
secular education, 114
secularization, 23
separation of church and state, 57
separatism, 155
settler churches, 17
skepticism, 29
small group discussion, 134, 146
Smith, Geoff (archbishop), 176
Smyrna, Ignatius' letter to, 33
society
  diversity, 17–18
  perceptions of character, 57
sola scriptura, doctrine of, 59
"sovereign" truth, 74

spirituality, 90
Spong, Jack, 4
Standing Committee, 92, 132, 147
  review, 134
Standing Orders, 184
State Church, transition to Established Church, 156
state paternalism, 122
Stillingfleet, Edward, 158, 178
  opposition, 159
Strategic Issues Advisory Panel, 131, 132–33
Strategic Issues and Other Bodies Canon, 147
Strauss, David F., 66
study groups, significance, 104–5
sub-atomic world, theory of, 43
subsidiarity, 75
Supreme Court of Western Australia, 143
Sydney, 87
  First Fleet in harbor, 86
Sykes, Stephen, 157
synods, 94, 116–17
  decision making, 103
  emergence of, 139
  purpose, 137–40
  structure, 127–28, 129
  Westminster Parliamentary style, 30

Tagung der deutschsprachigen katholischen Neutestamentler, 44
  1963 meeting, 45
Tannaitic Judaism, achievement of, 27
tariff, 121
Task Forces, 132
Tatian, 66
technology, 15
Temple, Frederick, *Saepius Officio*, 46–47
Temple, destruction, 27
Tertullian, 22
Thirty Nine Articles, 68–69, 165, 172

Thomas à Beckett, 58
trading companies, 19
Trinity, 75
    communion with, 76–77
Tudor imperialism, 108
Tudors, 58, 102

uncertainty, 43
uniformity, 107
unity, 95, 118
Unity and Authority document, 4
universal priesthood, 50
universal primacy, 159

values, 125
    transmission of, 120
Vatican I, 59
Vereker, Charles, xv
Victorian Act, 114
The Virginia Report (1998), 5, 6, 73, 74–76, 77, 81
    differences with other reports, 78–80
vision, 127
volunteer associations, 117
Vulgate translation, 59, 60

Wangaratta, Diocese of, xv–xvii, 151, 155
Wangaretta Blessing Service, 170
    doctrine and, 171–73

Wangaretta Move, and Appellate Tribunal, 167–68
Wangaretta Regulation, 170
Watson, Peter, 135
Webb, Paul, 13
weddings, 183
welfare agencies, 90, 128
Westcott, Brooke Foss, 62
Western Australia, Supreme Court of, 143
Western Christendom, beginning, 37
White Australia Policy, 89, 121
Whitlam government, 89
William I, 38, 58, 157
William Rufus, 58
Williams, Rowan, 30, 39, 40–41
    "Defining Heresy," 26–29
Windsor Continuation Group, 12
Windsor Process, 77
Windsor Report (2004), 8, 10
witness, 110
Wollaston College, 98
women
    as bishops, 8, 147, 155
    nurturing in leadership, 149
    ordination of, 5, 8, 141–43, 146, 155
    as priests, 4

Yong Pin Chung, 4

Zahn, Theodore, 62, 63, 65

Scripture Index

Matthew
10:37–38   106

Mark
10:41–45   xviii
10:42–45   70

John
13:35   22

Acts
15   137

Corinthians   107

1 Corinthians
12, 40–41   137–38
13   77
13:1–2   107
13:4–7   138
14   69

1 John   4:20, 109

www.ingramcontent.com/pod-product-compliance
Lightning Source LLC
Chambersburg PA
CBHW062025220426
43662CB00010B/1480